PRACTICAL INSURANCE GUIDES

Titles in this series are:

How to Manage Risk
2nd edition
by Jim Bannister

Insurance Solvency Analysis
2nd edition
by Jim Bannister

Introduction to Insurance
2nd edition
by D S Hansell

Professional Negligence and Insurance Law
by Neil F Jones & Co

Reinsurance: London Market Practice
by Carol Boland

Reinsurance Management
by Leslie Lucas, John McLean and Peter Green

The Nuts and Bolts of Reinsurance
by Keith Riley

PROFESSIONAL NEGLIGENCE AND INSURANCE LAW

PREPARED BY NEIL F JONES & CO

AND EDITED BY

JEFFREY C BROWN

LLB, FCIArb

FOREWORD BY JOHN L POWELL, QC

LONDON   HONG KONG

1994

LLP Professional Publishing
69-77 Paul Street
London EC2A 4LQ

EAST ASIA
LLP Asia
Sixth Floor
233 Hollywood Road
Hong Kong

First published 1994
Reprinted 1999

British Library Cataloguing in Publication Data
A catalogue record for this book
is available from the British Library

ISBN 1-85978-585-9

LLP Professional Publishing is a trading division of Informa Publishing Group Limited

Text set in 10 on 12pt Plantin by
Mendip Communications Ltd
Frome, Somerset
Printed in Great Britain by
WBC Ltd
Bridgend, Mid-Glamorgan

FOREWORD

The boom and bust of the late 1980s and early 1990s have engulfed the courts with an avalanche of claims against professional persons and insurers to a previously unprecedented extent. The avalanche is still unremitting, leaving a swathe of casualties. Only too often, the background to negligence claims against accountants, valuers, insurance brokers or solicitors has been an extensive fraud, the perpetrators of which are either untraceable or insolvent. Presumed to be insured professionals, though innocent of any moral wrongdoing, are then victim to secondary recovery actions brought by defrauded victims. All too frequently insurance cover has provided insufficient indemnity.

Common law principles relevant to professional negligence claims are long established and generally known. However, their application frequently gives rise to difficulty. To say that a professional's duty is to exercise reasonable care and skill is usually mere preliminary incantation before a journey through a discordant morass of rules and regulations, codes of conduct and different expert views as to what the competent professional would have done in the relevant circumstances. Nor have the courts lost their capacity occasionally to surprise.

The broad trends anticipated in the preface to the first edition to this book have become even more apparent in subsequent years. Courts continue to affirm the importance of contract, but not to the entire eclipse of tort as apparent from the survival of concurrent liability. "Service liability" continues to emerge as a recognisable classification for considering not only professional claims but also claims against other advisers and other service providers, especially in the context of financial service and computers. Claims against them continue to burgeon. Professional and regulatory bodies continue to promulgate new rules and guidance. Professional negligence policies are increasingly geared towards particular specialities and more accurately attuned to claims experience and expectation. Inapposite policies remain, however, a persistent virus.

The authors of the various essays in this book are again to be congratulated. Particularly refreshing is the prominence given to recent case law from which emerging trends are more apparent. As in the first edition, each of the essays contains a succinct, up-to-date and perceptive analysis of its subject and in terms which gives both lawyer and non-lawyer a clear account of the issues involved.

JOHN L POWELL*

* Q.C. Co-editor Jackson and Powell "Professional Negligence" and Lomnicka and Powell "Encylopedia of Financial Services Law" and President of the Society of Construction Law 1991–92.

PREFACE TO THE SECOND EDITION

It is some time since the first edition of this text was published in 1991. The law relating to professionals has indeed developed apace since this time and thus, there has been more than ample subject-matter to warrant a second edition. Again, the aim of the work is to be of interest and value to lawyers, those involved in the insurance industry and also the professionals themselves. The report is not written with the aim of being regarded as a standard text. Its aims are more modest.

As in the first edition, the intention has been in the first chapter to provide a broad analysis of liabilities of all professionals. This has been followed by a second chapter dealing with insurance law aspects. The following three chapters contain a more detailed analysis of the liability of surveyors, insurance brokers, architects and engineers. The specific issue of collateral warranties has not proved to be of such lasting topicality and thus, it has not been considered appropriate to include a specific chapter relating to this subject in this second edition. Apologies are offered to those professionals who had not been the subject of specific chapters. If all of the professions were to be the subject of their own separate chapters, it is to be doubted whether or not the completed text could have been accommodated within the required length of work. In any event, it is to be hoped that those omitted professionals and those who have interests in their legal liabilities will nonetheless find the contents of the first two chapters as being of interest.

Care has been taken, wherever possible, to include recent case law. This work aims to state the law applicable in England and Wales at the end of February 1994. However, care has been taken with the kind permission of the publishers to include specific decisions of the courts since this time.

Special thanks are proffered to John Powell for kindly agreeing to provide the Foreword. Thanks are also extended to Linda Vincent, Katrina Bevan, June Fazey and Lynn Fazey for their valued secretarial input and careful typing of the text.

Preface to the Second Edition

For the avoidance of doubt, Jeffrey Brown has been responsible for editing and Chapters 1 and 2—Liability of Professionals and Insurance Implications. Philip Harris has been responsible for Chapter 3—Liability of Surveyors: An Appraisal. Kevin Barrett has been responsible for Chapter 4—The Duties of the Insurance Broker. Ian Yule has been responsible for Chapter 5—Architects and Engineers: Professional Negligence.

The views as contained herein are those of the authors.

JEFFREY C BROWN, KEVIN J BARRETT,
PHILIP J HARRIS AND IAN R YULE
April 1994

CONTRIBUTORS

JEFFREY C BROWN LLB, FCIARB

Jeffrey Brown was born in Cardiff. He read Law at the University College of Wales, Aberystwyth. Upon qualifying as a solicitor he moved to Birmingham in 1981.

He joined Neil F Jones & Co. in 1984, was made a Partner in 1986, and as from 1 October 1993, is the Firm's Senior Partner. He practises in the fields of professional negligence and associated insurance matters, and construction law. He has published widely. He is a member of the Chartered Insurance Institute.

KEVIN J BARRETT LLB, ACIARB

Kevin Barrett is a Partner with Neil F Jones & Co. He practises mainly in the field of construction law, including related insurance aspects.

PHILIP J HARRIS MA CANTAB, ACIARB

Philip Harris was educated at Peterhouse, Cambridge. He graduated with Honours in 1980.

He was articled and practised as a solicitor in Birmingham before joining Neil F Jones & Co. as an associate in 1988. He became a Partner in 1990.

He has experience in a range of commercial litigation. He specialises in construction law. Several of his cases are reported in *Building Law Reports* and other Law Reports. He retains a keen interest in copyright and design law and is developing this aspect of the practice.

He is a member of the Licensing Executive Society of Britain and Ireland, which is concerned with the transfer of technology.

He contributes articles to a number of journals in the field of building and engineering.

Contributors

IAN R YULE MA OXON, ACIARB
Ian Yule read law at Worcester College, Oxford, and graduated with
Honours in 1980. After local government articles and general commercial
litigation work, he joined Neil F Jones & Co. in 1990, becoming a Partner
in 1992. He is specialised in construction litigation and arbitration and
professional indemnity work and has lectured and written on these
subjects. He is an Associate of the Chartered Institute of Arbitrators.

CONTENTS

Contents

TABLE OF CASES

Table of Cases

Table of Cases

Table of Cases

TABLE OF LEGISLATION, ETC.

CHAPTER 1

LIABILITY OF PROFESSIONALS

1   CONTRACTUAL LIABILITIES

Recent years have seen a change of emphasis from an economy based on manufacturing to an economy based on the services industry. The percentage of those employed directly in manufacturing has been falling while those engaged in the services industries has been increasing. Professionals are engaged in the services industry providing their services for wide ranges of clientele ranging from the domestic requirements of the consumer to the greater and more complex demands of the multi-national conglomerate.

Whatever the demands, the law is constantly evolving to meet them. Case law providing legal precedent is not always available in new areas of activity and it may be some years before case law will provide guidance as to the expected rights and liabilities of parties in given situations. Consumer awareness has also played its part and the body of litigation which has emerged in the last ten years alone relating to allegations of negligence against professionals is considerable. It is a tall order for the lawyer seeking to proffer advice and who has an interest in this field of law to be able to keep up to date with all cases which are reported in various journals and law reports.

Clients of professionals may feel that professional fees are substantial. Whilst the level of fees charged should have no direct bearing upon the legal duties and responsibilities incumbent, the existence of the obligation to pay substantial fees will often have a bearing on the mind of any client as to what his expectations are of the professional and will influence any remedial steps he has to take if he is dissatisfied or disappointed with the net result.

Consumer awareness also plays its part given the willingness on the part of a client to instruct specific professionals for specialist tasks taking into account expertise and perhaps cost implications. Where a client does not have inherent loyalty toward one single or group of professionals, there will be a greater willingness to go to law in the event of any dissatisfaction with the quality of service. Unfortunately also for the professional, whilst it

1

is a brave individual who practises without the benefit of insurance cover (and it is indeed mandatory for many professionals), any would-be plaintiff has the comfort of knowing that any claim made for damages is most likely to be honoured if liability is established given the presence of such cover.

Historically, the three main professions were medicine, the church and the law. However, the number of professions has now increased considerably and the number of distinct professions is increasing. There are also specialisations within existing professions which can in some instances be regarded as being separate from the main profession due to a separate professional body existing which regulates the respective affairs. An example would be the Royal College of Surgeons and a further example would be the Chartered Institute of Arbitrators which is a comparatively recently created body founded in 1915.

No great legal consequence follows from any decision as to whether an individual is a professional or not and the issue is unlikely to arise in practice since the existence of the various professions is reasonably well defined. The condition precedent must be the existence of a governing body for that same profession. In the decision of *Carr* v. *Inland Revenue Commissioners* [1944] 2 All ER 163, the Court of Appeal found that an optician was carrying out a profession. Du Parcq LJ stated:

"It seems to me to be dangerous to try to define the word 'profession', as Stratton LJ realised . . . I think that everybody would agree that before one can say that a man is carrying on a profession, one must see that he has some special skill or ability or some special qualifications derived from training or experience. Even then one has to be very careful because there are many people whose work demands great skill and ability and long experience and many qualifications who would not be said by anybody to be carrying on a profession."

The classic statement as to the standard of care that may be expected from a professional is provided by McNair J in *Bolam* v. *Friern Hospital Management Committee* [1957] 2 All ER 118 when he stated as follows:

"The test is the standard of the ordinary skilled man exercising and professing to have that special skill. It is well established law that it is sufficient if he exercises the ordinary skill of an ordinary competent man exercising that particular art."

The requirement to exercise the ordinary skill of the ordinary competent man exercising that particular art may well form the basis of the contractual relationship between the professional and his client as a consequence of a written contract which may make reference to such a duty. Professions often publish standard terms of engagement and a term will be included to this effect.

The aforementioned test as set out by McNair J in *Bolam* v. *Friern Hospital Management Committee* has been cited with approval in very many cases. The test of the skill and care has not since this time been seriously challenged. However, reference needs to be made to the recent decision in the Court of Appeal of *McManus Developments Ltd* v. *Barbridge Properties Ltd and Blandy and Blandy (a firm)* [1992] EGCS 50. This decision related to the conduct of a firm of solicitors having the conduct of a conveyance of property. It was argued on behalf of the solicitors that the test should be based upon whether or not the individual was "reasonably competent" or "reasonably well informed". Reliance was made upon the earlier comments of Lord Diplock in *Saif Ali* v. *Sydney Mitchell & Co.* [1980] AC 198 when he made reference (at page 220C, D and E) to the words "... unless the error was such as no reasonably well informed and competent member of that profession could have made". This argument was however rejected since the Court of Appeal rightly identified that to import this test would be to reduce the standard required to something lower than the lowest common denominator. They stated that one could always find, in this instance, an apparently reasonably competent solicitor who could say that he would have probably in similar circumstances have done the same.

In the absence of any express condition however, the law will always imply a term that the professional man will use his reasonable skill and care. The implication of such a term can always be justified on the basis of the requirement for business efficacy and also due to the clear but unexpressed intention of the parties to the contract.

A difficult question arises when one is asked to consider the practical application of the test of the exercise of all reasonable skill and care. Is it a case that a particular individual's experience and expertise need to be taken into account when assessing the requisite standard to be expected or, alternatively, is it more appropriate for the individual to be adjudged by the standards of his profession generally. In the past, the courts have tended to favour the latter approach, see for example, *Andrew Master Hones Ltd* v. *Cruikshank and Fairweather* [1980] RPC 16 in which Graham J stated:

"The degree of knowledge and care to be expected is thus seen to be that degree possessed by a notionally and duly qualified person practising that profession. The test is, therefore, if I may put it that way an objective test referable to the notional member of the profession and not a subjective test referable to the particular professional man employed."

In practice difficulties would arise in applying any other test since it could give rise to problems to ascertain the manner of deciding this subjective test. The courts would find difficulty in differentiating between standards of skill and care and how these would vary given age and experience. How could an expert witness viewing the actions of a fellow professional assist the court other than by assuming an objective view? There would also be the danger if a subjective test were to be applied of the courts favouring a strict liability approach, i.e. if there has been a mistake then there has to be

3

an inference that a breach of the duty of reasonable skill and care exists. However, the converse argument could be put forward. Clients of professionals, quite correctly, could expect to pay a larger fee to an individual which would reflect his skill and experience if he has, for example, spent 20 years in a particular field and is a renowned authority. Why then should this individual be judged by the same criteria as would a person with one year's experience. The dilemma was discussed by Megarry J in the case of *Duchess of Argyll* v. *Beuselinck* [1972] 2 Lloyd's Rep 172, a claim for negligence against a solicitor. He stated:

"No doubt the inexperienced solicitor is liable if he fails to attain the standard of a reasonably competent solicitor. But if the client employs a solicitor of high standard and great experience, will an action for negligence fail if it appears that the solicitor did not exercise the care and skill to be expected of him, though he did not fall below the standard of a reasonably competent solicitor? If the client engages an expert, and doubtless expects to pay commensurate fees, is he not entitled to expect something more than the standard of the reasonably competent? I am speaking not merely of those expert in a particular branch of the law, as contrasted with those practising in the same field of the law but being of a more ordinary calibre and having less experience. The essence of the contract retainer, it may be said, is that the client is retaining the particular solicitor of the firm in question, and he is therefore entitled to expect from that solicitor or firm a standard of care and skill commensurate with the skill and experience which that solicitor or firm has. The uniform standard of care postulated to the world at large in tort hardly seems appropriate when the duty is not one imposed by the law of tort but arises from a contractual obligation existing between the client and the particular solicitor or firm in question. If, as is usual, the retainer contains no express term as to the solicitor's duty of care, and the matter rests upon an implied term, what is that term in the case of a solicitor of long experience or specialist skill? Is it that you will put at his client's disposal the care and skill of an average solicitor, or the care and skill that he has? I may say that Mr. Arnold advanced no contention that it was the latter standard that was to be applied; but I wish to make it clear that I have not overlooked the point which one day may require further consideration."

The view presently taken by the courts is whatever a client's expectations may be when instructing a professional, in terms of experience and expertise which will no doubt be mirrored by the fees charged, and whatever the level of performance obtained in return the standard of care required of the professional should not thereby be affected and remains fixed.

Different rules apply when considering the liability of medical practitioners. In deciding whether or not due care and skill has been exercised it is necessary to consider the specialist skills of that individual and also the general level of expertise which that person has attained.

In *Wilsher* v. *Essex AMA* (Times Law Reports, 6 August 1986) the Court of Appeal by a majority held that the standard of skill and care expected of medical staff related not to the particular experience of the individuals involved, but to the posts which they occupied.

Similarly, in *Junor* v. *McNicol* (Times Law Reports, 26 March 1959) in deciding whether or not a junior doctor had failed to exercise proper skill and care the Lord Chancellor stated:

" ... there was a duty on her to display the care and skill of a prudent qualified house surgeon, it being remembered that such a position was held by a comparative beginner."

It is interesting to compare and contrast these rules which apply to medical practitioners with those which relate to other professions as discussed. The distinction may be explained by the historical divisions between the medical profession. Thus the distinction between a consultant gynaecologist and a consultant orthopaedic surgeon may be compared with the distinction between a chartered quantity surveyor and a chartered building surveyor. Both fall within the categories of medical practitioners and surveyors respectively, but their disciplines are completely different, which, in the examples quoted is recognised by the relevant professional bodies concerned. Furthermore, in being aware of the status of the medical practitioner, e.g. registrar or consultant, the courts have had regard to the distinct roles which such individuals perform and for which they are paid—more often than not by public funds. Other professions lack such a tier of advancement and this must have had a direct bearing upon the professional standards imposed by the courts.

However, to date, the prediction of Megarry J in *Duchess of Argyll* has not been implemented although it may yet form the basis of future judicial precedent. The issue of the standard of care that may be reasonably expected of a professional, in this event, an insurance broker, was discussed by Anthony Coleman QC sitting as a Deputy High Court Judge in *Sharp and Another* v. *Sphere Drake Insurance Plc and Others* [1992] 2 Lloyd's Rep 501. The Judge acknowledged the earlier judgment of Megarry J in *Duchess of Argyll* and concluding that the standard of skill to be expected of the broker was that of the typical non-specialist marine broker. However he added that this was not the same as the standard of a marine broker substantially inexperienced in the insurance of large yachts. He stated (at p. 523):

"It is rather the standard of a broker who has such general knowledge of the yacht insurance market and the cover available in it as to be able to advise his client on all matters on which a lay client would in the ordinary course of events predictably need advice, in particular in the course of the selection of cover and the completion of the proposal."

Thus, the effect of this statement must be that ignorance of precise areas of practice cannot be relied upon as a defence; a general knowledge will be assumed. It may be a matter of some speculation as to the stage, if any, whereby a broker's knowledge would cease to be a general one and become specialist. One assumes that this would occur with increased experience of that particular specialty. It must be however that the answer to this question is of no relevance to the issue of determining the standard of care. Recent years has seen a relaxation as to the professional rules which allow for the publication and distribution of brochures to clients and potential clients and individuals within the profession now freely market themselves as having specialist skills in specific areas. In these circumstances, would it be wrong to expect the standard of care from such individuals which would be expected from individuals professing to have those specialist skills as opposed to the ordinary skills which may exist within the profession at large? The argument that a higher duty of care in such circumstances is owed may be based on estoppel. If a professional has held himself out as having specialist skills then a court may prevent him from denying that he was a specialist in a given field and hence a greater measure of expertise could be expected. Similarly, if a representation is made as to the expertise of a professional either oral or written and this is relied upon by the client, then it may be incorporated as a term of the contract.

The words of Megarry J in *Duchess of Argyll* have provided a fertile ground for debate for lawyers. However, the decision is now over 20 years old and there has not been any tendency to follow the argument. Consumers show an increasing awareness and appreciation of any specialist skills of any professional and furthermore, there is an ever increasing tendency on the part of the professionals themselves to perfect specialist skills. The law has sensibly and properly distinguished the test for negligence being that of the ordinary skill and care from the reasonable expectation of the consumer. Two major consequences arise from this. On the one hand it is clear that the greater the degree of specialist skills of any professional and thus the narrower the field of expertise, the lesser the risk of any negligence. On the other hand however there will always be the risk that the non-specialist will be tempted to the areas of specialisation and in turn be found to have failed to comply with the standard of reasonable skill and care due to his having failed to comply with what may be considered an elementary requirement.

It is important to note that it is not every error of judgment which gives rise to a claim for a breach of the requirement for all reasonable skill and care, for example, see *Whitehouse* v. *Jordan* [1981] 1 WLR 246. The facts in this case related to a claim against a medical practitioner and was a decision of the House of Lords. To equate an error of judgment with negligence is a dangerous precedent indeed and would substantially extend the professional's liability for claims.

In considering the performance of a professional it is not necessarily a defence to any claim to demonstrate that other professionals in the same sphere adopt a similar practice. It could be that the profession as a whole has fallen short of proper standards of care and skill. In *Board of Governors of the Bethlem Royal Hospital* v. *Sidaway* [1985] AC 871, it is made clear that the practice of conduct called into question had to be judged not only against the generally accepted practice but also in accordance with a practice rightly accepted as proper by a body of skilled and experienced men. In other words, the judiciary reserves to itself the right to condemn certain practices or routines even if generally accepted as proper within the profession in question. A similar illustration may be found in *Edward Wong Finance Co.* v. *Johnson Stokes & Master* [1984] AC 296. This related to negligence on the part of solicitors. A practice in conveyancing known as "Hong Kong Style Completion" involved a foreseeable risk of embezzlement by the recipient of the money. It was therefore to be regarded as a negligent one.

The issue as to whether or not a professional has conformed with the requirement of all reasonable skill and care is often decided by a court only following the hearing of expert evidence. The importance to a court of law of expert evidence may be illustrated by comments made by the Court of Appeal in *Merrill Lynch Futures Inc* v. *York House Trading* (Times Law Reports, 24 May 1984). The court stated that exceedingly strong evidence from expert brokers in relation to individual transaction would become necessary to establish negligence. It is important to resist the temptation of adducing evidence from an individual whose standing is so great that he is not addressing his evidence as to the expected standard of the ordinary individual skill and care that would have been expected from an individual within that profession. The danger is that if the expert is out of touch then the risk is run that the evidence may be ignored by the court. This very same situation occurred in *George Wimpey & Co. Ltd* v. *D V Poole and Others* (1984) 27 BLR 58, a case involving allegations of negligence by engineers. Webster J made the following comments as to the evidence of one of the experts:

"Professor Rowe, Professor Emeritus of Soil Mechanics at Manchester University and a practising consultant in geo-technical engineering, gave expert evidence on behalf of Wimpeys. Throughout his life he has conducted original research: he has lectured on soils virtually throughout the world; he has published over 60 original papers; and he has advised on geo-technical aspects of the design or construction or remedial measures of over 300 civil engineering projects including large dams, nuclear power stations and off-shore platforms; he also gave the advice that resulted in the settlement of Venice beneath the waters being arrested. He has advised on a number of dock facilities. He is without doubt an outstandingly brilliant exponent of the complexities of soil mechanics and his work in that field has received international acclaim and recognition. He applies, however, both to himself and to others, the highest possible standards; and it can fairly be said that he is generous with his criticism. Few people connected with the case escaped it. For these reasons, and because his experience has given little contact with the ordinary day to day problems of designing structures in soil, I am able to place little if any reliance upon his evidence as to the standards to be expected of an ordinarily competent designer. On the other hand his analysis of the causes of the movement of the wall impressed me enormously, and I place very considerable reliance upon it."

Liability of professionals

The court will be influenced by the evidence of an expert witness who gives evidence in any dispute where the conduct of a professional is in issue. The evidence must however be that of the witness himself, as opposed to those instructing him. In *Whitehouse* v. *Jordan* [1981] 1 WLR 246 at p. 247 Lord Wilberforce warned:

> "While some degree of consultation between experts and legal advisers is entirely proper, it is necessary that expert evidence presented to the court should be, and should be seen to be, the independent product of the expert, uninfluenced as to form or content by the exigencies of litigation. To the extent that it is not, the evidence is likely to be not only incorrect, but self-defeating."

Thus, ultimately whilst an expert will invariably prepare a draft report which he will discuss with those instructing him, the report ultimately must reflect his own point of view and not of others.

Comments have been made by judges as to the responsibilities and expectations of experts. For example, Garland J in *University of Warwick* v. *Sir Robert McAlpine* (1988) 42 BLR 11 (QBD) made a number of positive statements as to what should be performed by an expert witness. In a similar context the decision of Mr Justice Cresswell J in *National Justice Compania Naviera SA* v. *Prudential Insurance Co. Ltd "Ikarian Reefer"* [1993] 3 CL 35, stated what he considered to be the duties and responsibilities of expert witnesses. It is important to note that expert witnesses themselves may be liable to their client should they fail to perform in accordance with the expected standard of care.

Where a professional has been involved with the designing and the manufacturing of a specific component the requirement upon him in the absence of any express term or implied term to the contrary is not to exercise the skill and care expected of the ordinary individual of his profession having those same skills but is a much more onerous requirement of warranting that the finished component works, i.e. that it is fit for its intended purpose. Lord Scarman in *Independent Broadcasting Authority* v. *EMI Electronics Ltd and BICC Construction Ltd* (1980) 14 BLR 1 summarised the situation as follows:

> "The extent of the obligation is, of course, to be determined as a matter of construction of the contract. But, in the absence of a clear, contractual indication to the contrary, I see no reason why one who is in the course of his business contracts to design, supply and erect a television aerial mast is not under an obligation to ensure that it is reasonably fit for the purpose for which he knows it is intended to be used."

In the Court of Appeal decision of *George Hawkins* v. *Chrysler (UK) Ltd and Burne Associates (a firm)* (1986) 38 BLR 36 (CA), the requirement of reasonable skill and care only affirmed as being the standard of care by which a professional would be judged when producing a design only. The court in Hawkins concluded that the earlier decision of the Court of

Appeal in *Greaves & Co. (Contractors) Ltd* v. *Baynham Meikle and Partners* [1975] 1 WLR 1095, in which a firm of consulting engineers responsible for the design only had been judged by the application of a test of fitness for purpose should not be considered as general authority for such a proposition and should be restricted to applying to its own facts.

A statutory modification to the requirement by a designer to exercise due care and skill only may be found in section 1(1) of the Defective Premises Act 1972. This imposes upon an architect, as indeed also a builder of a dwellinghouse, the duty to ensure that what is being produced is fit for habitation.

The legislature has obviously considered the policy value of ensuring that dwellinghouses should be fit for habitation. This legislation enacts in statutory form the earlier findings in *Hancock* v. *Brazier (B W) Anerley* [1966] 1 WLR 1317.

Difficulties can occur if a professional initially takes on a specific responsibility and then seeks to delegate it to others. It is important to recall that any party to a contract, and the professional can be no exception, cannot unilaterally seek to alter the terms of the contract, i.e. the terms of his engagement. If a professional seeks to engage specialist help then this can only be with his client's express consent. For instance in *Moresk Cleaners Ltd* v. *Hicks* [1966] 2 Lloyd's Rep 338, it was held that the defendant architect had no authority to delegate the function of design without the express agreement of his client. This issue has particular relevance when one is considering the liability of professionals involved in a construction project where a certain consultant may seek to provide a "package deal" for his client and then seek to delegate the tasks to other specialists. It is clear that he still remains liable for all of his own prime liabilities in the absence of his client's agreement to release him from such.

A cautionary tale was illustrated by the decision of His Honour Judge Newey QC in *Richard Roberts Holdings Ltd and Another* v. *Douglas Smith Stimpson Partnership and Others* (1988) 46 BLR 50 where the defendant firm of architects were found to be liable for negligence in the design of effluent tanks and they themselves genuinely did not believe that they were so liable. The court however found that the terms of their agreement with their clients was to act as architects for the creation of the Hinckley Dye Works which included the design of the tanks. If the architects had wished to limit their role they should have done so expressly and in writing. Had the architects felt that they could not form a reliable judgement about the linings to the effluent tanks then they should have informed their clients of this and advised them to take other advice, probably from a chemist. This decision illustrates the importance of identifying with certainty the terms of a professional's engagement.

It is unusual to condemn the performance by any professional without

Liability of professionals

suitably qualified experts being called upon to give evidence before a court. Thus, for example, it was stated by Slade LJ in *Investors in Industry Ltd* v. *South Bedfordshire District Council* [1986] 1 All ER at page 808, involving allegations of negligence by architects, that:

"Expert evidence from suitably qualified professional persons is, in our judgment, admissible to show what competent architects in the position of Hamiltons Associates could reasonably have been expected to know and do in their position at the relevant time. Indeed, in our judgment there could be no question of the court condemning them for professional negligence on account of their failure to appreciate points (3) and (4) and to take the suitable consequential action, unless there were appropriate expert evidence to support the allegation that their conduct fell below the standard which might be reasonably expected of an ordinarily competent architect ...".

Similar statements were made in the decision of *West Midlands Regional Health Authority* v. *Maynard* (1981).

In deciding whether or not a professional has exercised the requisite standard of reasonable skill and care that may have been expected of him, courts of law have increasingly referred to the professional rules which govern the conduct of the professions themselves. There has been a tendency to regulate the performance of its members by professional bodies who have argued that in codifying expected standards of performance their members are in turn assisted since they are able to observe exactly what is and what is not required of them in stated situations. The value of any such rules of conduct were appreciated by Mr Justice Oliver in *Midland Bank Trust Co. Ltd* v. *Hett Stubbs & Kemp (a firm)* [1979] Ch 384 when he stated:

"The extent of the legal duty in any given situation must, I think, be a question of law for the court. Clearly, if there is some practice in a particular profession, such accepted standard of conduct which is laid down by a professional institute or sanctioned by common usage, evidence of that can and ought to be received."

In *Harvest Trucking* v. *P B Davis* [1991] 2 Lloyd's Rep 638, Judge Diamond QC was able to make reference to the Association of British Insurers code of practice which became effective in 1989. The code which applies only to unregistered intermediaries made clear the intermediary's responsibility to bring to the attention of his client the existence of policy terms which were "unusual and onerous". Furthermore, in *PK Finans International (UK) Ltd* v. *Andrew Downes & Co. Ltd* [1992] 1 EGLR 172, allegations against a surveyor were considered to be unsustainable in view of the terms of guidance note 6 of the RICS "Guidance Notes of the Valuation of Assets". Whilst the judge made clear that these guidance notes were not to be regarded as having the force of statute and mere failure to comply with the guidance notes did not constitute negligence, the guidance notes were nonetheless to be considered as being powerful evidence of the conduct that may reasonably have been expected of the surveyor. Care should however be taken at all times to distinguish the standard of performance by the professional from the responsibility or the duty *per se*. This is a matter for the court to determine. This inference was clearly drawn by Mr Justice Oliver in *Midland Bank* v. *Hett Stubbs & Kemp (a firm)* [1979] Ch 384 (at 402e). The difficulties which the courts have to grasp as to extent of a professional's duty can be amply illustrated by the recent decision of the Court of Appeal in *White and Heath* v. *Jones and Philip Baker King and Co.* (*The Times*, 9 March 1993).

Nor is the reference to professional rules of conduct as an aid to the court to be perceived as an entirely English characteristic. In *Mirabito* v. *Liccardo* (Californian Court of Appeal, 1992) 92 Daily Journal DAR 2959, the California Appellate Court held it proper for a jury to consider the State Bar's rules of professional conduct on the issue of whether an attorney had breached his duty. It was argued that the Rules of Professional Conduct were not intended to impose civil liability but only for discipline; the court allowed the rules in evidence as bearing on the attorney's duty.

2 LIABILITY IN THE TORT OF NEGLIGENCE

The House of Lords delivered its judgment in *Caparo Industries plc* v. *Dickman and Others* on 8 February 1990. This decision cast doubt upon the single general principle of *Anns* v. *London Borough of Merton* [1978] AC 728 in which Lord Wilberforce put forward his test for liability in the tort of negligence, the requirements being foreseeability and any factor which sought to negative that. The decision nonetheless is of the greatest importance when considering liability in the tort of negligence alone. Following *Caparo*, the House of Lords in *Murphy* v. *Brentwood District Council* (1990) 50 BLR 1 has formally overruled *Anns*.

The facts of Caparo briefly were that the appellant accountants, Touche Ross, were auditors of Fidelity, a public company. The respondent Caparo made a successful bid for Fidelity in reliance, it alleged, on Fidelity's accounts. Caparo commenced proceedings against Touche Ross, amongst others, alleging negligence in certifying the accounts. Caparo alleged that Touche Ross owed a duty of care to investors and potential investors in respect of the audit. This question was tried as a preliminary issue assuming for this purpose the facts as set out in Caparo's Statement of Claim. The Court of Appeal by a majority had allowed Caparo's appeal against the decision of the trial judge holding that the auditors did owe a duty of care to individual shareholders who could therefore recover their loss in tort in acting in reliance of the accounts, but no duty to potential investors. Touche Ross appealed to the House of

Liability of professionals

Lords and Caparo cross-appealed against the rejection of its claim that they were owed a duty as potential investors. The House of Lords' findings were that Touche Ross's appeal was to be allowed and Caparo's cross-appeal was to be dismissed. The court's findings therefore were that the auditors did not owe a duty of care to individual shareholders and furthermore owed no duty to potential investors.

In his speech, Lord Bridge of Harwich drew strength from the decision in the High Court of Australia in the *Sutherland Shire Council* v. *Heyman* (1985) 60 ALR 143. In this decision Brennan J stated:

"The law should develop novel categories of negligence incrementally and by analogy with established categories, rather than by a massive extension of a prima facie duty of care restrained only by indefinable 'considerations which ought to . . . limit the duty'."

It was one thing to owe a duty of care to avoid causing injury to the person or property of others, it was quite another to avoid causing others to suffer purely economic loss. The spectre which the courts always had in their minds was the avoidance of quoting the classic words of Cardoso CJ in *Ultramares Corp* v. *Touche*, 174 NE 441 (1931):

"Liability in an indeterminate amount for an indeterminate time to an indeterminate class. This would confer on the world at large a quite unwarranted entitlement to appropriate for their own purposes the benefit of the expert knowledge or professional expertise attributed to the maker of the statement."

Lord Roskill in his judgment stated the dilemma in lucid terms. He relied upon *Hedley Byrne & Co. Ltd* v. *Heller & Partners* [1964] AC 465 in which it was stated that Denning LJ in *Candler* v. *Crane, Christmas & Co* [1951] 2 KB 164 stated the law correctly. It was clear that a duty of care could be owed by professional men to third parties where there was no contractual relationship between them. Subsequent attempts to define both the duty and its scope had created more problems than the decisions had solved. There was no simple formula or touchstone to provide in every case a ready answer to the questions whether, given certain facts, the law would or would not impose liability for negligence where in cases where such liability could be shown to exist, determine the extent of that liability. Phrases such as "foreseeability", "proximity", "neighbourhood", "just and reasonable", "fairness", "voluntary acceptance of risk" or "voluntary assumption of responsibility" were not precise definitions. At best they were but labels or phrases descriptive of their very different factual situations which had to be carefully examined in each case before it could be pragmatically determined whether a duty of care existed and, if so, what was the scope and extent of that duty.

Lord Oliver followed the same logic by stating that the extensions in the law of negligence since the decision in Hedley Byrne to cover pure economic loss not resulting from physical damage had given rise to a considerable and as yet unsolved difficulty of definition. The opportunities for the infliction of pecuniary loss for the imperfect performance of everyday tasks upon which people relied for regulating their affairs was illimitable and the effects were far reaching.

To search for any single formula as the general test of liability was to pursue a will-o'-the-wisp. Once one discarded, as one had to, foreseeability of harm as the single exclusive test—even a *prima facie* test—of the existence of a duty of care, the attempt to state some general principle served not to clarify the law but merely to bedevil its development. Thus, the essential requirements for establishing a duty of care in the tort of negligence are foreseeability, the relationship between the parties i.e. proximity and furthermore a requirement that it would be fair and reasonable in those particular circumstances to impose such a duty. The three matters overlapped with each other and as Lord Oliver pointed out (at p. 633) were in reality facets of the same thing.

The essential requirements for establishing liability for economic loss following *Hedley Byrne* was that a statement had to have been made with the knowledge of its maker and had been available to the recipient for the particular purpose upon which he had relied. The maker of the statement also must have actual knowledge or inferred knowledge that his advice so communicated was likely to be acted upon without any form of independent enquiry. Reliance upon any statement did not establish a duty of care of unlimited scope since regard has to be had to the transaction or transactions for the purpose of which the statement was made. It was a loss arising from such transaction or transactions rather than "any loss" to which the duty of care extended.

Lord Oliver in *Caparo* referred to the Privy Council decision of *Mutual Life & Citizens Assurance Co. Ltd* v. *Evatt* [1971] AC 793, from which a duty of care was confined to situations where advice was given in the course of a business or profession involving the giving of advice of the kind in question. Subsequent decisions, for example that of the High Court of Australia in *Shaddock and Associates Pty Ltd* v. *Parramatta City Council (No. 1)* (1981) 36 ALR 385, have not insisted upon this pre-condition of liability. However, in *Caparo* it was unnecessary to attempt a resolution of the difference of opinion resulting from the majority decision in *Mutual Life* and those dissenting decisions of Lords Reid and Morris since there was no question but of the certifying of the accounts done in the course of the ordinary business of the appellant accountants. On a general footing, liability of professionals in negligence will inevitably arise from advice given by them in their respective professional capacities.

Thus the impact of *Caparo* is that the liability in the tort of negligence will be extended by way of an incremental approach as opposed to any attempt to apply any specific definition as to whether or not any liability would exist. Thus no single formula can exist. Difficulties however may be posed by the adoption of the approach of Brennan J in the *Sutherland Shire*

Liability of professionals

Council v. *Heyman* (1985) 60 ALR 143. The incremental approach of Brennan J deals with the developing of novel categories of negligence by increments. No reference however is made of the manner in which the judges should decide whether or not there should be any retreat from allowing liability in those areas already established as giving rise to causes of action. No formula has been propounded for any such retreat. Judicial approaches to the tort of negligence have not always been consistent. Trends have been evolving during recent years and perhaps if the Sutherland Shire Council approach were to be extended and adopted universally existing areas of liability would become entrenched. Whatever the difficulties faced by the courts however in assessing whether or not duties are owed for pure economic loss, the principle that losses may be sustained for damages consequent upon either personal injury or damage to property remains unchallenged. This emphasis has recently been the subject of comment in *Nitrigin Éireann Teoranta* v. *Inco Alloys Ltd* (1991) 60 BLR 65 (QBD), a decision of May J.

Ultimately, allowing liability in the tort of negligence depends largely upon issues of public policy. The courts have already indicated that it is not the proper role for the tort of negligence to allow open-ended claims which would open up the flood gates to allow claims for economic loss. The difficulties of attempting to devise a precise formula were discussed in *Caparo*. Perhaps the most obvious illustration of allowing claims on the ground of policy may be seen from the decisions of *Smith* v. *Eric S Bush* and *Wyre Forest District Council* v. *Harris* [1989] 2 All ER 514. Consumer protection played its part in both of these decisions in the House of Lords which reinforced the right of a proposed purchaser to sue a surveyor on the grounds of a negligent survey or valuation undertaken by him on behalf of a building society, or in the case of *Wyre Forest*, a local authority where neither had a contract with the proposed purchasers notwithstanding that a fee was payable for the service by them. The law in this given situation has certainly developed to allow a remedy for the innocent purchaser and it is now a clearly established area of liability in the tort of negligence. The inference of *Caparo* must be, however, that the type of damage suffered, be it physical damage or purely economic loss is not the determining factor in resolving the issue of whether or not a duty of care exists. Whatever the damage sustained the court should approach the question in the same way.

Since the decision of the Court of Appeal in *Pacific Associates Inc and Another* v. *Baxter and Another* (1988) 44 BLR 33, an extensive area of potential liability for engineers, surveyors and architects in the tort of negligence no longer exists. This decision raised important issues as to the duty owed, if any, by an engineer appointed to supervise construction works to the contractor being the party responsible for the performance of these same works. This decision is of importance for professional firms engaged in construction work as architects, engineers or surveyors and for the companies which carry out such work or consent to know whether in a relationship as on the present facts between contractor, employer and engineer, the law imposed a duty of care upon the engineer to the contractor not to cause economic loss to the contractor in the process of certifying and of accepting or rejecting claims under the contract. The court stated that no duty of care was owed, but emphasised that each case would depend upon its own circumstances and upon the provisions of the relevant contract. However, it is likely that a large number of contracts are placed for construction or engineering works in which the contractual relationship of contractor and employer and the contractual duties of the engineer are substantially similar to this case. Accordingly, on the basis that this decision represents a clear statement by the Court of Appeal it should prove difficult for any contractor to allege that a duty of care is owed to him by an engineer or architect.

In *Pacific Associates* there was no request to the engineer by or on behalf of the contractor for the engineer to render any service of any kind to the contractor. Any relationship between the contractor and the engineer came into being as a consequence of the contractor entering into a contract with the employer and of the engineer having been engaged by agreement with the employer to perform the functions of the engineer under the contract. The engineer assumed that the obligation under his agreement with the employer was to act fairly and impartially in performing his functions. He was under a contractual duty to the employer to act with proper care and skill. Such risk as the engineer could reasonably foresee of the contractor suffering loss as a result of any want of care on the part of the engineer was remote. The contract provided for correction by arbitration of any error on the part of the engineer and it had not been suggested that there was any real scope for an error which would not be at once detected by the contractor.

The parties chose to structure their relationships so that there was no contract between the engineer and the contractor although there were contracts between the employer and the contractor and the employer and the engineer. The absence of any contract between the engineer and the contractor was not without significance. The test of proximity and foreseeability might be satisfied but it was not just and reasonable that there should be imposed such a duty upon the engineer. This Court of Appeal decision thus overrules the earlier decision at first instance of His Honour Judge Fox-Andrews QC in *Michael Salliss & Co. Ltd* v. *Calil* (1987) 13 CLR 68, in which the judge found that such a duty of care in not dissimilar circumstances existed.

In *Victoria University of Manchester* v. *Hugh Wilson and Lewis Womersley (a firm) and Pochin (Contractors) Ltd* (1984) 1 Const LJ 162, His Honour Judge Newey QC sought to discuss the duty on the part of the contractors to warn the employer of design defects in works which it was contracted to build which became aware. The judge confirmed that this duty arose by way of an implied term in the building contract and he also found that the duty arose in the tort of negligence. Toward the end of his judgment the judge turned his attention to the duty in the tort of negligence of architects employed by a building owner toward contractors and others. He said:

"Because of proximity an architect may sometimes owe a duty of care to contractors even in relation to how they carry out their work. If, for example, an architect knew that on a site with which they were concerned, contractors or sub-contractors were making a major mistake which would involve the contractors in expense, I think that the architect would probably owe a duty to the contractors to warn them."

He went on to say that in this case the architects had not discovered that bad work was being done so that they had no knowledge which they could communicate. This decision is fairly old when contrasted with recent judicial developments and it cannot be regularly reconciled with the decision of the Court of Appeal in *Pacific Associates*. The same logic would surely apply in this case which is that it is not for the courts to impose their own remedy where the parties had clearly defined their own parameters of legal responsibility and liability by entering into a contractual arrangement which excluded any direct contract between the contractor and the architect.

In commenting upon the effect of *Hedley Byrne*, Slade LJ giving the judgment of the Court of Appeal in *La Banque Financière* v. *Westgate Insurance Co. Ltd* [1988] 2 Lloyd's Rep 513 stated:

"While that case established that economic loss resulting from a negligent misrepresentation may be recovered in tort, there are two conditions for recoverability. The first is that the defendant should have assumed a voluntary responsibility towards the plaintiff in making the statement or representation. The second is that the plaintiff should have relied on it."

Similarly, in *Caparo* the court emphasised that in *Hedley Byrne* and the subsequent decisions of *Smith* v. *Eric S Bush and Harris* v. *Wyre Forest District Council* both reported at [1989] 2 WLR 790; [1989] 2 All ER 514 the emphasis was placed upon the defendant making a statement of fact or opinion, knowing that the advice or information would be communicated to him directly or indirectly and that he knew or reasonably should have known that the plaintiff would rely on that advice or information in deciding whether or not to embark upon a particular course of action. Thus, it could be summarised that it was an anticipation of reliance upon a statement made and communicated. Their Lordships in *Caparo* contrasted this situation with a statement which was put into general circulation and might foreseeably be relied upon by members of an "indeterminate class". This logic was at the root of the argument put forward by their Lordships in rejecting the plaintiff's claims in *Caparo*.

A number of decisions exist however where the negligence took place in the course of the performance of duties owed to a person other than the plaintiff and where no statement or representation express or implied was made by the defendant or acted upon by the plaintiff. Thus, this is not a situation which comes within *Hedley Byrne*. Thus, the plaintiff is a person foreseeably affected by the defendant's negligent performance of his duties owed to another. In the past, the courts have allowed such claims even where the claim is for purely economic loss and which is not consequent upon any physical damage or personal injury. Two notable examples may be found in *Ross v. Caunters* [1980] Ch 297 and *American Express Co. Ltd v. Hurley* [1985] 3 All ER 564. In *Ross v. Caunters* the court found a solicitor negligent where a will was prepared for a testator in which the plaintiff was a beneficiary. The solicitors sent the will to the testator for execution but failed to warn him that it should not be witnessed by the spouse of a beneficiary. They also failed to notice that when the will was returned to them, one of the attesting witnesses was the plaintiff's husband. Also, in *American Express*, a receiver was held to owe a duty of care to obtain the full market price for mortgaged property which he sold not only to the company (whose agent he was) and the mortgagee by whom he was appointed but also to the person who guaranteed the company's debt and therefore had been called upon to pay the balance due to the mortgagee. It may appear difficult on the one hand to reconcile these two decisions with the sentiments expressed by the Court of Appeal in *Pacific Associates*. The losses suffered in both *Ross v. Caunters* and *American Express* was economic or purely financial loss and these are claims which the courts have consistently since *Junior Books Ltd v. Veitchi Ltd* [1983] AC 520, set their face. However, if one adopts the incremental approach of *Caparo* it will be seen that the differences which on the one hand may appear irreconcilable may be reconciled. In some circumstances the same or similar factors may assume a different significance. Thus, for example in *Pacific Associates* the existence of the clearly defined contractual obligations of the parties and the ability on the part of the contractor to refer any issues to arbitration were clearly influential factors, and militated against the imposition of a duty. In *Ross v. Caunters* the fact that the plaintiff beneficiary could not have possibly pursued an action against any party other than the solicitor was a factor which influenced the imposition of a duty.

In *Ross v. Caunters*, counsel for the solicitors argued that the liability alleged against the defendants did not arise as a consequence of any negligent misstatement of fact or opinion and therefore fell outside the scope of *Hedley Byrne* which concerned itself with statements made only. Megarry J however did not think it essential when deciding this case to bring it within the *Hedley Byrne* formula. He stated (at p. 592):

Liability of professionals

"As to the ambit of *Hedley Byrne*, I can only say that I was unable to see what magic there was about law that would remove it from the sphere of *Hedley Byrne*, or, for that matter why all advice should be outside it. Counsel for the defendants was very patient with me when I attempted to ascertain why it was that *Hedley Byrne* was so circumscribed in its operation; but at the end of the day I was left without any cogent reason for this limitation, and without any authority. . . . In any event, on the view of the present case that I take, I do not think it matters much whether the scope of *Hedley Byrne* in this respect is narrow or wide; for, as I have indicated, my view is that the true basis of liability flows directly from *Donoghue* v. *Stevenson* and not via *Hedley Byrne*."

It will have been seen from *Caparo* that great significance was accorded to the decision of the High Court of Australia in *Shire of Sutherland* v. *Heyman*. The High Court of Australia in *Hawkins* v. *Clayton and Others* (1988) 78 ALR 69, had to consider the merits of a claim based on facts not dissimilar to *Ross* v. *Caunters*. The court by a majority of three to two in this instance allowed the appeal of the plaintiff who was both an executor and a beneficiary under a will against a firm of solicitors who had possession of a will. The respondent firm of solicitors were aware of the death of the testatrix and took some steps in the estate but they did not try to locate the plaintiff for some six years, by which time he alleged that he had incurred losses which included a fine on the late payment of estate duty, losses of rent of a property falling within the estate and also due to that same property falling into a state of disrepair which necessitated the performance of remedial works. The court concluded that the solicitors were in breach of their duty of care in the tort of negligence to the plaintiff in his capacity as executor. This decision would appear consistent with *Ross* v. *Caunters* but inconsistent with *Pacific Associates*.

In *Hawkins* it was emphasised that the only party to whom the solicitor owed a contractual responsibility was the estate which had not suffered a loss. Thus, there was no indeterminate class of potential litigants who could not claim for indeterminate amounts. Furthermore, one could foresee a situation whereby the "incremental approach" could operate given these unusual facts without espousing any significant increases in claims. The issue of whether or not a solicitor owed a duty of care in the tort of negligence to a beneficiary was decided in the affirmative by Judge Barnett QC in *Smith and Another* v. *Claremont Haynes & Co.* (*The Times*, 3 September 1991). The situation giving rise to a claim in this instance arose from a solicitor who had taken instructions from the testator as to the contents of an intended will. The will specified the plaintiffs as intended beneficiaries. However, the solicitor negligently failed to return promptly to take full instructions prior to the testator's death. It was held that the solicitor owed a duty of care to the plaintiffs.

This area of liability has more recently been the subject of the decision of the Court of Appeal in *White and Another* v. *Jones and Another* [1993] 3 All ER 481 (CA). The facts may be briefly summarised by stating that following a family row, a testator executed a will disinheriting his two daughters, the plaintiffs. Following a reconciliation he instructed the first defendant who was an employee of the defendant firm of solicitors to draft a new will directing payment of legacies of £9,000 to each of the plaintiffs who were privy to that arrangement. Instructions were given for the new will to be prepared in or about mid-July. Mr Jones did nothing to effect the will in accordance with the testator's instructions who died of a heart attack on 14 September. The courts stated that neither in *Caparo Industries* nor in *Murphy* v. *Brentwood District Council* [1991] AC 398 had the House of Lords expressly or implicitly doubted the correctness of *Ross* v. *Caunters* [1980] Ch 297. The position was simply that the House had left the matter open.

In relying upon the decision of *Caparo Industries Plc* v. *Dickman* the Court of Appeal in *White* recited the comments made which were that if there was to be a duty to take reasonable care to avoid causing damage of a particular type to a particular person or class of persons, three factors had to coalesce: foreseeability of damage, a close and direct relationship characterised by the law as "proximity" or "neighbourhood" and the situation had to be one where it was fair, just and reasonable that the law should impose the duty of the given scope upon the one party for the benefit of the other. The court concluded that it was inevitably foreseeable to a solicitor that if he failed to prepare a will as instructed by his client and arrange for it to be duly executed the disappointed beneficiaries would suffer financial loss. Furthermore, the court concluded that if there had been a failure by the solicitor on facts such as the present, justice required that there should be some remedy available. There was a good reason why the solicitor, the court stated, should be liable to a third party in this special situation since, otherwise, there was no sanction in respect of the solicitor's breach of his professional duty. Accordingly, the appeal was allowed and judgment awarded for each of the plaintiffs against the defendant for the sum of £9,000. It is understood that this decision may be the subject of an appeal to the House of Lords who in this event will take steps to finally dispose of the issue. In *White* v. *Jones* reference was made to the manner in which the Australian courts had determined a similar issue in *Hawkins* v. *Clayton*. In two separate decisions however being that of *Kirgan* v. *Parkes*, 478 A2d 713 (Md App 1984) and *Layman* v. *Layman*, 84 Md App 183, the Court of Special Appeals of Maryland rejected claims by aggrieved beneficiaries against attorneys due to their being deprived of the benefit which they would otherwise have hoped to have received under a will. In both cases, the court recited the standard and practice which had existed in Maryland and elsewhere in the USA for some years that an attorney's duty of diligence and care flowed only to his direct client or employer and that whether in an action of contract or tort only that client or employer could recover against him for breach of that duty. It would be difficult however to compromise the arguments based upon strict privity of contract with the decisions of *Smith* v. *Bush* and *Wyre Forest* v. *Harris* where the borrowers were considered to have a valid cause of action.

Recently Mr Justice Hirst in *Marc Rich & A G and Others* v. *Bishop Rock Marine Co. Ltd and Others (The Nicholas H)* [1992] 2 Lloyd's Rep 481, took the view that, upon the hearing of a preliminary issue, on the facts a marine surveyor employed by NKK, a classification society, owed a duty of care in the tort of negligence to the cargo owner with the consequence of authorising a vessel to proceed following the effecting of temporary repairs only. The vessel sailed, the temporary repairs failed and the vessel sank within a week of leaving port giving rise to loss on the part of the cargo owners. For the purposes of the preliminary issue, the defendants were prepared to admit those facts as pleaded in the points of claim which *inter alia* pleaded that the damage was physical damage. On this basis, the judge concluded that those facts did give rise to a cause of action in the tort of negligence. This matter, on appeal, was heard by the Court of Appeal who delivered a judgment on 3 February 1994 unanimously allowing the appeal ([1994] 1 Lloyd's Rep 492). The court emphasised that it was the shipowners and not the society who actually handled the cargo and were in a position to inflict damage upon it. There was no dealing whatsoever between the classification society and the cargo owners. It was not even suggested that they were aware that NKK had been brought in to survey the vessel, let alone that they relied on anything that the classification society did. It is interesting to note that in a not too dissimilar case being of the *Morning Watch* [1990] 1 Lloyd's Rep 547, Phillips J took the view that a Lloyd's surveyor did not owe a duty of care in the tort of negligence where a purchaser of a vessel relied upon a negligent classification of a vessel and thereby suffered economic loss. It is worthy to note furthermore that the individual employees themselves may owe a direct duty of care in the tort of negligence owed to the client notwithstanding that the client's contract is with the employer. In *Punjab National Bank* v. *DeBoinville and Others* [1992] 3 All ER 104, the Court of Appeal had to consider this issue. It took the view that the employees of a Lloyd's broking company did owe a duty of care in the tort of negligence toward their employer's client for whom they acted. The facts were that the employees had continued to act on behalf of the plaintiff when they moved from one Lloyd's broking company to another and thus the court concluded that the degree of proximity to the client was greater than that of the employer. Whilst the court concluded that it was not every employee of a firm or a company providing professional services who owed a personal duty of care to his client, the court took the view that in this instance the employees had been entrusted with the whole or nearly the whole of the task which they as employers undertook. The portion of the judgment relating to the personal liabilities of the employees does not depose to a great deal of detail. Thus, it is difficult to assess whether or not this decision will be perceived to relate to its own special facts or whether, in the alternative, it is to be considered of a more general application. It is difficult to see what benefit derives from finding additional and separate duties of care in the tort of negligence when the employer and the client have already defined the scope of their liabilities by means of a contract. There is scope for disrupting the contractual parameters of liability by alleging that the tortious liability owed by the employees is greater or lesser than the contractual liability. Furthermore, one sees potential difficulties if employers' insurers seek to exercise subrogation rights against individuals or employees when the relevant acts or omissions took place but have since moved away and are no longer employed.

Care should be taken against the adoption of the *Punjab Bank* decision as grounds for suggesting generally that employees of a professional firm or company owe independent duties of care in the tort of negligence to clients. The facts in *Punjab Bank* showed that the individuals concerned had a close relationship with the plaintiff so that they continued to be engaged by them notwithstanding the change of employer. If the ratio were to be applied generally, it may mean that employees of firms of professionals or limited companies which have been wound up would be faced by the spectre of having to insure themselves against "run-off" claims. The former employer would not have insurance cover for any period following an insolvency and thus any potential plaintiff would, leaving aside the remote possibility of a claim being made against former insurers pursuant to the Third Parties (Rights Against Insurers) Act 1930 have no other option other than to consider tortious remedies against the employees. Whilst such allegations may well be sufficient to overcome the foreseeability and proximity requirements it would be difficult to envisage courts of law finding that to allow such claims would satisfy the requirements of fairness and reasonableness. The difficulties caused by *DeBoinville* are clear nonetheless. If employees are not to be pursued independently claiming breaches of tortious liabilities, it will be necessary for the senior courts to emphasise that such remedies should exist only in exceptional circumstances. They failed to do this in *DeBoinville*. It is interesting to note that in any event no duties of care in the tort of negligence can be owed by professionals to directors of a client company. In *Verderame and Others* v. *Commercial Union Assurance Co. Plc and Another* (Times Law Reports, 2 April 1992), a decision of the Court of Appeal, Lord Justice Nourse was confronted with facts where insurance brokers acting as agents for a small private company in effecting insurance cover for it. He stated that it was accepted that there was a contract between the brokers and their client company and the company alone.

Liability of professionals

The proposition that the brokers also came under a duty of care to the directors was not only novel but startling. He added that if it were sustained, it would have wide-ranging consequences not only for insurance brokers but also for others providing services to such companies such as solicitors, accountants and so forth. He indicated that this would pierce the corporate veil on a vast scale and would lead to procedural impracticalities and rights, or potential rights of double recovery.

It is a highly dangerous pastime to make general predictions as to the future trend of tortious liability. It is also simplistic to refer to the general judicial trend in the tort of negligence during the past 10 years. There have been inconsistencies with the courts being prepared to allow liability in specific areas, e.g. building society valuations by surveyors but denying remedies in other instances.

However, the general trend following the high watermark in *Junior Books* following through to *Caparo* has been to limit the expansion of the tort of negligence.

Prior to *Hedley Byrne* the limits of tortious liability were only too clear; a claim for negligence would have to be based upon either physical injury or damage to property. The parameters of liability were fundamentally changed as a consequence of *Hedley Byrne* and the difficulties of devising a formula as a test of liability were graphically discussed in *Caparo*. Thus, it seems that certainty and clarity of defined limits cannot be reconciled with the stated aim and requirements for establishing a duty of care. Lawyers instinctively welcome and adopt tests in their quest for certainty and clarity albeit, as will be demonstrated by the preceding authorities, the impossibility of so doing.

Whilst it will have been noted that recent decisions have seen the ebbing of the tide of negligence, the decisions in the cases of *White* v. *Jones* and *Punjab National Bank* have shown that the waters have not yet altogether receded. The criticism of the incremental approach is that it leave established findings of liability in previous cases unchanged. Many of those decisions however were reached not by the adoption of incremental approaches but on Lord Wilberforce's two tier test in *Anns*.

3 CONTRIBUTORY NEGLIGENCE

Some professions cannot attract claims on behalf of the professional for contributory negligence whereas other professions are more susceptible. For example, it would be plainly impossible for a surgeon to claim that a patient had contributed to its own loss. In contrast, however, other professions are more susceptible. Insurance brokers in particular are more susceptible to allegations of contributory negligence due to the knowledge of the underwriters themselves on whose behalf the brokers may be appointed. It must be recalled that the existence of concurrent liability in the tort of negligence is a pre-requisite to being able to advance any claim based upon contributory negligence. Thus, it is no coincidence that the leading decision of *Forsikringsaktieselskapet Vesta* v. *Butcher* [1986] 2 All ER 488 is one where there was a finding by the court that the insurers were 75 per cent to blame for failing to answer enquiries of the brokers who had negligently failed to act on a request to contact reinsurers about an exclusion clause. It is important to draw the clear distinction between those brokers who act on behalf of underwriters who wish to lay off a portion of their risk by way of reinsurance as in the *Forsikring* case and brokers who merely act on behalf of a lay client when effecting insurance cover. The lay client will inevitably have little knowledge of the insurance market whereas an insurer obviously has. A broker acting on behalf of a large corporate client who has employees whose specific responsibilities are those of placing insurance will be in a similar situation to a solicitor instructed by a company's "in-house" legal department. It is submitted that a finding of contributory negligence could apply if the in-house personnel had actually been involved directly with the independent professional in either of the conducting of the legal work, or alternatively, of the placing of the insurance cover.

In *Youell* v. *Bland Welch (No. 2)* [1990] 2 Lloyd's Rep 431 the court had to consider whether or not the insurers should make a contribution on the grounds of contributory negligence. It had been held that the brokers were at fault in failing to inform the insurers of the existence of a 48th month clause under which the period of cover terminated in respect of any vessel 48 months after the commencement of its construction when inviting them to write to the original insurers and order reinsurance. Furthermore, having obtained the reinsurance which was subject to the cut-off, they were under a further duty to inform the insurers of what they had done clearly and unequivocally and furthermore, it was the duty of the brokers to obtain extensions of the reinsurance cover. Notwithstanding these breaches however, the insurers were unaware of the broker's breach of duty until after they had suffered the damage in respect of which they claimed. Their ignorance was due in part to their own negligence. The fact that the plaintiff's negligence occurred after the defendant's wrongful act was not a bar to apportionment under the 1945 Act. Extensions of the cover could have been obtained. The price at which the extensions would have been offered would have reflected the risk and bargaining position of the parties. The result of the insurer's negligence was that they failed to obviate the consequences of the broker's breach. Accordingly, the insurer's damages were reduced by 20 per cent, the brokers being liable for 80 per cent.

In *Sharp* v. *Sphere Drake Insurance Co. Ltd (The Moonacre)* [1992] 2 Lloyd's Rep 501, Mr Anthony Coleman QC sitting as a Deputy Judge of

Liability of professionals

the High Court had to deal with allegations of negligence against insurance brokers who had insured a large motor yacht. The judge found that the insurers were entitled to reject the plaintiff's claims for indemnity under the policy of insurance but the learned judge found for the plaintiff against the brokers who had been responsible for placing the risk by stating that they had failed to exercise the standard of care expected of them. The brokers in turn had raised contributory negligence as a defence but this was rejected by the court. The plaintiff had relied upon the broker's skill and judgement in answering the proposal form questions concerning the use of the yacht and was entitled to believe that the cover which he had sought was in place. No deduction could therefore be made. The broker had alleged that by failing to read the policy after it had been sent to him he had, through his own contributory negligence, not become aware of the restriction on cover where the vessel was being used as a houseboat. Thus it will be seen that it is a matter of the utmost importance to consider the degree of knowledge possessed by a client and the extent to which a broker has expressly passed the burden back to the client. Thus, one can properly contrast a lay person as in *The Moonacre* with that of the reinsured as in *Youell* v. *Bland Welch*.

In *Pryke* v. *Gibbs Hartley Cooper Ltd* [1991] 1 Lloyd's Rep 602, brokers alleged that the leading underwriter at Lloyd's had been contributorily negligent. This was due to his having been given an initial explanation which suggested that a policy issued was not a financial guarantee and was led to believe by the brokers that investigations in the USA supported that explanation. The underwriter had not been shown a copy of the offending policy which the brokers had nor was the underwriter shown a telex from the cover holder which showed that the brokers had a copy of the policy. Buller J held that the underwriter had not been negligent but indicated that had he seen the documents the position would have been different.

A further category of cases where findings of contributory negligence are a distinct possibility are those involving surveyors and valuers who are instructed by funding institutions. Surveyors and valuers, in particular, have been faced with increasing claims alleging negligence as a consequence of the significant reduction in property values experienced in the late 1980s. In *P K Finans* v. *Andrew Downes* [1992] 1 EGLR 172, Sir Michael Ogden QC sitting as a deputy High Court Judge, refused to find the valuer negligent. A defendant valuer had received a precis of a planning consent relating to a property the subject of a valuation by him. Appreciating that it was but a precis, the valuer reported to its client, a bank, that he had undertaken verbal planning enquiries but had made no official searches by way of verification. The bank subsequently alleged that it was negligent of the valuer either not to refer to the need for a verification and thus, give positive advice to this effect or alternatively, not to verify himself. The court was unwilling to find the valuer negligent, deciding that he had done all that could be expected of a reasonable and competent valuer. However, the judge indicated that had the valuer been negligent damages would have been reduced by 80 per cent on the basis that the bank had contributed significantly to its own loss by not referring the planning consent to its own solicitors for verification. Thus, it may be that the task of verifying the planning consent was considered to be one more suitable to solicitors than surveyors.

However, in the unreported case of *H I T Finance* v. *Lewis & Tucker*, a decision in March 1992 of Wright J, allegations that a secondary lender had been contributorily negligent was rejected by the court. The court concluded that lending, especially by a secondary lender as in this case, was a high risk area but, nonetheless, the client was entitled to rely upon the advice given to it by the valuer. If there were to be any finding of contributory negligence then this could only be on the basis that it could be demonstrated that the lender had not acted as a reasonably prudent lender in the same market at the time. Neither solicitors nor counsel were competent to perform this task and such questions had to be referred to expert banking evidence.

4   CONCURRENT LIABILITIES IN CONTRACT AND TORT

It has been questioned whether or not concurrent liability should exist both in contract and in the tort of negligence. Furthermore, it is clear that in those circumstances where claims in contract and in the tort of negligence exist, concurrently, the nature and extent of the duty of care in the tort of negligence is affected by the terms of the contract. It is submitted that it is not always easy to reconcile the numerous decisions relating to this area of law. It has to be considered that one of the principal reasons why the law has evolved to provide for concurrent causes of action in tort as well as in contract is that it may provide a remedy for a would be claimant in such circumstances where for various reasons a contractual remedy is denied.

It is important to recall that until recently it was considered that the relationship between the professional and his client gave rise to duties and liabilities in contract alone and that no concurrent duty of care in the tort of negligence existed. For instance, in *Bagot* v. *Stevens Scanlon* [1966] 1 QB 197, Diplock LJ (sitting at first instance) held that an architect who had carelessly carried out his supervisory duties under a contract with his professional client could be sued by him in contract alone. A further example of such a finding may be seen in the decision of *Clarke* v. *Kirby Smith* [1964] Ch 506. In this instance a solicitor was found to owe a contractual duty only to his client and not a duty of care in the tort of negligence as well.

Whilst it would appear that these two decisions were at variance with the earlier decisions of *Bowman* v. *Brown* (1884) 11 Cl & Fin and *Nocton* v. *Lord Ashburton* [1914] AC 932, the decisions were overruled some 12 years later by the Court of Appeal in *Esso Petroleum Co. Ltd* v. *Mardon* [1976] QB 801. Lord Denning MR delivering the main judgment compared the duty owed by the professional man, i.e. the duty to exercise all reasonable skill and care with the duty owed by a master to his servant or vice versa. He stated as follows:

"A professional man may give advice under a contract for reward; or without a contract in pursuance of a voluntary assumption of responsibility gratuitously without reward. In either case he is under one and the same duty to use reasonable care: see *Cassidy* v. *Ministry of Health* [1951] 2 KB 343. In the one case it is by reason of a duty imposed by law. For a breach of that duty, he is liable in damages: and those damages should be, and are, the same whether he is sued in contract or in tort."

This decision was subsequently followed by a decision at first instance of Oliver J in *Midland Bank Ltd* v. *Hett Stubbs & Kemp Partners* [1979] Ch 384 in which *Bagot* was specifically rejected. So long as the plaintiff can satisfy the test of being able to establish the existence of a duty of care in the tort of negligence then he should not be deprived of this remedy if he has a contractual remedy as well arising from the same facts.

Thus it may have been that these contentious issues had been finally resolved, but the arguments were raised afresh as a consequence of those observations of Lord Scarman in *Tai Hing Cotton Mill Ltd* v. *Liu Chong Hing Bank Ltd* [1986] 1 AC 80 where Lord Scarman observed (at p. 107):

"Their Lordships do not believe that there is anything to the advantage of the Law's development in searching for a liability in tort where the parties are in a contractual relationship. This is particularly so in the commercial relationship. Though it is possible as a matter of legal semantics to conduct an analysis of the rights and duties inherent in some contractual relationships including that of banker and customer either as a matter of contract law when the question will be what, if any, terms are to be implied or as a matter of tort law when the task will be to identify a duty arising from the proximity and character of the relationship between the parties, their Lordships believe it to be correct in principle and necessary for the avoidance of confusion in the law to adhere to the contractual analysis: on principle because it is a relationship which the parties have, subject to a few exceptions, the right to determine their obligations to each other, and for the avoidance of confusion because different consequences do follow according to whether liability arises from contract or tort, e.g. in the limitation of actions."

He then continued by stating:

"Their Lordships do not, therefore, embark on an investigation as to whether in the relationship of banker and customer it is possible to identify tort as well as contract as a source of the obligations owed by the one to the other. Their Lordships do not, however, accept that the parties mutual obligations in tort can be any greater than those to be found expressly or by necessary implication in their contract."

This passage was cited with approval in the judgment of the Court of Appeal delivered by Lord Justice Slade in *Banque Keyser Ullmann en Suisse SA* v. *Skandia (UK) Insurance Co. Ltd* [1988] 2 Lloyd's Rep 513 at page 563 who added:

"Lord Scarman's opinion contains a valuable warning as to the consequences of an ever expanding field of tort. It should be no part of the general function of the law of tort to fill in contractual gaps."

The facts in *Tai Hing* related to a forgery of a number of cheques and whether or not the bank was entitled to debit that customer's account for the total value of the forged cheques. The facts in *Tai Hing* do not concern allegations of negligence against a professional but the findings are directly referable nonetheless.

This passage may be construed in the first instance as giving rise to the inference that it is not in the interests of the development of the law to look for a tortious remedy where a contractual remedy already exists and thus one should ignore tortious aspects altogether. However, it should be seen that a close examination of the passage reveals that his Lordship is stating that there can be no purpose in looking for a tortious remedy where the parties have already clearly defined the scope of their respective duties and liabilities by entering into their contract. Accordingly, any tortious duty of care, if it exists, will have been defined by the scope of those contractual rights and liabilities which the relevant parties have agreed. Thus the contract between the parties is seen as being the issue which is of primary importance whereas the duty of care in the tort of negligence is at best relegated to a position of secondary importance. It is submitted that Lord Scarman cannot have been suggesting that no concurrent liability in tort can exist where the parties have agreed upon the scope of their contractual duties since such a concept would have resulted in a dramatic reduction of the effect of the Latent Damage Act 1986 to which he himself made a substantial contribution through his Chairmanship of the Law Reform Committee whose 24th Report on Latent Damage was published in November 1984. Furthermore, if Lord Scarman had intended to blow away completely any trace of the concept of concurrent liability both in contract and in the tort of negligence, then we may have expected a more detailed discussion of the existing case law and reasoning for this decision.

Tai Hing reflects the hallmark of a well considered statement of policy to which due regard must be paid. In deciding to regard the contractual relationship between the parties as being of primary importance and accordingly defining the extent of the duty of care in the tort of negligence, the court has had regard to the element of certainty. This is an important consideration. The parties know or should know the extent of their relative rights and liabilities and therefore it should not be too difficult to ascertain their true extent. In addition, the court is making clear that parties cannot seek to recover damages in tort where this remedy is denied them in contract. Thus the effect of this decision must be that courts should exercise some restraint in considering the effect of a breach of a duty of care where there is a contract between the parties which states the parties' respective rights and liabilities.

In *Youell and Others* v. *Bland Welch & Co. Ltd and Others (The "Superhulls cover" case) (No.2)* [1990] 2 Lloyd's Rep 431 at page 459, Phillips J referred to the earlier decisions of *Tai Hing* and *Skandia* by stating that they may well mark the start of a reaction by the English courts against the finding of parallel duties of care in contract and in tort. However, he confessed that it was not as yet open to a court of first instance to disregard the principle of concurrent liabilities which Lord Justice O'Connor in *Vesta* v. *Butcher* had considered to be "clearly established".

One can thus appreciate the logic that the respective rights and liabilities in the tort of negligence follow from those primary rights and liabilities in contract agreed between the parties. If a specialist professional is engaged by the client it has already been seen (see *Duchess of Argyll* v. *Beuselinck* [1972] 2 Lloyd's Rep 172) that the standard of care to be required of such a specialist would be higher than of the ordinary practitioner. In such circumstances, the standard of care to be expected and the tort of negligence would have to be increased since otherwise a novel situation would exist where the professional may in breach of contract on the basis of failing to observe more onerous requirements and yet not in breach of his duty of care in the tort of negligence. This situation could not be allowed to exist.

In instances of concurrent liability, it is interesting to ask whether or not in instances where a duty of care coexists side by side with contractual duties whether the extent of the duty of care is coextensive with those rights under the contract. The notable example must that of economic or purely financial loss. As *Caparo* demonstrates economic loss claims in the tort of negligence are frequently rejected. Thus for example in *Simaan General Contracting Co.* v. *Pilkington Glass Ltd* [1988] 2 WLR 761 and *Muirhead* v. *Industrial Tank Specialities Ltd* [1986] QB 507 which related to claims for economic loss in tort where there was no direct contractual relationship between the parties, and furthermore where no such relationship had ever existed the courts have had little difficulty in rejecting such claims for economic loss. However, the courts are yet to consider a situation where, for example, a contractual relationship had existed and thus, by implication, the parties had agreed that damages for economic or purely financial loss should be recoverable but is no longer capable of giving rise to a cause of action due to it being time-barred through limitation. This situation could raise complex issues for any court to consider. This situation could arise where, for example, an architect had failed to supervise building work which was defective and which had not been detected for a number of years or had negligently specified a type of material to be used in the structure which had proved to be unsuitable. Given these facts the architect and his client have entered into a contract and have defined the scope of their respective rights and liabilities and thus a client could, subject to commencing an action within the limitation period, include any claim for economic loss as a portion of his claim for damages, but if the contractual cause of action is time-barred and the tortious cause of action only remains, can these damages nevertheless be claimed? If *Simaan* and *Muirhead* were applied, the answer would be no. However, such a decision could not so easily be justified on the grounds of policy where the parties have defined the extent of their contractual relationship and therefore have accordingly defined the scope of the duty of care.

If it is accepted that claims for breach of contractual duties and duties of care in the tort of negligence are capable of existing concurrently, one may well question the significance of the existence of any tortious claim if it is governed by the primary contractual relationship between the parties and thus cannot confer any greater benefit/liability than that which the parties have contractually agreed. The importance of the existence of a concurrent duty of care is clear in the following four instances:

(1) The most obvious of these must be where the contractual cause of action has become time-barred. The primary period of limitation for breach of contract is usually six years and occasionally 12 years as from the date of the breach or breaches of contract complained of. In the tort of negligence, the primary period of limitation is again six years but this period does not start to run until the damage occurs. Whilst the courts have experienced initial difficulty in defining what is meant by damage, examples may be seen by the decision of *Forster* v. *Outred* [1982] 1 WLR 86 which may be contrasted with *Pirelli* v. *Oscar Faber and Partners* [1983] 2 AC 1. In most instances, the limitation periods for causes of action in the tort of negligence will expire later than those limitation periods for the contractual causes of action even though they may arise from the same facts. Thus, for example, in *London Congregational Union Incorporated* v. *Harriss and Harriss* (1987) 35 BLR 58, it was conceded that the cause of action against the architects in contract had expired whilst it remained to be argued whether the cause of action in the tort of negligence remained. The prospect of the continuation of causes of action in the tort of negligence following the expiration of contractual causes of action has been enhanced by the implimentation of the Latent Damage Act 1986.

(2) the existence of a concurrent duty of care is of importance when

Liability of professionals

deciding issues of contributory negligence. It has already been seen that the contractual relationship is responsible for limiting the scope of a duty of care. Conversely, by reference to contributory negligence, the existence of a duty of care can limit or reduce the potential contractual liabilities of the parties. In *Forsikringsaktielselskapet Vesta* v. *Butcher & Others* [1988] 2 All ER 43, the Court of Appeal considered the power to apportion blame under the Law Reform (Contributory Negligence) Act 1945. Even though this dispute went to the House of Lords on appeal from the Court of Appeal, the appeal did not relate to the Court of Appeal's findings on contributory negligence. The court identified three categories of cases when the question could be asked in each of the categories as to whether or not the 1945 Act applied. They were:

(a) where the defendant's liability arose from some contractual provision which did not depend upon negligence on the part of the defendant;

(b) where the defendant's liability arose from a contractual obligation which is expressed in terms of taking care (or its equivalent) but does not correspond to a common law duty to take care which would exist in the given case independently of contract;

(c) where the defendant's liability in contract is the same as his liability in the tort of negligence independently of the existence of any contract.

The court held that facts giving rise to claims falling within the third category only could give rise to a finding of any contributory negligence under the 1945 Act. The principal judgment of the Court of Appeal was delivered by O'Connor LJ who respectfully disagreed with the comments of Neil LJ in the earlier decision of *A B Marintrans* v. *Comet Shipping* [1985] 1 WLR 1270. He considered that he had to consider in detail the wording of the 1945 Act. Section 1 of the Act provides:

"1. Where any person suffers damage as a result partly of his own fault and partly of the fault of any other person or persons, a claim in respect of that damage shall not be defeated by reason of the default of the person suffering the damage, but the damages recoverable in respect thereof shall be reduced to such extent as the court thinks fit and equitable having regard to the claimant's share in the responsibility for the damage . . ."

By section 4:

"4. . . . fault means negligence, breach of statutory duty or any other act or omission which gives rise to a liability in tort or would, apart from this Act give rise to the defence of contributory negligence."

In his judgment, O'Connor LJ indicated that he was of the view that concurrent liability in contract as well as in tort existed. He stated as follows:

"... this is but a recognition of what I regard as a clearly established principle that where under the general law a person owes a duty to another to exercise reasonable care and skill in some activity, a breach of that duty gives rise to claims in tort notwithstanding the fact that the activity is the subject matter of a contract between them. In such a case the breach of duty will be a breach of contract. The classic example of this situation is the relationship between doctor and patient."

The crucial portion of this statement which needs to be analysed is his Lordship's reference to "general law". He proceeds to argue that there is power to apportion in contractual cases but only in the third category as cited above where liability in contract is the same as in tort independent of the existence of any contract. Therefore, one should assume that he is, by specifying the term "general law" making reference to a contractual duty to exercise all reasonable skill and care which arises irrespective of the existence of any express contractual provision to this effect. However, it is surprising that His Lordship did not consider proceeding further by holding that the Act could apply to the first and second category as well. His approach reveals a contrast and distinction from the views of Lord Scarman in *Tai Hing*. If the views of Lord Scarman were to be applied to these facts, the finding would surely have been that duties of care in the tort of negligence exist in the first and second category as well, albeit that the scope of that duty of care is governed and limited and is secondary to the scope of the contractual duty itself. However, even upon the basis of the reasoning of O'Connor LJ, the necessity for the existence of the duty of care in the tort of negligence may be clearly seen.

(3) The Law Reform (Married Women and Tortfeasors) Act 1935 provided a party with a right to claim a contribution from another tortfeasor but it did not provide a right of contribution between a tortfeasor and contract breaker or between two contract breakers. This situation was changed by the Civil Liability (Contribution) Act 1978 which repealed the 1935 Act. However, the 1978 Act preserves the position which prevailed before then. Thus, in order to obtain a right of contribution from a person in breach of contract where the contractual duty was assumed prior to 1st January 1979, it would be necessary to establish a concurrent duty of care in the tort of negligence which would allow the contribution proceedings to be made in the tort of negligence giving rise to a remedy under the 1935 Act. The effect and significance of the 1935 Act is diminishing given the passage of time which has elapsed since the 1978 Act.

(4) The English courts unlike their counterparts in the USA award exemplary damages in exceptional cases only. Reference can be made to *Rookes* v. *Barnard* [1964] AC 1129 and to *A B* v. *South West Water Services* [1993] 1 All ER 609 (CA). However, whilst there are instances when the courts will allow exemplary damages to tortious liability they will not where damages are claimed for breach of contract.

5   RECENT DEVELOPMENTS

The political mood prevalent throughout the 1980s has seen great emphasis placed upon de-regulation and the abolition of monopolies. It has been thought that the consumer derives a benefit from increased competition. Solicitors have lost their conveyancing monopoly; the city has experienced fundamental change. The bar's exclusive rights of audience in the High Court and the Crown Court has now come to an end with rights of audience having been granted to solicitor advocates. Thus, whereas 10 years ago, there may have been a greater degree of rigidity with each profession jealously guarding its own vested interest, this is no longer strictly true and there is greater competition between the professions for work with substantial overlap of expertise.

This competition can clearly be seen in the field of financial services where solicitors, building societies, banks, insurance brokers and accountants may all be competing in the same market. Similarly, surveyors and chartered accountants have been accorded the right of direct access to the bar, whereas formerly, in order to canvass counsel's views they had to proceed via an instructing solicitor. This evolutionary change in the work practice of the professions may well cause legal difficulties in due course. Where the number of the professions was finite, each having their own areas of expertise, it was easier to ascertain the standard of care to be expected from the ordinary skilled practitioner. For example, at present there are authorities as to the standard of skill that may be expected from a solicitor engaged in conveyancing, but no authority as to the standards that may be expected of a licensed conveyancer. Is there a difference in the standard of care to be expected and if so what should this be? The difficulties posed are two-fold. First, it is a question of ascertaining, with a degree of certainty, whether or not a duty or responsibility exists. Guidelines, if any, published by the professional bodies or institutions can help with this question but they cannot be considered conclusive. Secondly, it would be necessary to show whether or not the requisite standard of skill and care has been taken by the professional and this is a question which can only be resolved following the consideration of expert evidence.

It will be a number of years before the courts are able to catch up with the changing trend and provide some guidance by way of legal precedent. This has to be seen to be highly desirable.

A professional may often be required or requested by his client to advise in areas outside his normal area of expertise, for example, an insurance broker may be asked to advise as to a specific point of law. Whilst an insurance broker may be expected to have a basic knowledge of insurance law and an understanding of the meaning of various standard clauses to be found in insurance contracts, he is not customarily qualified or required to advise as to detailed legal issues. Therefore, he should justifiably decline the temptation to proffer such legal advice and indeed, his own policy of professional indemnity may preclude him acting and advising other than in the capacity of an insurance broker. If he strays outside this normal area of expertise and gives such legal advice nonetheless, then if he does not take reasonable care and if he does not take such reasonable steps and precaution in expressing that opinion, he may be held liable to his client. He could be found liable for failing to exercise the required standard of skill and care to be reasonably expected from one holding himself and proffering such legal advice, i.e., a lawyer.

A similar example may be found if an architect or surveyor is asked by his client to advise as to a point of law which may arise in a building contract to be entered into between the client and a building contractor. Thus, the extension of services to a client will not be without its inherent risk.

The courts have traditionally accorded some professions immunity from suit. Thus, for example, judges themselves cannot be sued by any disaffected litigant claiming a failure to exercise all reasonable skill and care on the part of the judge. The courts have always taken the view that any decision reached is the correct decision unless overturned on appeal and has refused to entertain, on the grounds of public policy, the notion of liability on the part of judges to litigants. To do so would surely undermine the authority of the court and could give rise to endless litigation with judges being sued and tried by their peers by disaffected litigants.

Similarly, barristers may not be sued on the basis of any failure to exercise due skill and care in the conduct of advocacy, though they can be sued for any defective advice given on the same basis as a solicitor may be sued—see *Saif Ali* v. *Sydney Mitchell & Co* [1980] AC 198. If barristers could be sued then this would place a responsibility upon them to exhaustively pursue all of the issues arising in a dispute. Advocacy calls for an instinctive grasp of the issues and knowing as to the best means of presenting a client's case given all of the circumstances prevailing at that time. It therefore cannot readily be assessed by means of expert evidence as to whether or not the barrister has failed to exercise all reasonable skill and care. To allow judges and barrister advocates such immunity from suit is a principle that has not been seriously challenged. This belief however would not appear to have deterred The Law Society from insisting that all solicitors who work only as advocates and thus do not perform any advisory work should nonetheless contribute to the Solicitors Indemnity Fund. They state that they had received opinion that in certain circumstances a solicitor advocate could be negligent. They however did not define what would be those circumstances.

Mr Simon Tuckey QC sitting as a Deputy High Court Judge reached the same view in *Palmer and Another* v. *Durnford Ford (a firm) and Another*

Liability of professionals

(*The Times*, 11 November 1991). It was acknowledged as being well settled that witnesses in either civil or criminal proceedings enjoyed immunity from any form of civil action in respect of evidence given during those proceedings. The reason for that immunity was so that witnesses might give their evidence fearlessly and to avoid a multiplicity of actions in which the value or truth of their evidence would be tried over again. However, this should not prevent an expert from being liable for failure to give careful advice to his client. The production or approval of a report for the purposes of disclosure to the other side would be immune; but work done for the principal purpose of advising the client would not. Similarly, a number of decisions in the USA has confirmed the actionability of claims against expert witnesses. For example, in *Murphy* v. *Mathews*, 841 SW 2d 671 (decision of November 1992) the Missouri Supreme Court allowed a suit against an expert witness, an engineering firm, which it had engaged in order to support its claim which it maintained had been prepared and presented negligently. It was claimed that there was no adequate documentation to support the claim of over £4 million and that, as a result of the negligence, the party engaging the expert had incurred damages of a sum in excess of $3.7 million. Furthermore, a Californian court in the decision of *Mattco Forge* v. *Arthur Young & Co.*, 6 Cal RPTR 2d 781, a decision of 1992 allowed a company to sue an accountancy firm for negligent preparation of data. See also the New Jersey case of *Levine* v. *Wiss & Co.*, 478 A 2d 397 (1984) and *James* v. *Brown*, 637 SW 2d 914 (1982) where a Texas court allowed an action to lie against an expert psychiatric witness.

Many professionals accept instructions to act as arbitrators, their authority being derived from the consent of the parties who have agreed that in the event of a dispute this should be referred to an arbitrator who should have the authority to make an award which is binding upon the parties. This course of action is adopted in preference to the alternative of pursuing an action through the courts.

The fees of an arbitrator are payable by the parties, usually on a joint and several basis, with the arbitrator ultimately deciding where the burden of costs should fall. Even though the arbitrator is performing a role not dissimilar to that of a judge, the difference is that he is paid for his expertise. He is thus but a paid professional engaged by the parties.

It is not clear whether or not an arbitrator may be sued if he fails to exercise reasonable skill and care. In *North Eastern Co-Operative Society Ltd* v. *Newcastle Upon Tyne City Council and Another* [1987] 1 EGLR 142, a decision involving the appointment of a surveyor to arbitrate in a dispute, the court expressly refused to comment whether or not the surveyor was immune from action for negligence in his capacity as an arbitrator. In *Arenson* v. *Arenson* [1977] AC 405 a majority of the House of Lords was prepared to assume that arbitral immunity existed but the point was not one on which a decision was directly called for. Until the issue is finally resolved, practising arbitrators would be well advised to retain professional indemnity cover with their insurers. This is especially so if it is borne in mind that an arbitrator may be personally liable for the cost of any proceedings to set aside or remit his award.

The category of professional activities in which the courts will grant immunity is limited. Obviously, the courts must take the view that they should not deprive a potential litigant from a remedy without there being good and valid reason. The obvious implication is that any professional may be pursued by his client, or possibly by a third party claiming a remedy in tort if it is alleged that there has been a failure to exercise the requisite standard of skill and care.

Recent trends appear to indicate that the volume of claims against professionals alleging negligence increases in times of recession. For example, the late 1980s has seen a surge of claims against surveyors alleging overvaluation of properties. This has led to them being liable not only to their clients, i.e. the fund, in contract but also, to the borrower in the tort of negligence. Similarly, on the basis that a high percentage of claims involving solicitors arise from either conveyancing or company and commercial business, they have also suffered as also have accountants. More recently it has been a time for the insurance industry itself to have faced the effect of direct claims. The action against the *R H M Outhwaite Underwriting Agency and Others* for allegedly failing to exercise reasonable skill and care in underwriting insurance risks giving rise to potential huge liabilities for asbestosis claims on the part of the members has been the subject of a well publicised settlement. The settlement was reached in March 1992 and a payment was made to the names' solicitors in the sum of £116 million. Subrogation issues arising as a consequence of the settlement were the subject of the decision of the Court of Appeal in *Lords Napier and Ettrick* v. *N F Kershaw Ltd* [1993] 1 Lloyd's Rep 197R. The settlement may be regarded by those working at Lloyd's as being an unwelcome new development since otherwise, relations existed on the basis of trust together with the willingness on the part of members to take the good years with the bad. It is likely that it is the sheer scale of the loss with which the members were faced which prompted such an action. The settlement of the disputes avoids any discussion by the court as to whether or not underwriters were immune from any suit against them by the members of the syndicates.

With the mounting losses within the insurance market, underwriters are adopting a very firm and rigid position when confronted by claims. In this climate, brokers need to be more vigilant and ensure that they have at all times advised their client properly. If a client's claim is rejected by an insurer, quite often, they will allege that the reason for such rejection, if valid, is a failure on the part of the broker. An example of this may be seen

Liability of professionals

from the recent decision in *Sharp* v. *Sphere Drake Insurance Co. Ltd (The Moonacre)* [1992] 2 Lloyd's Rep 501.

Neither has the corporation of Lloyd's itself been unable to avoid litigation. In *Ashmore and Others* v. *Corporation of Lloyd's* [1992] 2 Lloyd's Rep 620, Mr Justice Gatehouse sitting in the Commercial Court found that the Corporation of Lloyd's was under no duty either to take steps to alert names about matters of which Lloyd's became aware which might seriously affect their interests or to impose a premium income monitoring system. Additionally, Lloyd's had immunity from suit under section 14 of the Lloyd's Act 1982 from 23 July 1982 when it came into force. The claim was brought for breach of contract and/or breach of statutory duty by Patricia Ashmore and 32 other Lloyd's names who had lost more than £5 million. The claim was based on an implied contractual duty of care and also a statutory duty arising out of section 10 of the Lloyd's Act 1871 as amended by section 4 of the Lloyd's Act 1911. It was argued that there were three bases on which a term could be implied into a contract. The first two "implications in fact" depended on the presumed joint intention of the parties and arose either under the doctrine of *The Moorcock* (1889) 14 PD 64, that is the business efficacy test, or the officious by-stander test based on *Shirlaw* v. *Southern Foundries* [1939] 2 KB 206 at page 227. The third basis on which a term could be applied as was argued, was an "implication in law" and did not depend on the presumed joint interests of the parties but on a principle derived, as the plaintiffs said, from *Liverpool City Council* v. *Irwin* [1977] AC 239. The plaintiffs contended for two specific duties. They were, to take reasonable steps to alert the names about matters of which Lloyd's became aware which might seriously affect their interests and also to impose a premium income monitoring system even if it was only an ad hoc system of monthly monitoring of the syndicates. The plaintiffs failed to comply with any of those three tests and in any event, had it done so, the court held that Lloyd's was immune from action under section 14 of the Lloyd's Act 1982. In *Wood* v. *The Law Society (The Times*, 28 July 1993) the High Court held in reserved judgment that The Law Society did not owe a duty of care to complainants at common law or under statute when exercising its investigative or disciplinary powers in respect of its members. The court commented, *inter alia*, that the plaintiff was a member of an unascertained class which included those clients complaining about their solicitors. It was impossible to identify or ascertain within the class those sections or particular persons who could be afforded a duty of care and those who would be denied. The duties owed by The Law Society were not to safeguard the plaintiff against loss but rather to sanction conduct unbecoming a solicitor. The Law Society, furthermore, had no power to control the day to day activities of solicitors who by their activities caused loss. The dictates of good sense and consideration of what was fair and reasonable pointed clearly against the imposition of any duty of care.

Whilst it must be doubted as to whether or not a professional body may be held responsible for any shortcomings of its individual members by in some way failing to regulate their activities, these decisions must give rise to a greater awareness on the part of professional bodies and institutions that they must to a significant extent regulate their members' activities themselves failing which, some parliamentary intervention will be inevitable.

A further consequence of the recession has been, sadly, an increase in instances of fraud and embezzlement of client's money by professionals. The Solicitors Compensation Fund for example has seen an increase in the amount of its claims. The Solicitors Disciplinary Tribunal reporting on 13 July 1993 ordered that Graham Maurice Durnford Ford should be struck off the Roll of Solicitors. He was the founding partner of a firm of solicitors having offices in London and the South East of England which had had a staff of 152. Due to very many unlawful appropriations of the monies of clients which had not been repaid, it was stated that the Law Society's Compensation Fund was exposed to claims totalling between £5 million and £6 million. As at the date of the hearing, that is, 4 May 1993, £3.6 million had been paid out of the Compensation Fund.

6 LATENT DAMAGE

In *Iron Trades Mutual Insurance Co. Ltd* v. *Buckenham Ltd* [1989] 2 Lloyd's Rep 85, the judge at first instance reviewed the line of authorities relating to the accrual of causes of action in contract and in tort. The law as for limitation of action in contract is that the claim becomes statute barred within six years from the date of the breach of contract or 12 years if the contract is under seal. In tort, an action must be commenced within six years from the date when the cause of action accrues. This is defined as being the date when damage occurs. If the action relates to personal injury, the action must be commenced within three years of the date when the cause of action accrued or the date of knowledge (if later) of the person injured. The three year time limit is set out in Section 11 of the Limitation Act 1980. this time limit applies irrespective of whether the cause of action results from a breach of a duty of care in the tort of negligence or a breach of contract.

Tortious liability is distinguished from damages for breach of contract on the basis that there may be a breach of the duty of care but this is not actionable until there is actual damage. In property cases this has been interpreted to mean the date of the occurrence of physical damage which will not necessarily be the date of the discovery of the damage or when a reasonable person would have discovered the damage.

The decision of *Pirelli General Cable Works Ltd* v. *Oscar Faber & Partners* [1983] 2 AC 1 is an obvious example of this. In *Pirelli* the cause of action accrued on the date that the damage occurred, being cracks in a chimney. It is often difficult to pinpoint the date when the damage occurred. The burden falls upon the plaintiff at first instance to show that his action is not statute-barred. This issue was discussed by Ralph Gibson LJ in *London Congregational Union Incorporated* v. *Harriss and Harriss* (1987) 35 BLR 58 (CA) at page 83. Furthermore, in the decision of *London Borough of Bromley* v. *Rush and Tompkins and Others* [1985] 1 CLJ 374, Sir William Stabb QC considered that any damage had to be relevant or significant to give rise to a cause of action. On the facts in this case he decided that the cause of action accrued when hairline cracks to the exterior of the building first occurred. This needs to be contrasted with the authorities and line of argument based upon liability for negligent advice as represented by the decision of *Forster* v. *Outred* [1982] 1 WLR 86, where the court found that the damage occurred when the negligent advice was given and was relied upon.

The facts in *Buckenham* related to advice given by an insurance broker and the finding was that the cause of action accrued in the tort of negligence when the advice was given and relied upon by the client, thus following the *Forster* v. *Outred* precedent.

Thus it will be seen that where professionals are involved in any form of design process, the cause of action in the tort of negligence will inevitably accrue at a later date on the basis that it will take some time before the damage becomes manifest and until this time, no cause of action in the tort of negligence will exist. Thus, in damage cases, the cause of action in negligence may still exist some time after the cause of action for a breach of contract has long since expired. In instances involving advice, the cause of action in the tort of negligence will inevitably accrue at the same time as the cause of action in the breach of contract, being the date when the advice was tendered and subsequently relied upon.

The iniquities which can arise in instances of latent damage following advice, negligently given, may be seen by reference to the Court of Appeal decision of *Bell* v. *Peter Brown & Co.* (a decision delivered in April 1990 but as yet unreported). The facts related to the plaintiff consulting the defendant firm of solicitors following the breakdown of his marriage. One of the prime issues was to decide what was to happen to the matrimonial home. The house was registered in the joint names of the plaintiff and his wife Sandra. The house was alleged to be worth about £12,000 and was subject to a mortgage of about £8,000. Therefore, had the house been sold at this time the plaintiff would have received about £2,000, that is about one sixth of the gross proceeds. Mr Bell was agreeable to the house not being sold for the time being, but he was to receive one sixth of whatever might be the gross proceeds when the sale did take place. Subsequently the house was transferred into his wife's sole name, but no steps were taken by the defendants to protect his one sixth share in the proceeds of sale. In December 1986 the plaintiff learned from his former wife that she had sold the property in July 1986 for £33,000, that is almost eight years after the property had been transferred into her sole name. She had spent all the proceeds and so Mr Bell had lost his one sixth interest. The court reluctantly concluded that the plaintiff's claim in tort was statute barred as was also his claim against his former solicitors for breach of contract.

The unfairness resulting from the operation of the rules relating to latent defects has long since been known to exist. The need for reform was indeed acknowledged by Lord Scarman in giving his judgment in *Pirelli*. As a consequence of the conclusions contained in the Law Reform Committee's 24th Report (Latent Damage) in November 1984, the Latent Damage Act became law and came into force on 19 September 1986. The work of the Law Reform Committee had begun prior to the *Pirelli* decision, but the decision gave added significance and impetus to its work. The main provisions of the Act are as follows:

(a) There should be no change in the general rule of substantive law whereby a cause of action in negligence accrues at the date when the resulting damage occurs:

(b) In negligence cases involving latent defects, the existing six year period of limitation should be subject to an extension which would allow a plaintiff three years from the date of the discovery, or reasonable discoverability of significant damage;

(c) There should be a longstop applicable to all negligence cases involving latent defects which would bar a plaintiff from initiating court action more than 15 years from the defendant's breach of duty (irrespective of whether damage has occurred);

(d) The longstop should not apply to cases of latent damage involving fraud, deliberate concealment or mistake;

(e) It is important to note that this Act applies in instances of negligence only and does not apply to breaches of contract. The Act cannot apply to any action commenced prior to 19 September 1986 and it also is clearly specified as not being applicable to any cause of action which is time-barred as at 19 September 1986. Thus one has to look at the law already existing prior to 19 September 1986 to see whether or not the new Act can apply.

In *The Eras Eil Actions* [1992] 2 All ER 82, the Court of Appeal affirmed the view taken in the earlier decision of *Iron Trades Mutual Insurance Co. Ltd* v. *Buckenham Ltd* [1989] 2 Lloyd's Rep 85 confirming that the Latent Damage Act 1986 had no application to contract actions. Whilst the Act has not been without its critics, it will serve to reduce the unfairness and iniquity which would otherwise arise.

The decision of *Horbury* v. *Craig Hall & Rutley* [1991] EGCS 81 was the first reported decision involving the application of the Latent Damage Act 1986. Thus, it serves to provide a useful example of its application in practice. The court concluded that the Act applied on the basis that the cause of action was not time-barred at the date when the act came into force being 18 September 1986. However, the court concluded that the plaintiff who had brought a claim against the defendant surveyors should have considered the damage to the property sufficiently serious to justify instituting proceedings in 1984 when the plaintiff had to actually expend a sum of £132 to render chimneys safe. On the basis that the writ was not issued until February 1988 and therefore the action had to be considered time-barred.

A further more recent example of the application of the Latent Damage Act 1986 is *Campbell* v. *Meacocks* ((1993) CILL 886).

7 DAMAGES

The cases show the practical application by the courts of assessing damages for the negligence of the individual professions. This is to be seen within the context of the principle in the assessment of damages as enunciated by Lord Blackburn in *Livingstone* v. *Rawyards Coal Company* (1880) 5 App Cas 15, when he referred to damages within the context of compensation and placing the innocent party in the same position so far as was possible as he would have been if he had not sustained the wrong. Exemplary damages have never been considered as a remedy for breach of contract but have been considered in the context of a tortious remedy as a means of punishment. The Lord Chancellor Lord Mackay of Clashfern announced on 11 June 1991 that a review would be undertaken by the Law Commission which would deal with the principles of assessing damages in personal injury actions but the Law Commission was also given the mandate to assess and report on the wider issue of the principles relating to damages in civil proceedings, including whether or not it would be desirable to introduce into the English legal system the concept of awarding damages on a punitive basis. The Law Commission published its consultation paper in September 1993. Submissions are now being taken as to its contents. The Final Report is to be published in 1995. Exemplary damages may be currently awarded when the requirements as set out by the House of Lords in *Rookes* v. *Barnard* [1964] AC 1129 are met. The requirements are:

(1) the normal measure of damages would be considered inadequate. This arises where the application of the usual principles based upon the compensation of the injured party would still leave the party who had committed the wrong with a benefit which he should be entitled to retain;

(2) there has been oppressive arbitrary or unconstitutional action by the servants of government.

Thus, one will readily appreciate that the scope for awarding exemplary damages is limited.

In the English legal system there has not been hitherto the ability to award damages on a punitive basis on the basis as, for example, in the United States where there have been some four hundred verdicts during the past 25 years where punitive damages have been awarded. Whereas the origins of the American practice of punitive damages may be found in the eighteenth century English legal practices, the position today is markedly different in the two jurisdictions.

The outcome of the Law Commission's review will be awaited with interest. Consumer groups in the United States argue in favour of punitive damages invoking arguments based upon the remedies for product liability. Furthermore, they argue that the existence of punitive damages affects the standard of conduct of professionals including medical practitioners. Whether the reality would be that punitive damages if introduced into the English legal system would not punish the guilty party only but also those innocent parties who would be compelled to pay high insurance premiums for their policy cover. Thus, through the machinery of insurance the punitive effect would be largely dissipated. Thus, the principle would be largely obscured.

CHAPTER 2

INSURANCE IMPLICATIONS

1 WHAT IS A CLAIM?

It is usual and customary for professional bodies to insist upon their members holding approved professional indemnity cover up to a certain financial limit. There are obvious sound policy reasons for this insistence which may be perceived as being a part of the self-regulatory role which the professional body exercises on its members behalf. Policy wordings which cover professional indemnity risks are underwritten on a "claims made" basis. Thus the insured is covered for any claims which are made within any policy period. In this event, cover will apply irrespective of the dates of the commission of the negligent act or acts which may have given rise to the loss. A "claims made" policy wording is an obvious contrast to policies written on an "events occurring" basis where it is the occurrence of the event itself and not the claim which is the determining factor as to which policy period the claim relates.

The significance of underwriting policies on a "claims made" basis may be seen given the necessity for policies "run-off" cover where a professional either retires from practice or alternatively moves to a new position. The term "run off" is used to describe specific insurance against future claims albeit relating to previous events. The necessity for such cover is all the more necessary given the rules relating to joint and several liability of partners.

Problems can and often do result from any change of insurer. The difficulty is due to inability to determine the effective date of the claim which will thus decide which insurer is liable to indemnify the insured. Inevitably the second insurer will require full disclosure of all material circumstances prior to assuming the risk and may seek to exclude them from cover. Thus, it is possible that the insured will be faced with the prospect of being an uninsured litigant in the event of claims being made albeit relating to earlier events the existence of which had been disclosed and which had been the subject of specific exclusion by the second insurer. Given this market practice it will clearly be appreciated that it is not in the insured's best interest to change insurer unless considered absolutely necessary and even in this event care must be taken to ensure if at all possible, that there are no excluded risks.

A decision which illustrates the inherent dangers of changing insurers is that of *Thorman and Others* v. *New Hampshire Insurance Company (UK) Limited and Another* (1987) 39 BLR 45 (CA). This was a decision of the Court of Appeal given on 8 October 1987 which was stated by Sir John Donaldson MR as being concerned:

"with the problems which can arise when professional men, in this case a firm of architects, transfer their professional negligence insurance cover from one set of underwriters to another".

Transfer occurred at midnight on 30 September/1 October 1983 and was from the New Hampshire Insurance Company, the first defendant, to Home Insurance, the second defendant. The plaintiff was a firm of architects of which various allegations of negligence had been made relating to a housing development at premises known as Rose Duryard in Exeter. Whilst liability had been denied the decision was concerned with ascertaining which of the insurers, if any, were liable to indemnify the plaintiff, i.e., the insured against the risks the subject of the allegations. The two insurers stated that the other of them was liable and in addition the Home Insurance advanced a secondary contention based upon the grounds of material non-disclosure. The action brought by the building owners against the plaintiff architects was begun by a generally endorsed writ issued on 3 June 1982 but not served until 30 December 1983. Since then the building owners' claims had been particularised in a Scott Schedule which showed that they fell into two main categories, although there may be some overlap. These categories were (a) brickwork and (b) other matters, and in particular, roofing. Both companies provided what is known as "scheme" insurances, namely, insurance and terms approved by the RIBA and designed specifically for members of the architects' profession. Thus in the main the terms in both the Home and the New Hampshire Policies were identical, save that the Home policy contained additional terms under the heading of "Special Provisions".

"SPECIAL PROVISIONS
1. INNOCENT MISREPRESENTATION AND NON-DISCLOSURE:
The Company will not exercise its right to avoid this Policy where it is alleged that there has been non-disclosure or misrepresentation of facts or untrue statements in the proposal form, provided always that the Insured shall establish to the Company's satisfaction that such alleged non-disclosure, misrepresentation or untrue statement, was innocent and free of any fraudulent conduct or intent to deceive.

. . .

ALL OTHER TERMS, EXCEPTIONS AND CONDITIONS OF THIS POLICY REMAIN UNALTERED.

EXCEPTIONS
This Policy does not indemnify the Insured against liability:
...
7. Arising out of any circumstance disclosed in the proposal for this insurance as likely to result in a claim against the Insured."

The material terms common to both policies were as follows:
"SECTION 1 – PROFESSIONAL LIABILITY
The Company will indemnify the Insured against Loss arising from any claim or claims for breach of duty in the professional capacity stated in the Schedule which is made against them during the period set forth in the Schedule by reason of any neglect omission or error whenever or wherever the same was or may have been committed or alleged to have been committed by the Insured or any person now or heretofore employed by the Insured or hereafter to be employed by the Insured during the subsistence of this Policy.

CONDITIONS
4. The Insured shall as a condition precedent to their right to be indemnified under Sections 1 and 2 of this Policy give to the Company immediate notice in writing:
    (a) of any claim made against them
    (b) of the receipt of notice from any person of an intention to make a claim against them.
7. It is hereby agreed by the Insured that in the event of the Company being at any time entitled to void this Policy ab initio by reason of any inaccurate or misleading information given by the Insured to the Company in the proposal form the Company may at their election instead of voiding this Policy ab initio give notice in writing to the Insured that they regard this Policy as of full force and effect save that there shall be excluded from the indemnity afforded hereunder any claim which has arisen or which may arise and which is related to circumstances which ought to have been disclosed in the proposal form but which were not disclosed to the Company. This Policy shall then continue in full force and effect but shall be deemed to exclude as if the same had been specifically endorsed ab initio the particular claim or possible claim referred to in the said notice.
8. If during the currency of this Policy the Insured shall become aware of any occurrence which may be likely to give rise to a claim falling within Section 1 or 2 and shall during the period of this insurance give written notice to the Company of such occurrence any claim which may subsequently be made against the Insured arising out of the occurrence of which notification has been given shall be deemed to be a claim arising during the period of this Policy whenever such claim may actually be made.
12. There shall be no liability hereunder in respect of any claim for which the Insured are entitled to indemnity under any other policy."

It will seen by reference to Section 1 that the cover is stated to be on a "claims made" basis and not on an "events occurring" basis. This is subject to two qualifications the first is made in Condition 4 and makes a condition precedent to liability under the policy that not only shall the insured give immediate written notice of any such claim but that he shall also give such notice of any "receipt of notice from any person of an intention to make a claim against them". The second qualification is contained in Condition 8. Section 1 does not apply to claims made at a

Insurance implications

later time, of which advance notice has been given to the insured under the period of the policy and passed on to underwriters pursuant to Condition 4(b). In the absence of some further provision this would create a situation in which the architects were bound to inform underwriters of claims which were likely to be made during the currency of future policies but underwriters would, on the issue of those future policies, be able to exclude liability for those claims. This would be an impossible situation hence the need for Condition 8. Thus, the effect is to back-date any claim made to the date when the insured gave notice to underwriters of any "occurrence" which may be likely to give rise to a claim falling within Section 1. Thus, the effective date for the claim would be earlier than that date on which the claim will have actually been made. The Court of Appeal took the view that a generally endorsed Writ constituted a claim covering all matters subsequently particularised in the Statement of Claim and in the Scott Schedule. In its view the issue of the Writ as distinct from its service, constituted an "occurrence which may be likely to give rise to a claim falling within Section 1" within the meaning of Condition 8 the architects having informed underwriters of that occurrence any claim against them arising out of that occurrence would be deemed to have been made during the period of the policy. Thus, the Court concluded that the whole of the burden fell upon *New Hampshire*. It is emphasised by the Court that it was not possible to set out any clear binding definitions as to what would and what would not constitute a single claim. To the contrary Stocker LJ stated at page 60 when he concluded:

"It seems to me, therefore, that the question of whether there is one claim or a series of separate claims depends upon the facts of the case and the contexts in which the question falls to be decided. Furthermore, useful guidelines were given by the Master of the Rolls albeit the emphasis has to be on the circumstances of each particular case".

The guidelines (at p. 51) are set out below:

"Let me take some examples. An architect has separate contracts with separate building owners. The architect makes the same negligent mistake in relation to each. The claims have a factor in common, namely the same negligent mistake, and to this extent are related, but clearly they are separate claims. Bringing the claims a little closer together, let us suppose that the architect has a single contract in relation to two separate houses to be built on quite separate sites in different parts of the country. If one claim is in respect of a failure to specify windows of the requisite quality and the other is in respect of failure to supervise the laying of the foundations, I think that once again the claims would be separate. But it would be otherwise if the complaint was the same in relation to both houses. Then take the present example of a single contract for professional services in relation to a number of houses in a single development. A single complaint that they suffered from a wide range of unrelated defects and a demand for compensation would, I think, be regarded as a single claim. But if the defects manifested themselves seriatim and each gave rise to a separate complaint, what then? They might be regarded as separate claims. Alternatively, later complaints could be regarded as enlargements of the original claims that the architect had been professionally negligent in his execution of his contract. It would, I think, very much depend upon the facts."

This decision is of value since it clearly illustrates the distinction between a "claim" and any "circumstances" which may give rise to a claim.

Some policies of insurance seek to avoid the difficulty by including a definition of the term "claim" in the policy itself.

On the basis of the Court's finding that the *New Hampshire* was responsible, the allegations raised by the Home Insurance relating to material non-disclosure did not have to be the subject of lengthy debate. In *Normid Housing Association Limited* v. *Ralphs & Mansell & Others* (1990) 21 Con LR 98 there was an issue between the insurers and their insured who were architects as to the limit of the insurer's liability. The policy cover was limited to "£250,000 any one claim". The claims made against the Defendant architects amounted to some £5.7 million. The insurers sought to argue that there was effectively but one claim and thus the limit of any liability was to £250,000. The reported decision shows that this issue between the architects and their insurers had to be the subject of reference to an arbitrator for his decision. It would appear that similar difficulties of construction have bedevilled other jurisdictions as well. See for example the decision of the Manitoba Court of Appeal in *Reid Crowther & Partners Limited* v. *Simcoe & Erie General Insurance Co* (1991) 77 DLR (4th) 243.

2 MATERIAL NON-DISCLOSURE AND POLICY COMPLIANCE

All contracts of insurance are based upon the principle of the utmost good faith and if the utmost good faith is not observed by either party the contract may be avoided by the other. This is the broad general principle which is epitomised in the well-known passage from Lord Mansfield's Judgment in *Carter* v. *Boehm* (1776) 3 Burr 1905:

"Good faith forbids either party, by concealing what he privately knows, to draw the other into a bargain from his ignorance of that fact, and from his believing the contrary . . ."

Whilst the principle of the utmost good faith is more usually directed toward the insured since he is the party who could otherwise conceal facts within his own knowledge of which the other party is ignorant, it is quite clear that the principle extends to both parties. The conclusion of the Court of Appeal in *CTI* v. *Oceanus Mutual Underwriting Association (Bermuda)* [1984] 1 Lloyd's Rep 476 was that (see p. 492) the actual insurer was entitled to the disclosure to him of every fact which would

Insurance implications

influence the judgment of a prudent insurer in fixing the premium or determining whether he will take the risk. This test has since been the subject of much criticism since it ignores the issue of whether or not the insurer would actually have been influenced by such a fact. Furthermore, it places the emphasis upon the insured and his agent, his broker, to give exhaustive disclosure much of which may be irrelevant merely in order to avoid any argument that there has been a failure to disclose all material risks. This test would appear to have been the subject of some change as a consequence of the decision of the Court of Appeal in *Pan Atlantic Insurance Company Limited & Another* v. *Pine Top Insurance Company Limited* [1993] 1 Lloyd's Rep 496. In this decision Lord Justice Steyn indicated that his understanding of *CTI* v. *Oceanus* was to ask whether the prudent insurer would view the undisclosed material as probably tending to increase the risk. That did not mean that it was necessary to prove that the underwriter would have taken a different decision about the acceptance of the risk. Whilst the Pan Atlantic decision gives a change of emphasis and interpretation of the *CTI* decision the fundamental error remains which is that the actual underwriter is regarded as a legal irrelevance. There may be any number of sound commercial decisions why the underwriter could not afford not to underwrite a particular line of business. Alternatively, he would not wish to jeopardise any relationship with a particular firm of brokers. These considerations which may be motivating factors for the actual underwriter may be lost when one considers that the notional prudent underwriter. Pan Atlantic has recently been the subject of appeal to the House of Lords whose decision is eagerly awaited.

In any event the onerous requirements of disclosure have been reduced by the convention that an underwriter was waiving his right to rely upon any materiality if no questions on such issues were disclosed in a proposal form completed by the insured. This was the effect of the decision of the Court of Appeal in *Roberts* v. *Plaisted* [1989] 2 Lloyd's Rep 341. The decision related to insurance cover for an hotel in North Wales. The insurers alleged following a fire that there should have been disclosure by the insured as to the operation of a discotheque at the hotel. Whilst the Court of Appeal concluded that the activity of running a discotheque was a material fact which should have been disclosed by presenting the proposal form the insurers waived any right which they might have had to repudiate on the basis that the insured had failed to disclose that he was operating a discotheque at the hotel. The Court's view was that if it was considered to be material at the time when the existing proposal form was being prepared it seemed that it did not rate as an exceptional risk so as to be included in a supplemental condition. It was clearly waived by the questions proposed in the proposal form which did not touch upon any use as discotheque.

Forms which are for standard use by specific professions inevitably adopt a benevolent wording toward the professional when considering issues of material non-disclosure. For example, the Royal Institution of Chartered Surveyors Professional Indemnity Collective Policy has as its special Condition 1(a):

"Insurers will not exercise their right to avoid this policy where there has been non-disclosure or misrepresentation of facts or untrue statements in the proposal form, provided always that the Insured shall establish to Insurers' satisfaction that such non-disclosure, misrepresentation or untrue statement was free of any fraudulent intent."

Similarly the policy published by RIBA Insurance Agency Limited (reference APIA-RIBA/87) has as its special RIBA Conditions 1.

"Insurers will not exercise their right to avoid the Policy nor will Insurers reject a request for indemnity when it is alleged that there has been:
    (a) Non-disclosure of facts; or
    (b) Misrepresentation of facts; or
    (c) Incorrect particulars or statements; or
    (d) Late notification of a claim; or
    (e) Late notification of intention to make a claim; or
    (f) Late notification of a circumstance or event.
Provided always that the Assured shall establish to Insurers satisfaction that such alleged non-disclosure, misrepresentation or incorrect particulars or statements or late notification was innocent and free of any fraudulent conduct or intent to deceive."

Of other professions, solicitors have to insure losses up to £1 million for each and every claim through the Solicitors' Indemnity Fund on the basis of its own policy wording. Chartered Accountants are also bound to insure against their liabilities by reference to the standard policy wording endorsed by its own professional body. Insurance brokers however are not so constrained and may insure against their professional liabilities on the basis of any policy wording.

Insurers underwriting these policies will no doubt consider the effects of such generous wording when calculating premiums. However, they at all material times will need to be aware of those risks which they adopt which they would otherwise be entitled to avoid were it not for such wording reliant upon common law rules.

In any event, where professionals are not insuring on the basis of standard wording as imposed by the professional body they will obviously need to be made aware of their onerous disclosure responsibilities. Professionals need to be especially aware of the less benevolent attitude of a number of insurers who have faced declining premium income whilst being beset with an ever increasing quantity of liability by way of claims. Furthermore, whilst policies of insurance prepared with the assistance of professional bodies may favour the professional this will not obviate entirely the risk of non-compliance with the policy conditions as is demonstrated by the recent decision in *Summers* v. *Congreve Horner & Co. (a firm) and Independent Insurance Co. Ltd* [1992] 40 EG 144.

This decision related to an exclusion clause being exclusion 11 of the Collective Professional Indemnity Policy issued by the Royal Institution of Chartered Surveyors. The exclusion provided:

"The Policy shall not indemnify the Assured against any claim or loss arising from survey/inspection and/or valuation report of real property unless such survey/inspection and/or valuation shall have been made:

  (a) by [a person holding prescribed professional qualifications] or
  (b) by anyone who has not less than 5 years experience of such work or such other person nominated by the Assured to execute such work subject always to supervision of such work by a person qualified in accordance with (a) above."*

The issues before the Court dealt with the interpretation of this clause and whether or not there had been sufficient supervision where surveyors had nominated an employee who had just under 3½ years of practical experience and had carried out the inspection of the property on his own. The draft report prepared by the employee was submitted to his principal, who was a qualified person and who considered it and discussed it in detail with him. He also approved the final report but did not visit the premises surveyed at any material time. The Court of Appeal reversing the judgment of Judge James Fox-Andrews QC at first instance considered that the degree of control exercised by the principal was sufficient to justify a finding of supervision albeit that the principal had not attended the site with the employee. Thus, the surveyors in this instance somewhat fortunately were able to seek indemnity under their policy of insurance. However, this must serve as a salutary lesson and warning.

3 RIGHTS OF THIRD PARTIES TO BENEFITS UNDER INSURANCE POLICIES

Any third party will be anxious to discover whether or not a professional has the benefit of insurance and if so what the limits of such insurance cover is. It is indeed a matter of some debate as to whether or not the existence of insurance cover which, in many instances, is mandatory, merely fuels the fires of litigation. Many employers especially those who engage professionals involved in the construction industry insist upon there being full disclosure of their professional indemnity cover as a condition of appointment. Local authorities in particular have a tendency to insist upon this. If a claim is made against a professional then the claimant knows inevitably, his battle is with the insurer of the professional

* It is important to note that this wording relates to the previous edition of the Collective Policy and not the current edition included as an Appendix. The current edition has been used since 1 August 1993.

who will be indemnifying the insured albeit subject to the terms of the policy. It must be appreciated by third parties that the issue of insurance is one which is personal to the insured and the third party cannot in some way assume some beneficial interest in the proceeds of the insurance nor can it seek to interfere in the relationship between insurer and insured.

The Third Parties (Rights against Insurers) Act 1930 is unlikely to provide a claimant with a remedy against the insurer unless liability may be established either by a judgment of a court or an arbitrator's award or by an agreement between the insured and the third party. In addition thereto it is necessary for the insured to be an insolvent person. The purpose of the Act being designed to remedy the injustice where a creditor had no right to the proceeds as such of any third party insurance effected by an insolvent person when the insurance moneys became payable to meet the claim. Thus the Act confers a right to claim against the proceeds of the insurance policy and it is important to note that the creditor does not rank pari passu among all the unsecured creditors but may claim all the proceeds himself. In *Nigel Upchurch Associates* v. *The Aldridge Estates Investment Company Limited* [1993] 1 Lloyd's Rep 535, a counterclaiming defendant sought an Order against a Plaintiff firm of architects and the supervisor of his scheme of voluntary arrangement pursuant to Section 2 of the Third Parties (Rights against Insurers) Act 1930. The Defendant was most anxious to know whether or not the Plaintiff had appropriate insurance cover and what the limits of this cover were. However the request for information was refused on the ground that the request was premature since liability of the Plaintiff to the Defendant was not yet established. Whereas Counsel for the Defendant urged that commercial common sense required early information as to insurance cover to be given so that time and money were not wasted on what could turn out to be a fruitless effort, Miss Barbara Dohman QC sitting as an Official Referee was clearly of the view that the Act was not designed to deal with such mischief. To the contrary, it was designed to remedy the injustice that the creditor had no right to the proceeds thus, the application was dismissed.

A similar situation had arisen in the earlier case of *Normid Housing Association Limited* v. *Ralphs & Mansell Limited* (1990) 21 Con LR 98. It is surprising that no mention was made in the *Nigel Upchurch* decision to the earlier decision in *Normid Housing.* The issue which came before the Court of Appeal in *Normid Housing* was whether or not the client of a firm of architects had any rights to interfere with the proposed settlement of a claim by the architects against their professional indemnity insurers, having regard to the provisions of the Third Parties (Rights Against Insurers) Act 1930. The client of the architects commenced an action in the High Court against them claiming some £5.7 million. The insurers for the defendant architects made them an offer of £250,000 in settlement of

Insurance implications

the claims which the insurers considered as representing the limit of their liability to indemnify. The defendant architects were minded to accept this offer. The application was made for an injunction restraining the defendants from entering into the proposed settlement. However it was emphasised by the Court of Appeal that at present the plaintiff had no rights under the 1930 Act since the Act only applied in the event of the insured becoming insolvent. This had not taken place. Furthermore there was no liability which had been established which would have allowed the Act to operate. It was emphasised by the court that the issue of insurance was a matter entirely for the judgment of the professionals. Slade LJ in giving judgment also indicated:

"Likewise, however in our judgment, after they had in their discretion effected such policies, that duty placed them under no contractual obligation to the Plaintiffs to deal with the policies in any particular way. The policies were their own assets and they were as free to deal with their rights under them as with any others of their assets. They owed no professional duty of skill and care to the Plaintiffs to deal or not to deal with them in any particular way. Any such dealing would be right outside the course of their professional activities. Having rejected the arguments based upon the Third Parties (Rights against Insurers) Act 1930, the Court indicated that the only basis for the Plaintiff's claim could be on the basis of an application for a Mareva injunction to restrain the Defendants from dealing with or disposing of assets in cases where it appeared likely that the Plaintiff would recover judgment against them for a certain or approximate sum."

Having invited Counsel for the plaintiff to make an application on the grounds of an Mareva injunction the Court of Appeal upon further consideration rejected the application.

CHAPTER 3

LIABILITY OF SURVEYORS—AN APPRAISAL

1 NEGLIGENCE AND ECONOMIC LOSS

Whilst the liability of a surveyor may arise from a breach of contract, it is the debate as to the circumstances in which a duty of care in the tort of negligence may arise which has recently given cause for concern. A person is not liable in the tort of negligence for the purely economic loss which he causes by his negligent deeds. "In English law in general the fact that economic loss is the foreseeable consequence of a negligent act is insufficient to entitle the plaintiff who suffers that loss to recover damages" (*Winfield and Jolowicz*, 11th Edition, p. 82). Economic loss may be regarded as being purely financial loss which does not arise as a result of physical damage or personal injury. This principle is subject, however, to a notable exception in the case of negligent misstatement.

The law of liability for statements is a specialist area of the law. It is perhaps not surprising that one of the exceptions to the rule that economic loss is not recoverable in negligence actions relates to negligent misstatement. The case which introduced the principle of liability for economic loss arising out of negligent misstatement is the case of *Hedley Byrne and Co. Ltd* v. *Heller & Partners Ltd* [1964] AC 465. Hedley Byrne, who were advertising agents, wanted to know whether they could give credit to a company called Easipower for whom they acted in advertising contracts. They asked for bankers' references about Easipower. Hedley Byrne's bankers approached Heller & Partners, who were Easipower's bankers, and were given two favourable references. Hedley Byrne's bankers passed on the references to Hedley Byrne. It is important to appreciate that Heller & Partners did not know specifically that the information they revealed was being passed to Hedley Byrne. They had marked their letters to Hedley Byrne's bankers "Confidential. For your private use". Hedley Byrne relied on the references supplied. Easipower went into liquidation and Hedley Byrne suffered loss. The case went to the House of Lords. Again, it is important to appreciate that Heller & Partners were *not* found liable to Hedley Byrne. The reason for exonerating them was that their references had been given "without responsibility". In the

Hedley Byrne case, a denial of responsibility was sufficient to avoid liability.

However, the *Hedley Byrne* case established that people holding themselves out as being skilled advisers could be liable in negligence for the economic loss they cause to those who rely upon their advice. In certain circumstances (usually where the adviser is in the business of giving advice), a "special relationship" exists so that the adviser owes a duty of care to the person relying upon his advice, in the giving of information or advice. The precise circumstances in which a special relationship will exist have not been defined but the following words of Lord Morris in the *Hedley Byrne* case have been often quoted:

"It should now be regarded as settled that if someone possessed of a special skill undertakes, quite irrespective of contract, to apply that skill for the assistance of another person who relies on such a skill, a duty of care will arise. The fact that the service is to be given by means of or by the instrumentality of words, can make no difference. Furthermore, if in a sphere in which a person is so placed that others could reasonably rely upon his judgement or skill or upon his ability to make careful enquiry, a person takes it upon himself to give information or advice to, or allows this information or advice to be passed onto another person who, as he knows or should know, will place reliance upon it, then a duty of care will arise."

It should be emphasised that the *Hedley Byrne* case did not create liability for economic loss in the case of negligent acts but only negligent statements.

The courts have always been concerned that if they allow the recovery of economic loss in the tort of negligence, this will give rise to the spectre of liability in an indeterminate amount for an indeterminate time to an indeterminate class.

The House of Lords in the case of *Caparo Industries PLC* v. *Dickman and Others* [1990] 1 All ER 568 has considered liability in tort for economic loss and taken a restrictive view. It is important to bear in mind that the *Caparo* case post-dates *Harris* v. *Wyre Forest* and *Smith* v. *Bush* which are reviewed later in this Report. The House of Lords in the *Caparo* case considered recent attempts by the courts (up to 1990) to define the duty of care owed by a professional man to third parties with whom he did not contract and the scope of the duty. The House of Lords regarded criteria such as proximity, policy and the existence of a special relationship as simply convenient labels which could create more problems than they solved. The wisdom of allowing the law to develop novel categories of negligence incrementally and by analogy with established categories, rather than by principles creating massive extensions of the *prima facie* duty of care, had to be recognised.

Furthermore, the House of Lords in the *Caparo* case considered that, where a duty of care in respect of negligent statements did exist, the limit, or control mechanism, imposed on the liability of a wrongdoer towards those who have suffered economic damage as a result of his negligence, depends on the need to prove that the wrongdoer knew that his statement would be communicated to the plaintiff either as an individual or as a member of an identifiable class specifically in connection with that transaction or transactions of a particular kind.

The decision of *Yianni* v. *Edwin Evans & Sons* [1982] 1 QB 438 can be considered a milestone in the development of this area of law. The facts were that Mr and Mrs Yianni bought a house for £15,000 with an advance from the Halifax Building Society of £12,000. The total extent of their personal capital was £3,000. The house was valued on behalf of the Halifax Building Society at £12,000. Unfortunately, having bought the house, the Yiannis discovered the house needed repairs valued at £18,000.

Evidence was given to show that less than 15 per cent of the general public purchasing properties have an independent survey done. The evidence suggested that the public rely on the building society's valuation and that the public trust the building society, knowing that they have paid a valuation fee to the building society and that that fee will be passed on to someone who surveys the house on behalf of the building society. The trial judge followed the *Hedley Byrne* case and held that a duty of care was owed by the valuers of the property to the Yiannis if the valuers knew that the valuation would be passed on to the Yiannis who would, in the valuers' reasonable contemplation, rely on its correctness in deciding to buy the house. The valuers therefore perceived that because of their report, the building society would offer to lend the Yiannis £12,000 and by virtue of that offer, would pass on to the Yiannis the valuer's valuation. It was common practice known to the valuers for borrowers who were purchasing lower priced houses to rely on their building society's valuation and not have an independent survey. The trial judge concluded in the *Yianni* case that there were no policy considerations which required that the valuers' duty to the Yiannis should be negatived since:

(a) to hold that the valuers were liable to the Yiannis would not result in a valuer to a building society having unlimited liability to third parties, since his liability would be limited to liability to the purchaser named in the building society's instructions to value a property; and

(b) it would not be objectionable if the consequence of holding that the valuers were liable to the Yiannis was that applicants for building society mortgages would always rely on building societies' valuations.

The Court also concluded that the Yiannis had not been guilty of contributory negligence in failing to have the property independently surveyed. Following the decision in the *Yianni* case in 1981, it was plain to surveyors and valuers that the valuation which they carried out on behalf of building societies and which came to the knowledge of residential property purchasers could fall within the "*Hedley Byrne* umbrella", giving rise to potential liability for economic loss where negligent misstatements were made.

However, the *Yianni* case was specific to a residential property in the lower price bracket. It was not clear, following *Yianni*, whether valuers could be held liable for negligent misstatement to the wealthier house purchasers/borrowers, purchasing houses in the upper price bracket, who might reasonably be expected to seek independent surveys. There was no disclaimer of liability for the negligent misstatements of the valuers in the *Yianni* case.

2 VOLUNTARY ASSUMPTION OF LIABILITY

In cases involving potential liability for economic loss arising out of negligent misstatements, it has sometimes been argued that a duty to use due care where there is no contract arises only where there is a voluntary assumption of liability. In the case of *Ministry of Housing and Local Government* v. *Sharp* [1970] QB 223, Lord Denning rejected the "voluntary assumption of liability" argument. He stated:

"In my opinion, the duty to use due care in a statement arises not from any voluntary assumption of responsibility, but from the fact that the person making it knows, or ought to know, that others, being his neighbours in this regard, would act on the face of the statement being correct."

However, in the case of *Curran* v. *Northern Ireland Co-ownership Housing Association* [1987] 2 All ER 13, the Court of Appeal in Northern Ireland appeared to give credence to the view that, in cases falling under the *Hedley Byrne* principle, responsibility can only attach to the defendant in respect of his statement if the defendant's conduct implied a voluntary undertaking to assume responsibility. If the "voluntary assumption of responsibility" argument is a good argument, then it is difficult to see how, where a disclaimer is issued expressly denying responsibility in respect of statements contained in a house valuation, there can truly be a voluntary assumption of risk.

Lord Templeman, giving judgment in *Smith* v. *Bush* and *Harris* v. *Wyre Forest District Council* both reported at [1989] 2 All ER 514, in the House of Lords, dealt with the matter as follows. He stated:

"In my opinion the valuer assumes responsibility to both mortgagee and purchaser by agreeing to carry out a valuation for mortgage purposes, knowing that the valuation fee has been paid by the purchaser and knowing that the valuation will probably be relied upon by the purchaser in order to decide whether or not to enter into a contract to purchase the house. The valuer can escape the responsibility to exercise reasonable skill and care by an express exclusion clause, provided the exclusion clause does not fall foul of the Unfair Contract Terms Act 1977."

The court concluded both in the case of *Smith* v. *Bush* and in the case of *Harris* v. *Wyre Forest* that the disclaimers did fall foul of the Unfair Contract Terms Act and were unreasonable. However, with due respect to Lord Templeman's wise judgment, he does not answer the question "How can a man voluntarily assume responsibility where he expressly attempts to exclude liability?" That question is posed by surveyors' disclaimers and merits an answer. Lord Griffiths in his judgment in *Smith* v. *Bush* and *Harris* v. *Wyre Forest* rejected the voluntary assumption of responsibility as a prerequisite for duty of care arising. What mattered in his view was whether the law deems the maker of a statement to have assumed responsibility to the person who acts on that statement.

Smith v. *Bush* has now been reviewed by the House of Lords in *Caparo* v. *Dickman* [1990] 1 All ER 568. In the judgment of Lord Oliver of Aylmerton in the *Caparo* case, *Smith* v. *Bush* was regarded as establishing that the law might attribute an assumption of responsibility to the maker of a statement regardless of the expressed intention of the person making the statement relied on.

On the related point of knowledge or deemed knowledge by the surveyor that the purchaser would rely on his report, it now appears, following the review of the law in the *Caparo* case, that a surveyor will owe a duty of care to the intending purchaser either because he actually knew that the purchaser would rely on his report or because the court would infer such knowledge by the surveyor.

3 DUTY OF CARE AND DISCLAIMER

The House of Lords in *Harris* v. *Wyre Forest District Council* and *Smith* v. *Eric S Bush* [1989] 2 WLR 790, [1989] 2 All ER 514, delivered the long-awaited decision. In the words of Lord Templeman, these cases involved three questions:

(a) Whether a valuer instructed by a building society or other mortgagee to value a house, knowing that his valuation would probably be relied on by the purchaser and mortgagor of the house, owed to the purchaser in tort a duty to exercise reasonable skill and care in carrying out the valuation unless the valuer disclaims liability.

(b) Whether a disclaimer of liability by or on behalf of the valuer is a notice which purports to exclude liability for negligence within the Unfair Contract Terms Act 1977 and is therefore ineffective unless it satisfies the requirement of reasonableness.

(c) Whether in the absence of special circumstances, it is fair and reasonable for the valuer to rely on the notice excluding liability.

The answers were:

Liability of surveyors—an appraisal

(a) A duty is owed.
(b) A disclaimer would be within the Unfair Contract Terms Act 1977.
(c) It is unreasonable for the valuer to rely on the notice excluding liability.

In the *Harris* v. *Wyre Forest* case, Mr and Mrs Harris purchased 74 George Street, Kidderminster. They needed a mortgage so they applied to the Wyre Forest District Council which was authorised to advance the money for the purpose of their acquiring the house. They signed an application form supplied by the Council with which they enclosed the valuation fee of £22. The form that they signed contained a declaration saying that the valuation was confidential; that it was intended solely for the benefit of the Wyre Forest District Council in determining the value of the property as security and no responsibility was accepted by the Council for the value or the condition of the property by reason of the inspection and report. The declaration also stated that the valuation was the property of the Council and that the Harris's could not require its production. The house was valued at £8,505. by the Council's valuer. The Harris's purchased the property at £9,000. The property was defective and cost of repairs was quoted at £13,000. Wyre Forest District Council was found vicariously liable for the valuation carried out by their employee/valuer.

On appeal, the court allowed the appeal on the grounds that, by the disclaimer notice, the Council had avoided incurring liability. The case then went to the House of Lords.

The facts of *Smith* v. *Bush* were that Mrs Smith purchased 242 Silver Road, Norwich. Her mortgage was from the Abbey National Building Society. She paid an inspection fee of £37.89 and signed an application form which also contained a disclaimer of liability on behalf of the building society and the surveyor or firm of surveyors carrying out the valuation. Eric S Bush carried out the valuation, valuing the property at £16,500. In the valuation, a number of items of disrepair were noted but were not considered to be essential for mortgage purposes. It is interesting to note that in this case, Mrs Smith borrowed only £3,500 from the Abbey National, although she purchased the property for £18,000.

The property was substantially defective as the chimney breast and chimney were unsupported. Bricks from the chimney collapsed and fell through the roof into the main bedroom and ceilings on the first floor. This case also found its way through the appeal process to pose the aforesaid three questions before the House of Lords. It seems likely that, had the valuer simply ascertained the amount which Mrs Bush intended to borrow from the building society and stated in his valuation that the property was worth at least £3,500, then he may have incurred no liability. There may be a lesson in this for valuers in the future.

It must of course be recognised that purchasers often require to know the value of a property before they can fix their borrowing requirements. They can obtain an independent survey to ascertain the value. The purpose of the mortgage valuation is to tell the lender how much to lend, not the borrower how much to borrow. The Royal Institution of Chartered Surveyors has published a leaflet "Mortgage Valuation or Survey", highlighting to the consumer the different services provided on the valuation and the survey respectively.

The House of Lords' response to the first of the above three questions (whether a duty was owed) is unsurprising. The matter had been resolved in the *Yianni* case. Lord Templeman was able to link the *Harris* and *Smith* cases directly to the principle in the *Hedley Byrne* case. He quoted a passage from Lord Devlin's judgment in the *Hedley Byrne* case:

"The categories of special relationships which may give rise to a duty to take care in words as well as in deeds are not limited to contractual relationships or to relationships of fiduciary duty, but include also relationships which are 'equivalent to contract'."

Lord Templeman then pronounced that in the present case, the relationship between valuer and the purchaser is "akin to contract". There was sufficient proximity for the duty of care to arise.

Lord Templeman's answer to the second question (whether the disclaimers used fell under the Unfair Contract Terms Act), took the form of a simple and brief argument. The Court of Appeal had held that the relevant sections of the Unfair Contract Terms Act were confined to "situations where the existence of a duty of care was not open to doubt". Lord Templeman could find nothing to support this. The Court of Appeal held that the Act did not apply to negligent misstatements where a disclaimer has prevented a duty of care from coming into existence. However, this was to confuse the valuer's report with the work which he carried out in order to make his report. The valuer owed a duty to exercise reasonable skill and care in his inspection and valuation. If he had been careful in his work, then he would not have made a negligent mis-statement in his report. Did Lord Templeman, and indeed the House of Lords as a whole, lose sight of the point that the *Hedley Byrne* case did not, as stated earlier, create liability for negligent acts but only for negligent statements? Lord Templeman concluded that the Unfair Contract Terms Act requires that "all exclusion notices, which would in common law provide a defence to an action for negligence, must satisfy the requirement of reasonableness".

In answering the third of his questions, Lord Templeman reviewed the present state of the house purchasing market as at 1989, concluding that there was a great pressure on a purchaser to rely on mortgage valuations. He observed:

Liability of surveyors—an appraisal

"the valuer knows full well that failure on his part to exercise reasonable skill and care may be disastrous to the purchaser. If, in reliance on a valuation, the purchaser contracts to buy for £50,000 a house valued and mortgaged for £40,000 but in fact worth nothing and needing thousands more to be spent on it, the purchaser stands to lose his home and to remain in debt to the building society for up to £40,000. . . . The public are exhorted to purchase their homes and cannot find houses to rent . . . In these circumstances, it is not fair and reasonable for building societies and valuers to agree together to impose on purchasers the risk of loss arising as a result of incompetence or carelessness on the part of valuers."

Lord Templeman made several other biting comments. He noted that it was open to Parliament to provide that members of professions, or members of one profession, providing services in the normal course of the exercise of their profession for reward, should be entitled to exclude or limit their liability for failure to exercise reasonable skill and care. However, in the absence of any such provision, he stated that valuers were not entitled to rely on a general exclusion clause excluding the common law duty of care owed by valuers to purchasers of houses. Apparently, Lord Templeman found the prospect of a class of professional people excluding their common law duties by carefully worded contract terms unacceptable.

Lord Griffiths, in his judgment, made it clear that although he regarded the disclaimers given in the cases before him as unreasonable, he would not consider it unreasonable for professional men in all circumstances to seek to exclude or limit their liability for negligence. Where breathtaking sums of money may turn on professional advice, it may be reasonable to give the advice on the basis of no liability or liability limited to the extent of the adviser's insurance cover. He added that his decision was made in respect of a dwellinghouse of modest value, in which case it is widely recognised by surveyors that purchasers are, in fact, relying on their skill and care. He expressly reserved his position in respect of valuations of different types of property for mortgage purposes such as industrial property, large blocks of flats, or very expensive houses. "In such cases it may well be that the general expectation of the behaviour of the purchaser is quite different. With very large sums of money at stake, prudence would seem to demand that the purchaser obtain his own structural survey." In those circumstances, it may be reasonable for valuers to exclude or limit their liability. It should be noted that Lord Templeman stated: "I agree with the speech of my noble and learned friend Lord Griffiths and with his warning that different considerations may apply where homes are not concerned." It may well be the case that Lord Templeman thought that all homes were embraced by his decision, whether expensive or not.

4 THE TEST OF REASONABLE SKILL AND CARE FOR SURVEYORS IN THE RESIDENTIAL MARKET

Whilst the decisions of *Smith* and *Harris* related to the issue of a duty of care in the tort of negligence, it should be borne in mind that where a contractual relationship exists between a surveyor and his client, in the absence of any express term, there will always be implied a term in the contract that the surveyor has to exercise all the relevant skill and care that may be expected from such a surveyor. The standard of care that may be expected from the surveyor is the same irrespective of whether or not a cause of action is framed as a breach of contract, or, breach of a duty of care in the tort of negligence, or both.

Although the judgment of Lord Templeman may indicate that he is not the champion of the surveying profession, he was careful not to impose too high a duty of care upon the valuers in *Smith* and *Harris*. The valuer must exercise reasonable skill and care in recognising defects and being able to assess value. He must take into account "major defects which are or ought to be obvious to him in the course of a visual inspection of so much of the exterior and interior of the house as may be accessible to him without undue difficulty". Lord Templeman expressly agreed with the decision in the case of *Roberts* v. *J Hampson & Co.* [1988] 2 EGLR 181. In that case, the trial judge commenting on the building society valuation stated: "It is a valuation and not a survey, but any valuation is necessarily governed by condition. The inspection is, of necessity, a limited one."

On the other hand, if the average inspection time for a property would be half an hour but, in a particular case, the valuer needs to spend two hours in order properly to inspect a property, then he must devote two hours to the inspection. If the valuer has specific grounds for suspicion and the trail of suspicion requires him to move the furniture or lift the carpets, then the valuer must take all reasonable steps to follow the trail until he has all the information which he reasonably requires in order to make his valuation.

Whether there are grounds for suspicion is a question of fact as the case of *Bere and Parchment* v. *Slades* (1990) 6 Const LJ 30 illustrates. The case is of interest in demonstrating the standard of care required by the valuer. The plaintiffs purchased an Edwardian house relying on a valuation prepared by the defendant who was instructed to carry out a Scheme 1 valuation. The defendant/surveyor conceded that a duty of care was owed to the plaintiffs but denied breach of duty. The defendant failed to warn the plaintiffs of the existence of a defect in external cellar walls caused by the fact that some of the cement used in the building of the walls was unstable. It was conceded that the defect was not directly discoverable on a Scheme 1 valuation but the plaintiffs argued that the surveyor should have recommended detailed further investigations to be carried out. The plaintiffs stated that a number of factors, including external and internal cracking and the state of the walls and the presence of dampness, should have put the surveyor on notice of the defect.

The court decided that the surveyor's report was carefully done given the age of the property and the condition of other properties in the area. The damage stated by the plaintiffs to exist was not sufficient to create a duty to inform the plaintiffs of the need for a further investigation. The surveyor's liability for breach of duty would not extend to subsequent buyers of the property who could be expected to make their own investigations.

In summary, the inspection is a limited one but it must be the appraisal of a skilled professional man. The duty of the surveyor is to use reasonable skill and care. He must exercise the reasonable competence expected of a professional man and is judged against the standard of what others in his profession would reasonably have done in the same situation.

The principle is illustrated by the case of *Eley* v. *King and Chasemoor* (1987) 139 NLJ 791. This case indicates that a defendant surveyor who advises house purchasers that they should seek insurance cover against the possibility of defects may, by virtue of that advice, defeat a claim by the house purchasers grounded in negligence. The facts were that the surveyor carried out a full structural survey of a residential property, noting the existence of cracks in the walls. He advised the plaintiffs to seek insurance cover against subsidence, ground heave, settlement and landslip. The plaintiffs took this advice and purchased the house. The cracks worsened and remedial works cost £20,000, £15,700 of which was borne by the plaintiffs' insurers. The Court of Appeal accepted that the surveyor was not negligent. The advice to insure against subsidence was sufficient indication of a defect in the property and insurance was the best means of covering the risk.

The Court of Appeal decision of *Beaumont* v. *Humberts* (*The Times*, 17 August 1990) offers further interpretation of the surveyor's duty of care. A member of the defendant surveyors carried out a mortgage valuation for a bank. The defendant agreed that the valuation could be shown to the purchasers. The valuation was stated to be for insurance reinstatement purposes. The valuation was £175,000. This was the sum for which the purchasers insured the house in question. The house burned down three years after the valuation. The purchasers claimed that the reinstatement cost was in fact £300,000. A majority of the Court of Appeal decided that the surveyor had not been negligent. The expression "reinstatement" was ambiguous. It could mean replacing with an exact copy or it could mean replacing with as near as practicable an exact copy or it could mean replacing with a modern building, retaining the style and general shape of the old one. The defendant surveyors' valuation was based on modern building costs. The majority of the Court said that if the bank had required a direct replacement cost valuation, it should have asked for this. The majority considered that the extent of the duty of the surveyor to the purchaser is determined by the extent of his duty to the mortgagee. If it was reasonable to provide the bank with a reinstatement value based on the cost of providing the modern equivalent of the building, then no higher duty was owed to the purchaser. Lord Justice Dillon dissented, apparently on the grounds that the duty owed to the purchaser was a separate duty from that owed to the mortgagee. The expectations in respect of reinstatement may differ as between the purchaser and the mortgagee and the surveyor should have considered this.

Again, the Court of Appeal differed on the existence of a duty of care. A minority held that necessary reliance by the purchasers did not exist so as to give rise to a duty of care. The purchasers had arranged their own survey of the property prior to the valuation being obtained. It is interesting to note that the majority held that a duty of care did arise despite the fact that *Smith* v. *Bush* left open an exception in the case of expensive houses. The property in question, despite the figures referred to above, was not in the category of an expensive house.

The Royal Institution of Chartered Surveyors and the Incorporated Society of Valuers & Auctioneers, have published guidance notes with effect from 1 July 1990, called "Mortgage Valuations: Guidance Notes for Valuers", which set out the level of services to be expected from a valuation.

The recent case of *Preston* v. *Torfaen Borough Council, The Independent,* 24 September 1993 (CA) is proof that the court is prepared to limit the extent of the duty of care owed by a professional man in preparing a survey.

In that case, Torfaen Borough Council built a housing estate. Prior to doing so, they commissioned the defendant, a soil expert, to investigate the soil conditions and the foundations of the site and to report whether work could proceed safely. The defendant's report concluded that work could proceed safely.

Some years later, the plaintiffs were granted a weekly tenancy of one of the houses in the new housing estate. They then purchased the house from the Council. Cracks began to appear in the walls of the house caused by defective foundations and proceedings were brought by the plaintiffs against the Council and the Council's expert. It was alleged that the expert knew that the Council would rely on his advice relating to soil conditions and foundations and that the plaintiffs would suffer economic loss if the advice was wrongly given. The plaintiffs sought to impose liability on the expert under the *Hedley Byrne* principle on the basis of negligent misstatement. However, the plaintiffs did not see the report of the expert and could not have been said to have relied on it. There was insufficient proximity between the plaintiff purchaser of the premises and the expert. At the time of the negligent report, there was no complainant who could be identified other than as a member of a class of potential purchasers.

5   THE REASONABLENESS OF THE DISCLAIMER

A party may seek to avoid liability for a breach of a duty of care in the tort of negligence by giving notice purporting to disclaim any such liability. Lord Griffiths made it clear in his judgment in the *Harris* v. *Wyre Forest* and *Smith* v. *Bush* cases that the burden is on the surveyor to establish that in all the circumstances it is fair and reasonable that he should be allowed to rely on his disclaimer. In considering reasonableness, four matters should always be considered:

(a)   Were the parties of equal bargaining power?
(b)   Would it have been reasonably practicable to obtain the advice given from an alternative source, taking into account costs and time?
(c)   The difficulty of the task undertaken.
(d)   The practical consequences of the decision on the question of reasonableness—taking into account the sums of money potentially at stake, the ability of the parties to bear the loss involved and the insurance position.

Lord Griffiths also said: "Everyone knows that all prudent, professional men carry insurance and the availability and cost of insurance must be a relevant factor when considering which of two parties should be required to bear the risk of a loss."

Section 30 of the Building Societies Act 1962 provides that where a building society makes to a member an advance to be used in meeting the purchase price of a property, the society is deemed to warrant to the member that the purchase price is reasonable, unless, before any contract is made, the society gives notice to the member, in writing in the prescribed form, stating that the making of the advance implies no such warranty. In *Beaton* v. *Nationwide Anglia Building Society* (*The Times*, 8 October 1990), it was decided that a notice in writing in the prescribed form given by a society to a prospective borrower under section 30 of the Building Societies Act 1962, did not have any effect upon the liability of the building society for a negligent valuation of the property carried out by their staff surveyor pursuant to section 25 of the Building Societies Act 1962. The court decided that the valuation survey had been done negligently and went on to decide that the wording of section 30 of the Act was not appropriate to constitute a statutory exclusion of a duty of care. To decide otherwise would create an artificial distinction between the position of valuers directly employed by building societies and other valuers. The section was not concerned with negligence. It simply created an excludable statutory warranty that the purchase price was reasonable.

The decisions of the House of Lords in *Smith* and *Harris* were policy decisions which must be viewed in the light of the economic conditions pertaining in the residential property market in 1989. The state of that market was rehearsed in some detail in the judgments. The court had accepted that, faced with the heavy financial commitments involved in purchasing residential properties, the general public does not, as a general rule, go to the expense of having an independent survey performed. It followed that the reliance of the public on building society valuations could not be denied.

The House of Lords had, in effect, either to allow the surveying profession to avoid liability to the general public for negligent mis-statements in building society valuation forms, or else to deny the validity of such disclaimers. Given the wording of the Unfair Contract Terms Act, it was not unreasonable for the House of Lords to bring the disclaimers in issue within the requirement of reasonableness, provided by section 2(2) of the Unfair Contract Terms Act 1977. The doubts which existed after the *Yianni* case as to whether the house valuer would owe a duty of care to the purchaser of an expensive property, who could well afford the costs of an independent survey, remain. It may be that the judgment of Lord Griffiths is sufficient to enable valuers to escape liability where the property is expensive and the purchaser rich.

6 DAMAGES

(a) *Some principles for assessing damages*

Following the House of Lords decision in the case of *Swingcastle Limited* v. *Alistair Gibson (a firm)* [1991] 2 All ER 352, it is now clear that a lender who lends money in reliance on a negligent valuation is only entitled to be placed in the same position as if the negligence had not occurred. The lender is only entitled to present its claim on the basis that if the valuer had properly carried out the valuation, the lender would not have lent the money and accordingly the valuer is entitled to recompense for loss of use of the amount lent, since if the valuer had not been negligent and had advised the correct value, the lender would not have made the loan but employed the money elsewhere. The lender is not entitled to claim that the valuer, by his negligence, deprived the lender of the interest which the lender would have received from the borrower if the borrower (who in fact defaults) had paid up pursuant to the loan agreement. The security provided to the lender for the loan is the property of the borrower. The lender does not have a further security consisting of a guarantee by the valuer that the borrower would pay everything, or indeed anything, that was due to the lender at the date on which the loan transaction was terminated.

The facts of the *Swingcastle* v. *Gibson* case were that the lender specialised in lending money on mortgage to high risk borrowers. It agreed to lend £10,000. to the borrowers on the basis of a valuation of their house on a forced sale with vacant possession. The valuation was carried out negligently by the surveyor who valued the property at £18,000. The annual percentage rate of interest on the mortgage was 36.5 per cent with a default rate of 45.6 per cent.

In 1986, the borrowers fell in arrears; the lender obtained a possession order and sold the property in 1987 for £12,000. leaving a shortfall, including accrued interest under the mortgage at the default rate, of £7,136.41.

The House of Lords decided that the fallacy of the lender's case was that it was trying to obtain from the valuer, compensation for the borrowers' failure to pay the loan and not the proper damages for the valuer's negligence.

(b) Diminution in value or the cost of repairs?

In two first instance decisions dating from 1990, the courts considered whether the appropriate level of damages payable to a house purchaser in relation to a negligent survey was the cost of diminution or the cost of repair and concluded that the appropriate measure of damages was the cost of repair.

The two cases in question are the case of *Pamela Syrett* v. *Carr and Neave* (noted at (1990) 54 BLR at p. 121) and *Watts and Watts* v. *Morrow* at first instance.

The first instance decision in the case of *Watts and Watts* v. *Morrow* was overturned by the Court of Appeal and the Court of Appeal judgment is reported at (1991) 55 BLR 86 (CA). The judgment of the Court of Appeal in the *Watts and Watts* v. *Morrow* case also overturned the judgment in *Syrett* v. *Carr and Neave*.

The facts of the *Watts and Watts* v. *Morrow* case are that in 1986, a wealthy couple, a stockbroker and a solicitor living in London, decided to buy a country residence. They had budgeted for a purchase price of £170,000 but eventually offered £177,500. Because they were buying a property which stretched them financially, the purchasers decided to have a full and detailed survey carried out. The survey was carried out by Ralph Morrow and was a detailed and long report. The gist of the report was that any repairs which were needed were not substantial in cost terms. Mr Morrow confirmed to Mr and Mrs Watts that the price of £177,500 was fair.

Mr and Mrs Watts purchased the property in April 1987.

Defects were soon discovered. The roof was due for a major overhaul including stripping tiles, repairing or replacing the roof structure, rebuilding the top courses of brickwork, woodworm treatment, felting, rebattening and retiling. There were other defects. The property in its true condition was valued at £162,500.

One of the consequences of having the repair works carried out was that Mr and Mrs Watts spent almost every weekend staying in their country residence which was described as "a building site". They were unable to entertain friends and clients and instead of spending their summer holiday in their new country residence, took their holidays elsewhere.

Ralph Gibson LJ concluded in his judgment that the financial loss of the plaintiffs in law was limited to the diminution in value of the property which was £15,000 with interest thereon.

Mr and Mrs Watts had entered into a contract with Mr Morrow for the survey of the property. There were no special terms beyond the usual undertaking of the surveyor to use proper skill and care.

The principle that a plaintiff is entitled to a sum which will place him in as good a position as if the contract for the survey had been properly discharged underlay the decision of the Court of Appeal in *Philips* v. *Ward* [1956] 1 WLR 471 and was applied by the Court of Appeal in the *Watts and Watts* v. *Morrow* case. At first instance, the Judge had awarded £33,961 in respect of the cost of repair. This award had to be set aside and the diminution in value of £15,000 substituted.

If the survey contract had been properly performed, Mr and Mrs Watts would either not have bought the property, in which case they would have avoided any loss, or, after negotiation, they would have paid the reduced price. If the plaintiff, in such a case, extricates himself from the transaction by selling the property then, in the absence of any point on mitigation, he will normally recover the diminution in value together with costs and expenses thrown away in moving out and of resale.

If the situation was that the plaintiffs, had they been properly advised, would have bought the property anyway, then the fact that after purchase they discovered that the unreported defects would cost more than the diminution in value, did not entitle the plaintiffs to recover the excess. If the survey contract had been performed properly, the plaintiffs would still have done no better than to reduce the market value of the property to its value in its true condition.

(c) Distress and inconvenience

In *Hayes* v. *Dodd* [1990] 2 All ER 815 (CA), Purchase LJ said with reference to a claim for damages for mental distress in a claim against a surveyor, that: "Damages of this kind are only recoverable when the subject matter of the contract or duty in tort is to provide peace of mind or freedom from distress."

In the *Watts and Watts* v. *Morrow* case, the Court of Appeal decided that a contract to carry out a prepurchase survey was not a contract to provide peace of mind or freedom from distress. General damages for mental distress were not recoverable except to the extent that they were caused by physical discomfort or inconvenience. Some measure of damages was recoverable where plaintiffs move into a property and live there in physical discomfort because of the existence of unreported defects. At first instance, Mr and Mrs Watts had been awarded damages of £4,000 each for inconvenience, vexation and distress. The Court of Appeal reduced the award to £750 for each plaintiff.

However, in the hitherto unreported case of *Ezekiel* v. *McDade and Others* [1994] 10 Const LJ 122 His Honour Judge Peter Bowsher QC has again shown himself willing to award plaintiffs significant and substantial damages for distress and inconvenience. He awarded £6,000 to a husband and wife whose property had been negligently overvalued. Whilst the events which befell the plaintiffs following the discovery of defects within their property must be described as very sad indeed, the sum of £6,000 awarded (i.e., £3,000 each) shows a marked increase upon the amounts awarded by the Court of Appeal in *Watts* v. *Morrow*. This decision was itself an appeal against Judge Bowsher's earlier decision at first instance.

7 PROPERTY VALUATION

In recent years there have been very many examples of actions brought against the surveyor by lenders and funding institutions where it has been alleged that there has been an overvaluation. As a consequence of this overvaluation the lender has advanced money and the property which has been charged by way of security has been found to be insufficient to reimburse the lender following default by the borrower. These examples relate both to domestic and also to commercial property. However, on the basis of the amount of the losses, most of the reported decisions of the courts are concerned with commercial property. In the past where there has been a general rise in property values this would not have mattered since the lender's security was appreciating in value. Any overvaluation on the part of the surveyor was unlikely to give rise to an actionable cause since in the event of a default by the borrower the property would more often than not have increased in value during the interim and thus would not have given rise to any claimable loss. Whereas in previous years any overvaluation would in all probability have been due to a failure to observe and identify defects, the more recent claims against surveyors have mostly been due to allegations that surveyors were somewhat calculating values, buoyed by the excessive optimism prevailing at that time which subsequently was shown to be capable of being quickly reversed.

Property prices reached their maximum limit in 1990 and thereafter with the rise in interest rates started to fall. Increasing interest rates furthermore gave rise to increasing difficulty to meet monthly repayments and many borrowers who had purchased in the previous "boom" were unable to meet their commitments. The result was that lenders increasingly had to seek security of their loans only to find that it was inadequate to meet those amounts due and owing. As a result they looked to the surveyors who had given valuations at the time of purchase. In many instances surveyors have been found to have given inflated opinions upon the valuation of property. In many other cases however this has not been so but lenders who have suffered considerable losses have been faced with little alternative other than to sue the valuer unless they are prepared to bear all the losses themselves.

Thus, the ingredients existed which have given rise to a tide of claims against surveyors. The profession is currently paying the price by the imposition of dramatically increased professional indemnity insurance premiums.

Once it became apparent that the property market was in a state of decline, surveyors were undoubtedly cautious when making property valuations. Thus, the tendency was to undervalue properties. Prospective purchasers whilst concerned that they could not secure borrowing for any property purchase of which was being sought would encounter legal difficulties in suing a surveyor alleging undervaluation. Not surprisingly, there have been no reported decisions concerning such claims alleging undervaluation. It could be argued that with the tendency to undervalue, albeit for obvious reasons, surveyors were themselves contributing to the decline in property values. There have been a significant number of decisions alleging overvaluation.

Four decisions of the courts which illustrate the principles adopted by the courts and the difficulties encountered in dealing with allegations of overvaluation are:

  (i) *Mount Banking Corporation Ltd* v. *Brian Cooper & Co.* [1992] 35 EG 123;
 (ii) *Private Bank & Trust Co. Ltd* v. *S (UK) Ltd* [1993] 09 EG 112;
(iii) *Banque Bruxelles Lambert FA* v. *John D Wood Commercial Ltd and*

Others (21 December 1993). (Times Law Reports, 8 March 1994)

(iv) *United Bank of Kuwait* v. *Prudential Property Services Ltd.* (10 December 1993).

The facts in each case are discussed in turn.

In *Private Bank & Trust Co. Ltd* v. *S* the allegations arose from a valuation performed in March 1989 of premises in London which were valued at £1.7 million. Subsequently in April 1990 the surveyor advised that the value of the property was at that time between £1.35 million and £1.45 million. An advance was made of £1.25 million and a mortgage secured on the property by the lender. The borrower subsequently defaulted. His Honour Judge Rice, sitting as a Deputy High Court Judge, found in dismissing the claim against the surveyor that in making his valuation the surveyor was entitled to a permissible margin of error of 15 per cent either side of his valuation of £1.35 million to £1.45 million. His valuation was within this margin and, thus, he was not found to be negligent.

In *Mount Banking Corporation Ltd* v. *Brian Cooper & Co.* the court was again involved, *inter alia*, with discussing the legitimate margin of error. This involved an action by a bank who had lent monies to a borrower which was secured on premises known as 117–119 Hartington Road, Stockwell, South London. The case was concerned solely with the allegation that the existing open-market value at £530,000 was negligent. Upon receipt of a valuation the plaintiff advanced a loan of £370,000 with two further payments being made of £1,928.50 and £8,072.70, such amounts being paid between September 1989 and January 1990. The borrower totally defaulted on the loan and was made bankrupt in November 1990. The property was eventually sold for £125,000. The plaintiffs' loss in respect of the loan was a loss of a principal of £248,638.13 and £23,471.95 being loss of interest and various expenses. The claim by the bank failed. The judge, Mr R M Stewart QC, sitting as a Deputy High Court Judge, sympathised with the bank over their massive loss but said that this was no basis for finding liability when none lay. The huge fall in the property was to be attributed to the collapse of the property market in 1990. Their inability to recover anything from the borrower was due to his bankruptcy which was no doubt attributable largely to the same cause.

The judge stated: "I should avoid seeking a mean figure between valuations and applying a margin of error, even a broad margin of error to that."

The correct approach was to assess whether the valuer's approach was proper and what a competent approach could properly have resulted in. If the valuer's figure was higher than the sensibly acceptable figure, then the question had to be asked whether it was within an acceptable margin of error.

A competent valuer must consider all relevant factors and evidence in reaching his valuation.

Relevant factors to be taken into account by the valuer in the *Mount Banking* case were:

(a) the size, condition, tenure and location of the property;

(b) planning permission and permitted user;

(c) the value and use of adjoining and neighbouring premises;

(d) the value, particularly rent and capital, of other offices in the general location and their comparability and any consequent adjustments to be made when applying that information to the property in question;

(e) the state of the property market;

(f) increases in bank base rates;

(g) the realism of the projected development and its costing;

(h) the proposed purchase price for the property.

In all the circumstances, the judge concluded that the defendant valuer had acted correctly and had reached a valuation which was within the acceptable bracket.

In the *Banque Bruxelles* decision (a hitherto unreported decision of Mr Justice Phillips of 21 December 1993) the facts concerned a series of loans made by the plaintiff bank in the first half of 1989. These loans which were syndicated by the plaintiffs to a number of other banks, ranged in size from £4.77 million to £92.7 million. In every instance the loan in question was made to a property company and secured on a single property which that company had recently acquired. Further, in most cases the property concerned represented that company's only asset. Before making a loan of this kind the plaintiffs routinely insisted on being shown a professional valuation of the property concerned and it would then lend a maximum of 90 per cent of the open market value shown therein. Moreover, the plaintiffs required a mortgage indemnity guarantee insurance policy from Eagle Star for the full amount of the loan. Before deciding to issue the required policy Eagle Star would also be shown the valuation. The reported decision was, in the end, only part of all the disputes which had arisen out of these transactions, the remainder having been resolved or left in abeyance. It concerned three loans involving three substantial London properties—Trevelyan House, Cambridge Circus and Crusader House. In each of these cases a valuation was obtained from the defendants which exceeded by a large margin from 30 per cent to 73 per cent of the price at which the property had just been acquired. Notwithstanding these excessive valuations, the Banque lent 90 per cent of the valuation sum in each event. The property market collapsed in 1990 and the borrowing companies defaulted on their loans and the properties proved to be insufficient security. The lenders and the insurers sought to recover their losses from the valuers concerned alleging that they were guilty of overvaluing the properties.

An issue which greatly concerned the judge was the relative cogency of two difference kinds of evidence in assessing a commercial value. He considered:

(a) the price that a property recently sold had realised; and
(b) the evidence of the prices achieved by similar properties sold on the open market and of factors taken into account in achieving those prices ("valuation by comparison").

The judge began his deliberation on this issue by stating:

"When a property is marketed on the open market it is almost axiomatic that the price which it realises represents its open market value at the time that the price is agreed. Where market value cannot be established in this way, it can only be estimated by comparison with prices achieved by similar properties sold on the open market."

The judge dealt at length with the various complexities of valuation by comparison but the thrust of his judgment was that when valuing a property that had just been sold, the sale price is the most cogent evidence of the open market value. It was possible that a seller might not have achieved the full market value. The valuer is, therefore, under a duty to check carefully that the property has been properly exposed to the market and competently marketed. If it has, then the market price will demonstrate the market value. It followed, in the judgment that the valuer who gives an open market valuation without considering the implications of a recent sale of the property is negligent. The judge found on the facts that John D Wood had been negligent.

Expert evidence was given and accepted that a reasonable banker would discount the security offered by the top 30 per cent of a property valuation. However, Banque had lent 90 per cent of Wood's valuations. This was because Banque had 100 per cent insurance cover. It was argued that since Banque relied on insurance cover in advancing the top slice of the loan rather than relying on the value of the security Wood was not liable for the top 20 per cent of the loan. This argument was rejected by the court. The amount of the valuation was the factor which determined how much was lent, given the top slices of the loan. Banque believed that the valuation was reliable. Banque took the risk of advancing more than 70 per cent of the valuation because they believed that the risk was transferred to Eagle Star but that did not mean that they did not rely on the valuation. If Banque had been imprudent in lending the top slice it did not break the chain of causation linking the valuations and the totality of the sums advanced.

In *United Bank of Kuwait and Prudential Property Services Ltd* (a hitherto unreported decision of Mr Justice Gage of 10 December 1993) the facts related to a claim for damages for breach of contract and negligence arising from a valuation of property made in the Summer of 1990. The property was known as "Coachmans Court" in Ipswich. The property was valued by a Mr Spettigue in September 1990 as being worth £2.5 million. Subsequently a loan was made by the plaintiff to the borrower. The property was subsequently sold on 3 February 1982 for £950,000 following the appointment of a receiver to SDL, the borrower. The judge having listened to the evidence formed the view that the valuation had been negligently performed and did not fall within an acceptable bracket for margin of error. Thus, the plaintiff succeeded.

There are a number of important issues which were resolved by these decisions. They are as follows:

(1) It is important to consider not only the sum total of the valuation but also the method employed in arriving at this figure. However, in the *Mount Banking* decision the judge made clear that if the valuation could not be impeached as a total then, however erroneous the method or the basis by which the valuation had been reached, no loss had been sustained. Similarly, in *Private Bank* whereas the judge made a number of criticisms of the valuation the surveyor was not found to be negligent. The judge said that whereas the surveyor may have used the wrong approach, if it was wrong, it did not in effect make much difference to his conclusion and the valuation fell within the legitimate margin for error. Notwithstanding this finding, any judge must have regard to the methods used in reaching a valuation.

(2) It was emphasised in the *United Bank of Kuwait* decision by Mr Justice Gage that "valuation of a property is an art and not a science". The best he could do was to arrive at a determination on the basis of an analysis of the evidence before him. A valuer was not to be judged negligent merely because others disagree with his figures or merely because with hindsight his valuation was shown to have been too high or too low. One could determine an acceptable bracket of valuation by consensus between experts. It was accepted that the margin for error in a volatile market would be greater. For example, in *Mount Banking* it was conceded by counsel for the plaintiff that the margin for error was a maximum of 17.5 per cent either side of the actual value. The test was whether or not a reasonably competent valuer using proper skill and care could properly have reached the valuation given by the defendant. If it was

higher than the sensibly accepted figure was it within an acceptable margin of error? In finding the defendant surveyor liable in the *Kuwait Banking* decision, Mr Justice Gage was influenced by the expert witness for the plaintiff who said that any figure above or below 15 per cent of the actual value of the property would be a negligent valuation. The surveyor on those facts had valued the property some 40 per cent greater than the actual property value.

(3) There is an apparent conflict of authority between *Mount Banking* and *Banque Bruxelles* albeit that the facts in each case are obviously different. In *Banque Bruxelles* the surveyors were asked to provide a valuation following the acquisition of the property by the borrower. The judge stated his views as to the complexities of valuation but he indicated that when valuing a property that had just been sold the sale price was the most cogent evidence of the open market value. It was possible that a seller might not have achieved the full market value. The valuer is therefore under a duty to check that the property had been properly exposed to the market and properly marketed. If it had been, then the market price would demonstrate its market value. Thus, it must follow that a valuer who gives an open market valuation without considering the implications of a recent sale of the property was negligent. The judge found on the facts in *Banque Bruxelles* that the defendant had been negligent. This creates a conflict of authority since in *Mount Banking* the learned judge stated ([1992] 35 EGLR at p. 128) that he was satisfied on the expert evidence that "a body of competent valuers considers it proper to make a valuation without ever knowing the purchase price". Phillips J in *Banque Bruxelles* recited this passage from *Mount Banking* but disagreed with it.

(4) Judges have to make decisions as to what constitutes the value of a property at any given time on the basis of expert evidence adduced. As previously conceded, this is not a science but an art. Furthermore, they are prepared to concede that there is a legitimate margin for error so that accordingly, a surveyor is not negligent so long as his valuation falls within this legitimate margin. On the basis of this concession it must follow that the court's test is highly artificial. It is in no better position to make a judgment as to the value of a property than is the surveyor. Therefore, it must follow that the court's assessment of a valuation at any one time must also be subject to some margin for error. This issue has not however been grasped by the courts who have been prepared to state with exact precision the values

of properties at any given time. It is not possible to be so definite and specific.

(5) In *Banque Bruxelles* with regard to one of the properties in dispute, the defendant Wood carry out only a corroborative or "franking" valuation to support a valuation by another defendant valuer, Lewis & Tucker. The judge found that the franking valuation was not relied on by Banque in making the loan. Banque had already decided to proceed on the basis of Lewis & Tucker's valuation. However the franking valuation was really provided by Wood for the benefit of Banque's insurers, Eagle Star. Wood knew that Banque might leave it to Eagle Star to decide whether its valuation was satisfactory and that Banque would advance the loan if Eagle Star was satisfied.

The judge found as a matter of fact that Eagle Star did not substantially rely on Wood's valuation. Nevertheless, he concluded that had Eagle Star relied on Wood's valuation, he would have decided that Wood induced Banque to enter into a loan transaction and he would therefore have held Wood liable for the legal consequences.

Could a borrower/purchaser who commissions his own separate valuation or survey and relies exclusively upon it, nevertheless succeed in a negligence claim against another valuer or surveyor whose report he has seen and which has induced a lender to lend him money to effect a purchase of the property?

This example demonstrates that there may be liability to a second party where there is reliance by a first party on a statement, or opinion and a second party relies upon any acts or omissions of that first party. Thus, it is not necessary for the statement to have been made directly to the second party. An analysis of this concept should not give rise to too much surprise. For example, in *Wyre Forest* v. *Harris*, the borrower did not see the valuation report but relied upon the willingness on the part of the Council to advance the monies. It is submitted that the prime determinant must be that of reasonable foreseeability.

(6) The judge found that Banque's failure to have regard to the implications of the discrepancy between the price at which the properties were purchased and the valuation given to each property (by Wood and in one case also, by Lewis & Tucker, their co-defendant), constituted a serious lapse from the standard of reasonable care expected of a merchant bank. Although the fault by Wood was more serious, comprising a fundamental professional error, Banque's damages were

reduced by 30 per cent. An important factor taken into account by the judge was that Banque had lent to companies with no assets other than the properties securing the loans and that the borrower companies made no cash injections which would have shown some confidence in Wood's valuation.

Banque used the insurance cover which they had obtained from Eagle Star as a defence to the contributory negligence claim. However, a plaintiff must be considered as uninsured when his losses are assessed. It would, said Phillips J, be paradoxical if Banque could be treated as uninsured when claiming against Wood so that Wood could not claim any credit by reason of the insurance but, nevertheless, Banque could rely on insurance to argue that it was not guilty of contributory negligence. Phillips J. said:

> "If the risk is one that it was negligent to incur, the fact that the plaintiff has transferred it to the insurer, should not rebound to the insurer's benefit."

If it were not for the principle that a plaintiff, even when insured, must be regarded as uninsured when pursuing a liability claim against a third party, the third party could escape or avoid liability. In the event of a claimant electing to be indemnified by his insurer, the insured could elect to pursue the original claim against the third party by means of subrogation.

CHAPTER 4

THE DUTIES OF THE INSURANCE BROKER

1   VICTIMS AND VILLAINS

Conventional wisdom has it that he who pays the piper calls the tune. Not so in the case of the insurance broker. While, the law generally regards the insurance broker as acting on behalf and in the best interests of the insured, nonetheless, generally, the broker derives his remuneration from insurers. This traditional arrangement contains the seed of conflict of interest and begs questions as to the nature of the broker's duties and responsibilities in law particularly as in *Kenneth Roberts* v. *Patrick Selwyn Plaisted* [1989] 2 Lloyd's Rep 341 Lord Justice Purchas, in the Court of Appeal, was driven to observe that:

"To the person unacquainted with the insurance industry it may seem a remarkable state of the law that someone who describes himself as a Lloyd's broker who is remunerated by the insurance industry and who presents proposal forms and suggested policies on their behalf should not be the safe recipient of full disclosure."

Purchas LJ also affirmed the view of Hodgson J at first instance who had regarded the insured as a victim of the insurance industry:

"Before I come to examine this contract it is clear that, if the insurer's contention is correct, this plaintiff is yet another victim of the insurance industry. He made the fullest disclosure to the broker. Like the majority of laymen he probably thought that that was enough and that the broker was the agent of the insurers by whom he was remunerated by way of commission; that mistake was one which, unhappily, is all too common and all too often used by insurers to escape liability."

The experience of Mr Roberts is salutary. He claimed on a policy only to have the insurers attempt to avoid it due to alleged non-disclosure of material facts even though he had disclosed those facts to the broker. It is, perhaps, not an uncommon experience and one that raises the spectre of the broker as villain. Yet it will be seen that it is not so much that the insured is the victim of the industry as that both are hostages to the common law which has long been active in defining the role and duties of the broker with the effect that the so called victim is not always without a remedy. Added to this, Parliament and increasingly the European

Commission have sought to establish a regulatory framework for the conduct of the insurance broker's affairs.

2 THE BROKER AND THE COMMON LAW

The broker in the insurance industry acts in the capacity of intermediary between the insured and the insurer. In so doing, it is the function of the broker to effect and advise upon the policy and to assist in handling claims. Insurance brokers normally act as agent of the insured for the purpose of effecting insurance policies and in making claims but this is not always so and the "perennial problem", as the editors of the (now defunct) Insurance Law Reports put it, remains one of "whether at a critical juncture the brokers were acting as agents for the insurance company or simply as agents for the insured." Much litigation has turned on this problem.

In *Rozanes* v. *Bowen* (1928) 32 Ll L Rep 98, Wright J was in no doubt that "... throughout the business the brokers are simply the agents of the assured ...". However, this alluringly simple analysis has proved too much for the common law to maintain without innovation as, for example, in *Woolcott* v. *Excess Insurance Co. Ltd and Miles Smith Anderson & Game Limited* [1978] 1 Lloyd's Rep 633 where because the broker was authorised by particular insurers to act on their behalf (and as such was their agent) the broker's knowledge in relation to certain material facts was imputed to the insurers.

The innovative inroad into the general principle was further developed in *Stockton* v. *Mason* [1978] 2 Lloyd's Rep 430 (CA), where Diplock LJ, as he then was, found that:

"A broker in non-marine insurance has implied authority to issue on behalf of the insurer or enter into as agent for the insurer contracts of interim insurance, which are normally recorded in the cover note. The essential nature of the contract of interim insurance is that it is for a temporary period, generally a maximum of 30 days or so, but is terminable by notice by the insurer at any time during that period. The implied authority of the broker does not extend to entering into the complete policy of insurance which is substituted for the temporary one and is for a fixed period."

Stockton demonstrates that the broker can in certain circumstances find himself acting as agent for both parties, albeit at different times, in relation to the same insurance contract.

Even where the broker is authorised by insurers to act on their behalf the status of the broker can vary depending upon the circumstances. For instance, in *Newsholme Bros* v. *Road Transport & General Insurance Co.* [1929] 2 KB 356 insurers employed an agent to canvas and procure proposals for them. In so doing the agent completed a proposal form for the insured yet in spite of being given the true facts wrote down answers that were untrue. The agent was not authorised by the insurers to complete the proposal form, therefore, for the purpose of completing the form he was the amanuensis of the insured and as such his agent so that the insurers were entitled to repudiate the policy. However, in *Stone* v. *Reliance Mutual Insurance Society Ltd* [1972] 1 Lloyd's Rep 469 a broker employed to solicit business for the insurer was, by virtue of an express term of the proposal, to be regarded as the agent of the insured for the purpose of completing the proposal form. Nonetheless, the Court of Appeal disregarded the declaration because it was company policy that the proposal be completed by the company's agent so that he was acting within the scope of his authority and therefore remained the agent of the insurer when he completed the proposal.

It is not just the proposal stage that has thrown up anomalies in the broker's role. The broker's role in claims handling has given rise to the potential for double employment. The resultant conflict of interest is well illustrated in *Anglo-African Merchants* v. *Bayley* [1969] 1 Lloyd's Rep 268 and *North & South Trust Co.* v. *Berkeley* [1971] 2 Lloyd's Rep 467 where in each case after claims had been made the broker acted upon the insurer's instructions to obtain a report from loss adjusters. The question then arose as to whether the insured was entitled to insist upon disclosure of the loss adjuster's report once it had come into the possession of the brokers. In *Anglo-African* Megaw J (as he then was) found that it would be a breach of duty for a broker to accept instructions of this type from the insurer without the express authority of the insured. Later in the *North & South* case Donaldson J (as he then was) held that the brokers:

". . . in acting for the [insurers], were undertaking duties which inhibited the proper performance of their duties towards the [insured], but in so far as they acted for the [insurer], they were not acting in the discharge of any duty toward the [insured]. [Brokers] wore the [insured's] hat and the [insurer's] hat side by side and in consequence, as was only to be expected, neither hat fitted properly. The [insured] had a legitimate complaint on this account and can claim damages if and to the extent that the partial dislodgment of their hat has caused them loss or damage. But what the [insured] ask in these proceedings is to be allowed to see what [the brokers] were keeping under the underwriter's hat and for that there is no warrant."

In each of the previous cases, the Court placed reliance upon *Fullwood* v. *Hurley* [1928] 1 KB 498 which shows that:

"No agent who has accepted an employment from one principal can in law accept an engagement inconsistent with his duty to the first principal, from a second principal, unless he makes the fullest disclosure to each principal of his interest, and obtains the consent of each principal to the double employment."

In the circumstances, although the agency status of the broker can vary brokers should never be in any doubt as to the party for whom they act and to whom they are responsible. The decision in *London Borough of Bromley* v. *R A Ellis and A Lough & Son* [1971] 1 Lloyd's Rep 97 (CA) indicates

Duties of the insurance broker

that the broker can have responsibilities to the insured even though he is the agent for the insurer. Lord Denning expressed the unanimous view of the Court that:

"The brokers were, I think, under a duty of care to look after Mr Ellis's interest. I know that the brokers were not his agents. They were agents for the insurance company: but, nevertheless, they were also under a duty to use reasonable care to Mr Ellis. He had asked them to arrange the transfer of the insurance. They had undertaken the duty of arranging the transfer. They had taken the proposal form from him and got it filled in. They were clearly under a duty to arrange the transfer with reasonable care so as to see that he was protected."

In such circumstances, the broker's duty will lie in tort and may amount to no more than a duty not to make negligent misstatements or misrepresentations to the insured. Also, the insurance broker may have responsibilities to the client even after the broker's retainer has been terminated as occurred in *Cherry Ltd* v. *Allied Insurance Brokers Ltd* [1978] 1 Lloyd's Rep 274 where a broker whose retainer had been terminated failed to tell his former clients when certain policies were cancelled. In this case, Cantley J based his finding of liability on the part of the brokers on the tort of negligent misstatement without committing himself as to the existence of a residual contractual liability after termination of the retainer. He put it this way:

"Whatever may have been the position in contract, the situation seems to me to have been covered by the principles as stated by Lord Morris of Borth Y Gest in the well known case of *Hedley Byrne & Co. Ltd* v. *Heller & Partners Ltd.*"

In the field of reinsurance the broker acts as intermediary between the insurer and the reinsurer. In many respects the writing of reinsurance is similar to direct insurance. A special feature of reinsurance, however, is the practice whereby a broker instructed to obtain primary insurance will, on his own initiative, approach potential reinsurers to obtain from them, in advance, a binding promise to provide reinsurance for whatever person may subsequently write a line on the primary cover. The practice, which is explained in *General Accident Fire and Life Assurance Corporation and Others* v. *Tanter and Others (The Zephyr)* [1984] 1 Lloyd's Rep 58, enables the broker to offer underwriters a package, i.e., the opportunity to take part in the primary insurance and to place an order for reinsurance at the same time. In *The Zephyr*, Hobhouse J considered that the broker, when dealing with reinsurance, generally acts as the voluntary agent of the reassured: "The relationship of principal and agent is in the present context a voluntary one." Later, in *Youell and Others* v. *Bland Welch & Co. Ltd and Others (the "Superhulls Cover" case) (No. 2)* [1990] 2 Lloyd's Rep 431 at 446 Phillips J. considered *The Zephyr* to support the proposition that:

". . . the broker who approaches an insurer with an offer of reinsurance, is offering to act as agent of the insurer. If the insurer accepts the reinsurance offered he thereby constitutes the broker his agent to obtain the cover offered."

In view of the broker's pivotal role at the heart of the insurance web it is perhaps not surprising that the broker may find himself the servant of two (or more) masters either simultaneously or sequentially in the course of a single transaction. What is important is that the broker should realise that the circumstances of the particular transaction or, indeed, the brokers conduct itself may give rise to duties on the part of the broker breach of which may result in loss or damage being suffered for which the broker may ultimately be liable.

3 THE NATURE OF THE BROKER'S DUTIES AT COMMON LAW

The liabilities of a broker can arise by means of contract. The broker will be bound to perform the terms of the contract with his client, generally the insured. The terms of the contract may be express and/or implied. For instance, in the absence of an appropriate express term, there will generally, pursuant to section 13 of the Supply of Goods and Services Act 1982, be implied a term that the broker will exercise reasonable skill and care in the performance of his services.

In addition, the liabilities of a broker can arise independently of contract, by virtue of a duty of care in the tort of negligence. It has been accepted for some time that where a contract exists between a broker and his client, then, the broker may be liable concurrently in contract and in tort. However, in *Tai Hing Cotton Mill Ltd* v. *Liu Chong Hing Bank Ltd and Others* [1985] 2 Lloyd's Rep 313 PC, the Privy Council questioned whether the law can provide any greater protection than the parties have contracted for. Subsequently, the Court of Appeal adopted this proposition in *Banque Keyser Ullman en Suisse S A* v. *Skandia (UK) Insurance Co.* [1988] 2 Lloyd's Rep 513. Notwithstanding *Tai Hing* and *Skandia*, the attitude of judges at first instance to the question of concurrent liability in contract and tort of brokers may yet remain characterised by the comment of Phillips J. in *Superhulls*:

"There are in my judgment concurrent remedies in contract and in tort. The *Tai Hing* and *Skandia* cases may well mark the start of a reaction by the English Courts against finding parallel duties of care in contract and tort but it is not yet open to a Court of first instance to disregard the principle of concurrent liabilities held by Lord Justice O'Connor (see *Forsikringsaktieselskapet Vesta* v. *Butcher* [1988] 1 Lloyd's Rep 19 (CA)) to be 'clearly established'."

While this may remain the position in relation to primary insurance, it appears from the Court of Appeal's consideration of *The Zephyr* [1985] 2 Lloyd's Rep 529 that the broker acting on behalf of insurers in

Duties of the insurance broker

reinsurance transactions could not be treated as owing tortious duties to reinsurers except in very limited circumstances.

Except where the contract expressly provides for a higher standard, the standard of care required of the broker will be the same contract as in the tort of negligence, i.e., the degree of skill and care of reasonably competent insurance brokers as explained in *Chapman* v. *Walton* (1833) 10 Bing 57 where Tindal C. J. found that:

"... the most satisfactory mode of determining this question, [i.e. whether the broker had exercised reasonable skill and care] to show by evidence whether a majority of skilful and experienced brokers would have come to the same conclusion as the defendant."

It is important, nonetheless, to bear in mind that Tindal CJ's finding is not to be equated with a more general proposition that adhering to accepted, though bad, practice will exempt the broker from liability. In this respect, in *Lewis* v. *Tressider Andrew Associates Pty Ltd* [1987] 2 Qd R 533 a broker was found to be negligent in spite of evidence that the average broker would not have taken any steps to satisfy himself of the solvency of a new insurance company which subsequently became insolvent so that the broker's client suffered loss. Conversely, in *Pryke & Excess Insurance Co. Ltd* v. *Gibbs Hartley Cooper Ltd* [1991] 1 Lloyd's Rep 602 evidence of established practice was held not to be evidence of the existence of a legal duty.

If the broker acts in breach of his duty he will be obliged to pay damages to the injured party. The general principle of the assessment of damages will apply so that the measure of damages is, in the words of Lord Blackburn in *Livingstone* v. *Rawyards Coal Co* (1880) 5 App Cas 25 at page 39:

"That sum of money which will put the party who has been injured, or who has suffered, in the same position as he would have been in if he had not sustained the wrong for which he is now getting his compensation or reparation."

Applying the general principle to insurance brokers usually means that damages are assessed as the amount that the broker's client would otherwise have recovered under the policy of insurance but for the broker's breach of duty as occurred, for example, in *British Citizens Assurance Co.* v. *L Wooland & Co* (1921) 8 Ll L Rep 89. If the policy limits the amount recoverable this will act as a limitation on the broker's liability except where the broker was required to effect a policy without limitation or with a higher limitation than that obtained. The cases on damages usually arise because the broker's default is discovered after the loss that was to be insured against has occurred. However, if the client were to discover the broker's error before any loss had occurred and as a result were to effect fresh insurance of the type required, then the measure of damages would be the extra cost by way of extra premiums incurred as a result of the broker's negligence.

The damages claimed must be proximate to the breach of duty alleged, i.e., they must be caused by, and be foreseeable consequences of, the broker's breach of duty.

Where an intervening error or omission by the client is the cause of the loss rather than the default of the broker then the broker will not be liable. However, in *Dickson & Co.* v. *Devitt* (1916) 86 LJKB 313 it was held that the client, who had failed to check the cover note after receiving it from the broker, was entitled to rely on the broker carrying out his instructions (which in this case the broker had not) and is not bound to see whether those instructions have in fact been followed.

In *Superhulls* it was held that the Law Reform (Contributory Negligence) Act 1945 operates to reduce the client's damages where the client does examine the cover note or other document but fails to notice a patent error and as a result liability was apportioned between the broker and the client. At first sight *Superhulls* appears to contradict *Dickson*. However, the judge in *Superhulls* concluded that *Dickson* was decided on its own facts and does not lay down some inflexible rule of law as to what a broker's client can properly be expected to do in the exercise of reasonable care to protect his own interests. Where the client does examine the cover note and notices the error or omission and approves of it, the broker will not be liable if it can be established by the broker that the client ratified the broker's action. The case of *Sharp and another* v. *Sphere Drake Insurance Plc* [1992] 2 Lloyd's Rep 501 puts a limit, however, upon the ability to claim contribution by way of contributory negligence and in so doing adopts the *Dickson* approach. Sharp had relied upon the brokers' skill and judgment in answering the proposal form questions concerning the use of his yacht and was entitled to believe that the cover which he had sought was in place:

"Mr Sharp as a layman was clearly entitled to rely on [the broker's] skill and judgment as a professional broker in identifying what kind of information was required from Mr Sharp in order to answer the question. Having given [the broker] precisely the information for which he was asked he was entitled to assume, when he subsequently received the proposal form and the policy that what he had told [the broker] was all that was needed to bring about effective cover. It was no part of his duty to second-guess his own professional adviser and there was thus no 'fault' on his part. He had no share in the responsibility for the damage he sustained."

The facts of *Sharp* are clearly distinguishable from *Superhulls*, whereas *Sharp* was a layman in *Superhulls* the client was an insurer.

Superhulls (pp. 448–454) also confirms that in appropriate circumstances the broker may be entitled to invoke the defences of waiver, estoppel and reliance.

Duties of the insurance broker

In *O'Connor* v. *B D B Kirby & Co.* [1972] 1 QB 90 the Court of Appeal held that it was the client's failure to properly check the proposal form completed by the broker that was the sole cause of the loss even though the broker had incorrectly completed the form before submitting it to the client for checking and signature. In the Judgment of Megaw LJ "When Mr Kirby took it on himself to fill in the proposal form, the duty upon him was to use such care as was reasonable in all the circumstances towards ensuring that the answers recorded to the questions in the proposal form accurately represented the answers given to Mr Kirby by Mr O'Connor. But the duty was not a duty to ensure that every answer was correct."

The Insurance Brokers Registration Council Code of Conduct at paragraph 3(14) (see later) provides that "The client should always be asked to check the details and told that the inclusion of incorrect information may result in a claim being repudiated." In the light of the Code of Conduct, failure by the broker to give this warning might itself now constitute breach of duty by the broker and as such be the sole or a contributory cause of the loss. O'Connor might therefore be differently decided if heard today.

Where the proposed insurance that the broker was instructed, but failed, to effect would not have been effective in any event due to, e.g. misrepresentation or non-disclosure by the client, the chain of causation is broken. However in *Fraser* v. *Furman* [1967] 2 Lloyd's Rep 217 it was confirmed that the broker can only rely on this defence if he can prove that the circumstance was one that would have entitled the insurers to repudiate and that the insurers would actually have exercised their right to do so. In addition, *Everitt* v. *Hogg Robinson* [1973] 2 Lloyd's Rep 217 has confirmed that if it is uncertain whether the insurers would have avoided the policy or if the outcome of litigation or negotiations in relation to the avoidance would be uncertain then the client is entitled to damages representing the value of the lost opportunity or prospect of settling the dispute.

Where the required insurance would not have been granted if the full facts had been known then in principle the broker's negligence will not be the cause of the loss subject, however, to questions of whether or not some limited cover might have been obtainable had the full facts been known. Therefore, by analogy with *Fraser and Everitt*, the courts may find themselves called upon to assess the likelihood that insurance might have been obtainable and to award damages based on the amount of cover that might have been obtained.

4 LIABILITY TO THIRD PARTIES AT COMMON LAW

The tort of negligence is of particular importance for third parties to whom the broker may, both in the absence of a contract or a direct relationship, be liable in some limited circumstances. One example, *London Borough of Bromley* v. *Ellis*, has already been discussed. In recent years, however, a number of attempts have been made to extend the scope of the broker's liabilities to third parties, albeit with relatively limited success.

It was held in *The Zephyr*, at first instance, that a Lloyd's broker who gives a "signing indication" to underwriters owes a duty of care in tort to the underwriter to take reasonable steps to see that the signing indication is achieved. This duty was found to exist in circumstances where the court at first instance also found that no contract existed between the broker and the underwriter. On appeal to the Court of Appeal *The Zephyr* [1985] 2 Lloyd's Rep 529, the finding by the trial judge that a duty of care existed in such circumstances, although not directly raised in the appeal, was doubted. The Court of Appeal did find, however, that if the signing indication had been a representation of present fact relied upon by the representees to their detriment the representor would have been liable, except there was nothing in the circumstances of the particular transaction (the broker had promised to use his best endeavours to achieve the signing indication) that could be the subject of the law of negligence. Further, the Court of Appeal also found that the signing indication (such as it was) was not, in any event, directed to anyone other than the actual recipient (in this case the lead underwriter) and therefore the following underwriters (who were third parties in the true sense) could not rely upon the promise (had it been actionable) as it had not been made directly to them.

The effect of *The Zephyr* appears therefore to be that while the broker when dealing with re-insurance is agent of the insurer, nonetheless, a relationship which is contractual in nature may well arise as between the broker and the reinsurers in relation to specific signing indications given by the broker to any particular reinsurer. However, in the absence of a direct contractual promise the broker will, it would appear, have no liability to the re-insurers other than that arising from the principles to be derived from *Hedley Byrne & Co.* v. *Heller and Partners* [1963] 1 Lloyd's Rep 485.

Another partially successful attempt to extend the scope of the broker's liabilities to third parties is to be found in *Duncan Stevenson MacMillan and Others* v. *A W Knott Becker Scott Ltd and Others* [1990] 1 Lloyd's Rep 98, third parties were found to have suffered purely economic or financial loss that was the foreseeable consequence of negligence by E & O brokers who had allegedly failed to effect valid errors and omissions insurance and give timely notice of claims on behalf of other brokers (their clients) so that the E & O insurers denied liability. The client brokers went into liquidation. A group of claimants against the client brokers sued the E & O brokers for negligence claiming that the E & O brokers owed them a duty of care as it was foreseeable that they would suffer loss if they failed to exercise reasonable skill and care in effecting the errors and omissions insurance. The third parties were found to be sufficiently proximate because:

". . . the claimants are the very persons whom the errors and omissions insurance is designed to protect in the event that the insured broker proves financially unsound."

However, in spite of being found to be proximate to the E & O brokers so that a duty of care was owed the court would not permit direct recovery by the third party claimants from the negligent E & O brokers because it was also found that there were no compelling reasons why direct recovery should be permitted. As a result the third party claimants who had suffered loss had to claim through the liquidator of the insolvent broker who in turn could make a direct claim against the negligent broker. The cause of action against the liquidator of the insolvent broker was, however, of little or no value. *MacMillan* may be seen as another example of the court's reluctance, as a matter of policy, to allow claims for purely economic or financial loss. Both *MacMillan* and *The Zephyr* reinforce the importance of the contractual relationship and emphasise the limitations of reliance upon the tort of negligence. Both cases suggest that the categories of persons to whom the broker owes a duty of care are very limited indeed. Claimants must either bring themselves within the traditional categories of persons to whom the broker owes a duty of care or alternatively establish a direct contractual relationship or a relationship of the type occurring in *Hedley Byrne*.

Finally, the *Pryke* v. *Gibbs Hartley Cooper* case provides an example of how a broker may by his actions create obligations where they might not otherwise exist. In this case, the court had to consider whether, *inter alia*, it could be held that a duty of care existed and was owed by Gibbs as brokers to Lloyd's underwriters, namely Pryke and Excess. Pryke and Excess had, through Gibbs as brokers, authorised Atlas Underwriting to enter into insurance agreements on their behalf. The binding authority of Atlas did not extend to financial guarantee business but Atlas, acting outside the scope of their authority, entered into a contract of financial guarantee insurance. This matter was of particular importance to Pryke as under Lloyd's rules he was not permitted to offer financial guarantee insurance. At a later date a representative from the brokers, without any contractual obligation, visited the United States to investigate and discovered that Atlas had in fact issued financial guarantee insurance. The brokers reported to both Pryke and to Excess that Atlas had indeed issued a financial guarantee policy but that it had been cancelled in November 1983 and there were unlikely to be any claims under it. The report turned out not to be correct as the policy had not been cancelled and substantial claims eventually arose and had to be met by Pryke and Excess who consequently brought proceedings against the brokers. The court concluded that in voluntarily despatching a representative the brokers had assumed a duty of care towards Pryke and Excess to investigate Atlas's conduct in the United States. However, the court concluded that Excess had sufficient knowledge to be aware that Atlas had issued a financial guarantee policy prior to the despatch of the brokers' representative to the United States and was not convinced that Excess would have acted in any different manner had the brokers reported the true position. The importance of this decision may be no more than that it provides an example, within the insurance context, of a voluntary assumption of a duty of care in the tort of negligence.

5 THE BROKER'S RESPONSIBILITIES AT COMMON LAW

The insurance broker has a number of responsibilities at common law arising from his position and he must exercise reasonable skill and care in relation to each of them. The insurance broker's responsibilities have traditionally been seen as requiring the broker:

(a) to effect insurance on the terms specified by the client so as to meet with the client's requirements, and

(b) to act with reasonable speed in all the circumstances in connection with his instructions;

(c) to disclose material facts to the insurer;

(d) not to make misrepresentations;

(e) to give proper advice.

It has long been established, for example, in *Smith* v. *Cologan* (1788) 2 TR 187, that the broker has a responsibility to effect insurance though this is not generally, subject to express agreement, an absolute responsibility. In exercising the responsibility to effect insurance *Bromley* v. *Ellis* and *Cock*, *Russell & Co.* v. *Bray, Gibb & Co. Ltd* (1920) 3 Ll L Rep 71 confirm that the broker must act with reasonable speed having regard to all the circumstances.

Callander v. *Oelrichs* (1838) 5 Bing NC 56 confirms that where the required insurance is unobtainable, it appears to be the act of reporting this fact to the client that relieves the broker of his responsibility. The broker's reporting responsibility may be subject to the client establishing, (in the event that he seeks damages from the broker) either that it would have been possible to obtain insurance of the type required elsewhere, or, that he would have desisted from the activity had he known that the insurance required was unobtainable. Where the client's instructions are clear and unambiguous the broker will be under a duty to implement them as in, for example, *Dickson & Co* v. *Devitt*.

Dixon v. *Hovill* (1828) 4 Bing 665 and the later decision of *Enlayd Ltd* v. *Roberts* [1917] 1 Ch 109 establish that, if the client's instructions are ambiguous the broker will not be liable if he interprets them in a reasonable manner or in accordance with the usual practice of insurance brokers. In *Waterkeyn* v. *Eagle Star and British Dominions Insurance Co. Ltd* (1920) 4 Ll L Rep 178 and 5 Ll L Rep 42, it was found that it will be a good defence for the broker to show that insurance on the terms required by the client was not available but that he effected insurance on the best terms he reasonably could. In the current era of near instant worldwide communication the relaxations of the broker's duty, which the *Dixon, Enlayd* and *Waterkeyn* cases permit, may have little application. The modern approach is illustrated by the findings of Philips J in *Superhulls* that:

"... authorities ... establish that an insurance broker's duties include the following: (i) He must ascertain his client's needs by instructions or otherwise. (ii) He must use reasonable skill and care to procure the cover which his client has asked for, either expressly or by necessary implication. (iii) If he cannot obtain what is required, he must report in what respects he has failed and seek his client's alternative instructions."

An example of the modern philosophy can be found in *Harvest Trucking Co. Ltd* v. *P B Davis* [1991] 2 Lloyd's Rep 638 where brokers engaged in negotiating the renewal of a policy failed to notify the insured that insurers would only renew the policy on terms that the cover would only apply to one of the insured's vehicles while it was individually attended. Following theft of the vehicle the insurers denied liability due to the absence of individual attendance. His Honour Judge Diamond QC found that the broker was under a duty either to obtain the insurance instructed or to exercise reasonable care to bring the insurer's requirements to the express notice of his client, to ascertain whether they met the client's requirements and to obtain further instructions with the effect that the failure to obtain the client's informed consent to any further action amounted to negligence by the broker.

The decision of *Strong & Pearl* v. *S Allison & Co. Ltd* (1926) 25 Ll L Rep 504 is one of many authorities which shows that the broker must ensure that the risk the client wishes to insure against is correctly described in the policy so that the client will be entitled to claim should the need arise. Decisions such as Strong may be regarded as no more than a further example of the fundamental responsibility of the broker to ascertain the client's needs by instructions and implement them to the extent that the required insurance is available.

The broker must, where he acts for the insured, disclose material facts to the insurer which are or should be within his own knowledge. In the *Container Transport International Inc.* v. *Oceanus Mutual Underwriting Association (Bermuda) Ltd* [1984] 1 Lloyd's Rep 476 (CA) Kerr LJ stated that in determining whether a fact is material the question to be asked is whether:

"Having regard to all the circumstances known or deemed to be known to the insured and to his broker and ignoring those which are expressly excepted from the duty of disclosure, was the presentation in summary form to the underwriter a fair and substantially accurate presentation of the risk proposed for insurance, so that a prudent insurer could form a proper judgment ... whether or not to accept the proposal, and, if so, on what terms ..."

The question posed by the *Oceanus* case was clarified further in *Pan Atlantic Insurance Co. Ltd and another* v. *Pine Top Insurance Co. Ltd* [1993] 1 Lloyd's Rep 496 to that of whether the prudent insurer would view the undisclosed material as probably tending to increase the risk. Thus the issue becomes whether or not the undisclosed material would have influenced the judgment of the insurer. The *Pan Atlantic* decision will be welcomed by brokers because it provides a workable and practical judicial guideline as to what constitutes material facts which is to be based upon the objective standpoint of the prudent insurer and therefore avoids the need for endless disclosure of trivia but still requires the broker to exercise proper professional judgment both in taking instructions from his client and in passing on information to the insurer. It is understood, however, that the *Pan Atlantic* is destined for the House of Lords whose decision is awaited with interest.

Cases such as the *Litsion Pride* [1985] 1 Lloyd's Rep 437, *The Captain Panagos D P* [1986] 2 Lloyd's Rep. 470, *La Banque Financière de la Cité* v. *Westgate Insurance Co. Ltd* [1988] 2 Lloyd's Rep 513 demonstrate that the duty of disclosure of material facts applies before and throughout the currency of a policy. Further, *Lambert* v. *The Co-operative Insurance Society Limited* [1975] 2 Lloyd's Rep 485 confirms that the duty also applies at renewal.

If there is a material non-disclosure defence available to underwriters they are likely to avail themselves of it. Brokers are most vulnerable when an underwriter rejects the claim for material non-disclosure because if the insured has to sue his insurers then he may often be compelled to sue his brokers as well. The difficulties which brokers may encounter are graphically illustrated by the *Sphere Drake* case. In this decision, the insurer's entitlement to avoid the policy for material non-disclosure was upheld, however, the insured was able to successfully recover against his brokers. The Court held that since the broker had forged the signature of the client this was a material non-disclosure which entitled the insurers to avoid the policy. The insurer was also entitled to avoid the policy on the ground of an exclusion whereby the insurer was not liable for any period during which the vessel was "used as a houseboat". The Judge ruled that the brokers ought to have advised the insured that in answering the proposal form question as to whether the yacht would be used as a houseboat, the permanent presence of any person on the yacht was to be disclosed. It was not enough for the brokers to assert that it had not occurred to them that there would be a permanent crew. The existence of other allegations advanced, albeit unsuccessfully, by the insurer in *Sphere*, relating to material non-disclosure and lack of insurable interest demonstrate the need for brokers' vigilance.

It is submitted that the insurance broker should make sufficiently detailed enquiries of his client to ascertain or decide upon the facts that are material and which ought to be disclosed and must do so before inception, upon renewal and in handling claims under, a policy.

The broker when acting for the insured must not make misrepresentations to the insurer. In *Warren* v. *Henry Sutton & Co.* [1976] 2 Lloyd's Rep 276, a broker converted a vague response to a question into a positive assertion that was not justified by the client's response. As a result the insurers avoided the policy but the broker was found liable to pay damages to the client.

The giving of advice in connection with insurance matters is, perhaps, the broker's most important responsibility and in discharging this responsibility he must have a basic knowledge of insurance law. For example, in *Sarginson Bros* v. *Keith Moulton & Co.* (1942) 73 Ll L Rep 104 brokers who gave incorrect advice as to the application of a statutory war insurance scheme were held liable.

Furthermore, the broker must be familiar with the policies he deals with. For example, in *McNealy* v. *The Pennine Insurance Co.* [1978] 2 Lloyd's Rep 18 from which it is clear that the broker must be sufficiently familiar with the policies he offers so that he can properly take the client's instructions to ascertain whether the particular policy is available to him.

Sometimes it will be the responsibility of the broker to draft cover notes, slips or policy documents and where he does so, Superhulls confirms that the broker must exercise reasonable skill and care in drafting these documents so as to ensure that they give clear expression to the terms agreed.

In summary, it can therefore be said that the need to take clear and sufficient instructions at the outset and throughout his retainer is at the heart of the broker's responsibilities. The instructions should be promptly implemented and proper advice should be proffered at all times. It must, however, be emphasised that the broker may by contract assume an absolute responsibility to obtain insurance of the particular type required by the client and may take on more specific and more onerous obligations than those the law will otherwise impose.

6 STATUTORY AND VOLUNTARY REGULATION

For a long time, the common law was the sole regulator of the broker's conduct. As a result, the development of the broker's duties and responsibilities has been somewhat ad hoc. Latterly, the influence of statutory and voluntary regulation has increased so that, in common with many other fields of commercial endeavour, a plethora of regulations and voluntary codes of conduct exist. It is not the purpose of this work to engage in an in depth analysis of the regulatory minefield, nonetheless, they cannot be ignored in the context of a consideration of the insurance broker's liabilities.

The Insurance Brokers (Registration) Act 1977 is the principal legislative measure concerning insurance brokers. A great deal of secondary legislation has been produced under the Act in the form of regulations and have involved the establishment of the Insurance Brokers Regulation Council to maintain a register and to regulate the business of insurance brokers; the requirement of registration as a pre-requisite of the use of the title "insurance broker" (unregistered persons may not call themselves "insurance brokers", although they may call themselves brokers and act as such in connection with insurance); the requirement that all registered insurance brokers maintain professional indemnity insurance; and the establishment of a disciplinary procedure.

Section 10 of the Act required the Council to draw up and issue statements as to what it regards as unprofessional conduct. A code of conduct for the guidance of insurance brokers has been drawn up by the Council pursuant to Section 10 and is contained in the Insurance Brokers Registration Council (Code of Conduct) Approval Order 1978. It lists three fundamental principles and 19 examples of the application of these principles. The fundamental principles are as follows:

(1) insurance brokers shall at all times conduct their business with utmost good faith and integrity;

(2) insurance brokers shall do everything possible to satisfy the insurance requirements of their clients and shall place the interests of their clients before all other considerations. Subject to these requirements and interests, insurance brokers shall have proper regard for others;

(3) statements made by or on behalf of insurance brokers when advertising shall not be misleading or extravagant.

Apart from the Code of Conduct, insurance brokers involved in the life insurance sector operate subject to the various rules arising from the regulatory framework established under the Financial Services Act 1986. In January 1989 the Association of British Insurers introduced its own Code of Practice for all intermediaries other than registered insurance brokers. This Code of Practice applies to insurance brokers and their employees. It applies to general insurance business excluding re-insurance business. The ABI Code states that there is an overriding obligation upon an intermediary at all times to conduct business with the utmost good faith and integrity so that its starting point is similar to the statutory code. Other bodies concerned with the insurance industry have also produced voluntary codes of practice.

A Code of Practice for Lloyd's Brokers issued by the Council of Lloyd's came into force on 1 November 1988. The Code of Practice seeks to define guidelines by which Lloyd's Brokers are required to act. Of particular interest is paragraph 8 which deals with "Binding Authorities" in which the primary relationship between the broker and his client is emphasised. The code accepts the potential conflict of interest which can arise where a broker deals with his client's business under a binding authority. The primary purpose of a binding authority is to facilitate prompt and efficient acceptance of business. The effect of the Code of Practice is that Lloyd's brokers, when accepting a binding authority, should remind insurers granting the authority that the Lloyd's broker's first duty will be to his client.

During recent years, insurance brokers have been the target of financial institutions who are attracted to the brokers since they represent outlets in the area of financial services. Many brokers have been acquired by insurance companies, thus circumstances may arise where a broker is owned by a particular insurer yet is approached by a client for independent advice on his insurance requirements. In spite of the various codes putting the client's interests first, concern must be expressed as to whether this relationship sits easily with the necessity for the proper discharge of the broker's duties toward his client. The Financial Services Act 1986, does impose a requirement for disclosure by an agent to his client if he is a tied agent which may be seen as offering some protection to the insured.

Other insurance intermediaries are also subject to regulation under the "connected intermediaries" regulations provided for in the Insurance Companies Regulations 1981. These regulations require the connected intermediary to inform the prospective policy holder of his connection with the insurance company and require the company to declare all connected persons selling insurance on its behalf to the Department of Trade.

The European Union has been active in the regulation of insurance intermediaries. The principal standpoint of the European Commission is harmonisation of law across the Union to facilitate the free movement of services. Part of the process of harmonisation is seen as providing an equal level of consumer protection in the member states. The Insurance Intermediaries Directive of 13 December 1976 is the principle measure concerned with insurance intermediaries. This was developed further by the Commission Recommendation (92/48/EEC) on insurance intermediaries of 18 December 1991 which defines the professional requirements of insurance intermediaries in relation to independence, knowledge, professional indemnity, fitness (i.e., good repute) and minimum capital requirements. Currently, in England and Wales the existing common law and statutory framework appears to amount to compliance by the UK with its obligations arising from the Directive and the Recommendation.

7 CONCLUSION

It will be observed that in spite of much litigation and a great deal of statutory and self-regulation over recent decades, the essential relationship between the parties to an insurance transaction is largely unchanged. The insured remains the principal and the broker (for the most part) his agent who is nonetheless remunerated by the insurer. The common law is unable to change this arrangement and Parliament has seen fit not to interfere with the basic nature of the relationship. To the extent that Parliament has sought to intervene with legislation this has been limited to regulating the conduct of brokers within the framework of the historical relationship.

The regulatory provisions may be seen as reinforcing the contractual relationship between the broker and his client. They make clear to the broker where his responsibilities lie and may in this respect be seen as codifying, albeit in a very limited way, the essential common law principles. The obvious conflict between professional responsibility and financial gain remains. It is important, however, to note that the Code of Conduct is to be regarded as guidance only as to the professional conduct that may be expected from the broker and a failure to conform while amounting to unprofessional conduct which may give rise to disciplinary sanctions may not necessarily be construed as conclusive evidence of breach of duty at common law. Indeed, and fundamentally, neither the Act nor the regulations adopted under it displace the common law as the forum for obtaining compensation from brokers as a result of breach of duty.

In the context of the "victim and villains" analogy it may be concluded that all parties remain in a state of relationship that is not strictly of their own making. It is the web of the common law that Parliament has not seen fit to unravel. Nonetheless, in so far as the insured becomes the victim of

Duties of the insurance broker

the insurance industry a remedy may be at hand in the form of an action against the broker for damages for breach of contract or negligence. In so far as the broker should ever prove to be the "villain" (which in truth will hopefully be comparatively rare), whether wilfully (by fraud or greed) or by professional neglect the broker nowadays faces both the prospect of paying damages and of disciplinary action under the regulatory framework.

CHAPTER 5

ARCHITECTS AND ENGINEERS—PROFESSIONAL NEGLIGENCE

1 INTRODUCTION

The word "architect" like the word "solicitor" is a term of art. It can be used only by those who are registered by the Architects' Registration Council under the Architects' Registration Act 1938.

The word "engineer" is not a term of art.

Since a large part of the functions of architects and engineers is to design things and to oversee or advise on the construction of whatever it is that they have designed, this chapter will concentrate on their obligations in those two separate areas.

The test of whether an architect or an engineer is negligent (whether in tort or in contract) is the test that is applied to any professional, namely the test of whether he has exercised the reasonable skill and care to be expected of a member of his profession, often known as the "Bolam" test after the medical negligence case of *Bolam* v. *Friern Hospital Management Committee* [1957] 1 WLR 582.

In cases of "contractual" negligence (i.e., involving client and architect/engineer, as opposed to the issue of negligence in relation to third parties) the general test must be applied in the light of the specific terms of the contract between the parties. The main architects' body, the Royal Institute of British Architects, has issued a form "the Architect's Appointment" (1982) which comes in standard form and also in an adjusted form for design and build works and for small works. There is now also the Standard Form of Agreement for the Appointment of an Architect (SFA/92), again published by the RIBA. The standard form for engineers is the Association of Consulting Engineers (ACE) Conditions of Engagement 1981, which again comes in various forms.

The Architect's Appointment states that the architect will exercise reasonable skill and care in conformity with the normal standard of the architect's profession (part 3, paragraph 3.1). The ACE form states similarly that the engineer will "exercise all reasonable skill, care and diligence in the discharge of the services to be performed by him".

2 DESIGN LIABILITIES

Richard Roberts Holdings Ltd v. *Douglas Smith Stimson Partnership* (1988) 46 BLR 50 at page 52 is a "cautionary tale" for architects.

The facts were that the plaintiff retained the defendant architect to design an effluent tank for use in a dye works which was being rebuilt after a fire. It was accepted by both parties that the tank would need to be lined and the architect's design assumed that this would be with stainless steel. There then followed discussions between the plaintiff and the defendant's representatives regarding the choice of lining. The parties jointly investigated a number of possible firms to supply the lining including ECC, also defendants in the action. At the plaintiff's suggestion, the architects asked ECC to quote. Their quotation was accepted after the architect had confirmed to the plaintiff that he felt that the plaintiff's outstanding queries had now been answered. The plaintiff then entered into a direct contract with ECC (since the works at this stage were otherwise almost complete). Subsequently large areas of the lining became detached causing erosion of the concrete walls.

The architects argued that they had no legal responsibility for the lining. The plaintiff was aware that they had no knowledge of linings; the plaintiff had taken independent advice from a trade association about the linings; the architects had not charged any fee for their work in relation to the choice of linings; and their input had mainly been directed to helping the plaintiff to perform its part in the project. However Judge Newey QC held that the architects were employed as architects for the creation of the whole dye works (and contrasted their position in this case with their position in an earlier project to construct another dye works for this plaintiff where they had not designed the effluent tank).

"The lining was I think an integral part of the tank. The architects did not know about linings, but part of their expertise as architects was to be able to collect information about materials of which they lacked knowledge and/or experience and to perform a view about them. If the architects felt that they could not form a reliable judgement about a lining for the tank, they should have informed [the plaintiff] of that fact and advised them to take other advice, possibly from a chemist."

The architects were in breach of duty in failing to investigate alternative linings when they first designed the tank; and subsequently, when their investigations were limited to conversations with other dye works' owners (they did not seek advice from specialists or trade associations etc). Despite certain "alarm bells" such as a suspiciously cheap quotation from ECC, they did not warn the plaintiff in any way. As between ECC and the architects, Judge Newey QC held both parties equally to blame.

Holland Hannen and Cubitts (Northern) Ltd v. *Welsh Health Technical Services Organisation* (1985) 35 BLR 1 (CA) is a useful decision for two reasons. First, it provides an illustration of the way in which a court approaches the problem, typical in construction cases, of apportioning liability between a number of parties. Here the Court of Appeal substantially altered the apportionment that the trial judge had made. Secondly, and more importantly, it is some authority for the view that a professional such as a structural engineer, concerned with functional matters, is not liable for aesthetic matters where there is an architect in the employer's design team who might normally be expected to deal with such matters. In this case, there was held to be no overlapping of the function of assessing the aesthetics of this particular scheme as between the two professionals involved.

WHTSO engaged Cubitts to construct two hospitals. CED were to design the floors. They entered into a direct warranty with WHTSO agreeing to use all reasonable care and skill in the design of the floors, and they then became nominated sub-contractors to Cubitts. Their design work was carried out in conjunction with Alan Marshall & Partners (AMP), structural engineers, with whom they had previously patented a type of concrete floor called Arbigrill (CED and AMP had previously failed to persuade the WHTSO to use this floor in this project). WHTSO's design team consisted of Percy Thomas Partnership (PTP) as architect, and Wallace Evans & Partners (WEP) as structural engineers.

PTP amended the specification part way through the design phase, without reference to AMP, so that higher tolerances were required. PTP later condemned the floors as not being in accordance with the (amended) specification. The works were delayed for some 20 weeks. Cubitts commenced proceedings against WHTSO and CED. WHTSO brought in CED, PTP and WEP as third parties, CED brought in AMP as fourth parties, and AMP joined Costain, their suppliers, to the action. CED, PTP and WEP settled with Cubitts by paying them £396,681 for delay costs attributable to the floor problems. CED admitted that part of the delay was due to a design error on their part. CED then pursued AMP for a contribution towards the settlement sum. There were also issues as to the proper contributions of PTP and WEP (the design team) jointly as against CED, and also *inter se*.

The trial judge held the design team to be one third responsible (WEP and PTP to contribute equally *inter se*) and CED to be two thirds responsible. He also held that AMP should pay 75 per cent of CED's "two thirds" liability.

The Court of Appeal unanimously reapportioned the responsibility so that the design team were two thirds responsible and CED only one third. This was on the basis that the judge had not taken into account (except on the issue of the contribution as between WEP and PTP *inter se*) PTP's failure to grapple with the floor problem at a much earlier stage.

By a 2–1 majority, the Court of Appeal also allowed AMP's appeal so that they had to make no contribution to CED's own liability. The issue was whether it was part of AMP's duty to CED to foresee and warn them of the visual appearance that the floors might have when laid with tiles.

Lawton LJ held that it was not, on the relatively narrow basis that CED had had no such duty when advising the WHTSO regarding the Arbigrill floor. Dillon LJ also held that it was not, on the basis that:

"... Matters of visual appearance or aesthetic effect are not within the province of the structural engineer. It is for the structural engineer to work out what the deflections of a floor will be; it is for the architect to decide whether a floor with those deflections will be visually or aesthetically satisfactory when the finishings chosen by the architect has been applied"

Robert Goff LJ dissented on this point. He felt that the structural engineer had to consider not merely the strength of the structure, but also the profile of the flooring:

"The structural engineer may not know precisely what is to be the function of a particular part of the floor ... though he should know in general terms at least for what purposes [the floor] is likely to be used. But he should be able to ascertain, with his expertise, the likely profile of the floor as constructed from the design submitted to him; and he should be able to assess whether there is any significant risk that the floor, with the ascertained profile, will be unacceptable to a reasonable building owner or his architect. This is not a matter of aesthetics, nor is it a matter of finishes, nor is it a matter of subjective judgement. It is a matter of objective judgement founded upon professional skill and experience"

The fact that Lawton LJ's view was partly influenced by the particular facts relating to the Arbigrill floor, and the well argued nature of the dissent by Robert Goff LJ makes it impossible to state conclusively either that:

(a) structural engineers need not be concerned with aesthetics; or
(b) more generally, that professionals need not be concerned with matters outside their own sphere (particularly when their client has retained another professional adviser who might be expected to deal with the point).

However this case clearly provides some authority, and at Court of Appeal level, for both propositions.

It should be noted that if an architect or engineer actually does take on obligations outside his own field, being obligations normally undertaken by another professional, he will probably be judged by the standards of that other profession. For example, the ACE Conditions of Engagement provide for the consulting engineer to take on certain quantity surveying duties in some circumstances, e.g., preparing a cost plan, preparing bills of quantities, negotiating and agreeing prices with sub-contractors, reporting on valuations for the purpose of preparing interim certificates, measuring variations and preparing a final account.

Both the Architect's Appointment and the ACE Conditions of

Engagement contain provisions for the architect or engineer to appoint appropriate specialists or otherwise sub-contract work, but in both cases only with the consent of the client. Both forms also provide that the architect/engineer will not be liable for the sub-contractor's negligence.

(a) Delegation of duties

The question of the delegation of an architect's duties is important. It is important to separate two issues.

(a) Can an architect delegate his duties in any way?
(b) If he does, to what extent might he remain liable for the delegate's negligence?

As to the first issue, it is not generally permissible for a professional either to assign the burden of his contract with his client (i.e., to divest himself fully of his obligations) without the client's consent. Nor is it permissible to sub-contract (i.e., to arrange for someone else to carry out his obligations while still retaining primary liability to the client) without the client's consent.[1] This is because, in both cases, a professional retainer is generally seen in law as falling within a category of contracts that are of a personal nature (using that term to cover situations where a corporation or partnership is instructed) i.e., within the first of two types of category outlined by Bingham LJ in *Southway Group Ltd* v. *Wolff & Wolff* (1991) 57 BLR 33 (CA) at page 52:

"In some classes of contract, as where B commissions A to write a book or paint a picture or teach him to play the violin, it would usually be clear that personal performance by A was required. In other cases, as where A undertakes to repair B's shoes, or mend B's watch or drive B to the airport, it may be open to A to perform the contract vicariously by employing the services of C."

In *Moresk Cleaners* v. *Hicks* (1966) 4 BLR 50 the plaintiff employed the defendant architect to design an extension for a laundry. Unknown to the plaintiff, the architect invited the main contractor, whom he was clearly acquainted with, to design the shape of the building. The building failed because of the design of the portal frame and of the purlins in the roof. The official referee robustly rejected the architect's arguments:

(a) that there was an implied term that he would be entitled to delegate "certain specified tasks" to a relevant specialist; and
(b) that he had implied authority to act as the plaintiff's agent in employing the contractor to design the structure.

---

1. This does not mean that an architect's firm cannot, for example, have someone other than the person who took the instructions from the client actually carry out at least some of the work. If a client instructs a partnership or practice, rather than a specific architect within that practice, subject to any contractual stipulations by the client, it would not be unusual for mundane work on a project to be carried out by a member of staff at an appropriate level. But this would not amount to sub-contracting.

Architects and engineers—professional negligence

As to the first argument, there was no implied power to delegate his duty at all, and certainly not to a building contractor whose interests might well be opposed to those of the plaintiff. As to the second argument, no authority could be implied, and there were clearly no express powers.

It is important to note that *Moresk* is a case on the issue of the architect's power to delegate itself, and not on the issue as to what liabilities are retained by an architect who properly delegates (i.e. as against his client) – this is confirmed by Slade LJ at (1985) 32 BLR 37, line 8, in *Investors in Industry* v. *South Bedfordshire District Council*.

The official referee went on to say that if the architect had felt out of his depth in dealing with the form of reinforced concrete construction that was, in technical terms, relatively new at the time of this case, he might pay for a structural engineer himself to carry out that work, thus having the "satisfaction" of knowing that he would have a similar case against that engineer for negligent advice that the employer might ultimately have against him. In view of the personal nature of an architect's retainer in such cases, it is questionable whether this is correct.

Where either the Architect's Appointment or the ACE Conditions are used, the matter is provided for. Both forms allow delegation only with consent. In cases where the standard forms are not used, the architect or engineer may be in difficulties if he has taken on an unqualified obligation to perform a task and then finds that, because of the specialist skills required to perform at least part of it, he is unequipped to do so. He cannot force the client to employ a specialist and he will be in breach of contract if he cannot perform the task as promised. If he has alerted the client to the problem however, the client would have to choose between employing a specialist or abandoning the project. At this point, the client's obligation to mitigate his damages would come into play. If the costs of employing the specialist are less than the costs of abandonment, only the former would be recoverable as damages.

As to the second issue stated above, many cases will be covered by the terms of the Architect's Appointment or the ACE Conditions. Other cases will depend on their facts and it is difficult to lay down propositions of law in this area.

One case that provides some interpretation of the Architects Appointment, albeit *obiter*, is *Investors in Industry Commercial Properties Ltd* v. *South Bedfordshire District Council* (1985) 32 BLR 1 (CA). Slade LJ stated as follows:

"[Clauses 1.20, 1.22 and 1.23 of the Architect's Appointment] clearly contemplate that where a particular part of the work involved in a building contract involves specialist knowledge or skill beyond that which an architect of ordinary competence may reasonably be expected to possess, the architect is at liberty to recommend to his client that a reputable independent consultant, who appears to have the relevant specialist knowledge or skill, shall be appointed by the client to perform this task. If following such a recommendation a consultant with these qualifications is appointed, the architect will normally carry no legal responsibility for the work to be done by the expert which is beyond the capability of an architect or ordinary competence; in relation to the work allotted to the expert, the architect's legal responsibility will normally be confined to directing and co-ordinating the expert's work in the whole. However, this is subject to one important qualification. If any danger or problem arises in connection with the work allotted to the expert, of which an architect or [sic] ordinary competence reasonably ought to be aware and reasonably could be expected to warn the client, despite the employment of the expert, and despite what the expert says or does about it, it is in our judgement, the duty of the architect to warn the client. In such a contingency he is not entitled to rely blindly on the expert with no mind of his own, on matters which must or should have been apparent to him."

In cases not involving the standard forms, there is some authority for the view that, assuming delegation in a particular case is permissible, the fact that an architect's choice of a specialist is reasonable may be enough to discharge his design obligations. The case in question is *Merton LBC* v. *Lowe* (1981) 18 BLR 130 (CA).

The facts were that the defendant architects were retained to design a swimming pool and supervise its erection. Their design incorporated the use of Pyrok, a material for the suspended ceilings. This was a proprietary product produced by Pyrok Ltd who became nominated sub-contractors. The ceilings later developed cracks. This was because the mix used in the Pyrok coat was stronger than that used in the underlying coat; and also because of poor workmanship. The architects were held liable because they failed in their duties of supervision. But they were not held liable for the design error, even though it had undoubtedly been their obligation to design the pool.

Waller LJ distinguished *Moresk Cleaners* v. *Hicks* on the basis that the architect had "virtually handed over to another the whole task of design" in that case. However, as stated above, the true distinction appears to be that in *Moresk* there was found to be no contractual right to delegate at all, whereas in *Merton*, it does not seem to have been suggested that the architect was in breach of contract merely in employing nominated sub-contractors to carry out part of the design work. Waller LJ, the only member of the court to deal with the point in any detail, said:

"It was the defendant's duty to use reasonable care as architects. In view of successful work done elsewhere, they decided that to employ Pyrok was reasonable. No witness called suggested that it was not at the beginning."

It appears therefore that, for Waller LJ, the architect was acting reasonably in employing Pyrok to design the ceilings and that (leaving aside the breaches in supervision) its obligations of design of the ceilings were discharged simply by that reasonable selection. Matters would be different if the architect had no contractual right to delegate (*Moresk*) or if the selection itself had been unreasonable (i.e., falling below the standard to be expected of an architect in exercising such powers of selection).

(b) Fitness for purpose

Does the design liability of an architect/engineer include an implied obligation to achieve a result? A question closely linked to this is whether a design liability can include an implied fitness for purpose obligation. A promise that something will be fit for its intended purpose is only one type (though a very important one) of a promise to achieve a result. Other examples of such promises are that a house will achieve a certain insulation value, or a bridge withstand a specified load. In general such terms will be incorporated expressly (if at all) rather than as implied terms.

The question at the head of this subsection is important. The professional's duty is normally to exercise reasonable care and skill. An obligation to produce something that is fit for its intended purpose is a higher obligation. From the claimant's point of view it requires him only to prove something that is primarily a matter of fact (whether something is fit for its purpose) rather than something which is much more a matter of opinion (whether the professional has fallen below the standard of skill and care to be expected of him), and which correspondingly tends to require expert opinion evidence in support (see later in this chapter). It is easier for a claimant to show, for example, that a building is simply incapable of use due to condensation, than it is to show that the problem is due to a lack of care and skill on the part of the designer.

The answer to the question posed above is, in general terms, in the negative. The obligation of a professional is the lower duty of reasonable care and skill. That is to be contrasted with the obligation of a tradesman or a supplier of goods. He is held to promise that his goods are fit for any purpose expressly or impliedly made known to him by virtue of section 14 of the Sale of Goods Act 1979. (Although this Act does not apply to a building contract, which is a contract for the supply of work and materials and not just materials alone, the warranty is likely to be similar in practice. In *Young* v. *Marten Ltd & MacManus Childs Ltd* (1968) 9 BLR 77 the House of Lords held that there is normally an implied warranty in such a contract that the work and materials will be fit for the purpose for which they were intended.)

However, where a professional supplies as well as designs goods, the position is that he takes on the higher obligation of fitness for purpose. There is Court of Appeal authority for this view and also endorsement from the House of Lords, although admittedly *obiter*.

The House of Lords' decision is *IBA* v. *EMI and BICC* (1980) 14 BLR 1 (HL) which concerned a collapsed television aerial mast on Emley Moor in Yorkshire. The mast was constructed for the Independent Television

Authority by EMI through their nominated sub-contractors, BICC. The House of Lords held that BICC were negligent in their design and that, on the facts, EMI had accepted contractual responsibility for the design of the mast.

It was because of this finding of negligence that remarks concerning fitness for purpose were *obiter*. However, Lord Scarman referred to the words of du Parq LJ in *Samuels* v. *Davis* [1943] KB 526, where he stated that where a dentist (i.e., a professional) fixes a denture, he warrants that the denture will be fit for its purpose. The crucial point is that he is designing and supplying an item of goods and thus comes under the higher duty (fitness for purpose) applicable to tradesmen selling goods, rather than the lower one of professionals supplying a service. Lord Scarman said:

"In the absence of any terms (express or to be implied) negativing the obligation, one who contracts to design an article for a purpose made known to him undertakes that the design is reasonably fit for the purpose. Such a design obligation is consistent with the statutory law regulating the sale of goods."

In two special cases, a designer has been held to have an implied fitness for purpose obligation even where goods were apparently not supplied. But both cases can be explained on their facts.

The first is *Greaves (Contractors)* v. *Baynham Meikle & Partners* (1975) 4 BLR 57 (CA).

Baynham Meikle were structural engineers employed by a design and build contractor to design a structure of a warehouse. After construction it was found that the first floor was unable to take the weight of fork lift trucks carrying drums of oil, as required by the building owner. The trial judge found that the floors were not designed with sufficient strength to withstand the vibrations produced by these trucks.

Lord Denning began by noting that the professional man does not usually have an implied obligation of result. The surgeon does not promise to cure his patient or a solicitor that he will win his case. However there were two reasons why in this case the engineers were held to have taken on a higher duty:

(a) Mr Baynham for the defendants had admitted as follows in cross examination:
   "Q And it was your job, was it not, to produce a building which was going to be fit to be used as a store for oil drums and for stacker-truck use?
   A Yes.
   Q That was what you were being engaged to do and that is what you were being paid your fee for?
   A Correct."

(b) In their pleading, the defendants had originally admitted the implied term alleged. They amended the pleading on the second day of the trial. This was clearly nevertheless at least evidence that at one point they had accepted that the term alleged was part of the contract and to that extent, the admission was damning evidence.

Geoffrey Lane LJ regarded the case as deciding "no great issue of principle" and the trial judge's view that a professional designer took on higher duties than other professional men was rejected.

The second case is *CGI* v. *John Worman Ltd* (1985) 9 Con LR 46. Worman, who were building contractors, were engaged to renovate an abattoir for Turner. The judge held that Worman warranted to Turner that the works would be fit for their intended purpose, which, in this case, he held, meant that the works would comply with certain UK and EC standards necessary for Turner to obtain a grant. Worman had engaged architects, CGI, to provide design services. Even though they were not themselves supplying goods, Judge John Davies QC held that the architects undertook that the works as designed by them would be fit for their purpose, i.e., would comply with these standards.

The decision was based on the unusually close relationship between Worman and the architects. The architects were the "prime movers" in the project from start to finish. Worman relied heavily on the architects throughout and their relationship with them was more in the nature of a joint venture than a retainer. Having found that Worman took on an express (alternatively implied) fitness for purpose obligation with Turner, it was perfectly possible to construe the architects' contract with Worman as including the same obligations.

George Hawkins v. *Chrysler (UK) Ltd and Burne Associates* (1986) 38 BLR 36 (CA) illustrates the orthodox view that designers will rarely take on fitness for purpose obligations.

The second defendant engineers, Burne, designed a shower room for a foundry belonging to Chrysler, the first defendant. The plaintiff, a foundry worker employed by Chrysler, slipped and fell on the shower room floor. His action against Chrysler was settled but Chrysler continued their third party action against Burne.

It was found as a fact that the floor was unsafe. However, the trial judge held that the decision by Burne to use this particular type of flooring (called "Altro Standard"), while it may have been the wrong decision, was not negligent. Mr Burne had, amongst other things, specifically considered alternatives, considered the conditions of work in the foundry, tested the floor himself, and consulted a specialist flooring firm before reaching his decision. The Court of Appeal agreed with that view.

However, the trial judge had also held that Burne had warranted the floor's safety, i.e., undertaken a fitness for purpose obligation. The Court of Appeal overturned this finding. It is interesting to note two of the defendants' arguments that were rejected.

The first was that a professional man who designs is in a different category from a professional man who advises on some other matter, e.g., a doctor or solicitor. The argument was that the professional man who is advising on design is really producing a product, and that it would be anomalous if a contractor who constructed a building in accordance with an architect's proposals should be liable for fitness for purpose, whereas the architect who had designed the building was to be liable only if he had failed to exercise reasonable care and skill. Nourse LJ acknowledged that there might be anomalies between contractors or sub-contractors on the one hand, and professional men on the other. However, the court was unanimous that the distinction was established in law, and that it could not be said that a designer is in some way supplying a product.

The second argument was based on a particular answer given in cross examination by Mr Burne. He was asked:

"It was your job to produce a floor that was safe in those circumstances?"

and answered

"As safe as I possibly could, yes."

Dillon LJ dismissed the significance of this, and in doing so illustrated the distinction between the professional's admitted objective in doing his best for a client, and actually warranting that he will produce a result.

"It seems to me that that is the sort of answer which might be given by any professional man.
   'Question : it was your job to provide medicines which would cure the patient's illness?
   Answer : in so far as I possibly could, yes.
   Question : it was your job to provide a tax avoidance scheme which would save your client an enormous amount of tax?
   Answer : in so far as I possibly could, yes.'
The answer indicates the objective which the professional man would have in advising—what he would be hoping to achieve—but I cannot think that it is, just by itself, enough to extend his obligation, from an obligation to use reasonable care and skill in his profession, to a guarantee that his advice would be successful if any advice could be successful."

It may be noted in passing that Mr Burne's answer in cross examination was not so far removed from the answer given by the unfortunate defendant in *Greaves*, and which contributed to his downfall.

In summary:

(1) An architect/engineer carrying out design work does not generally impliedly warrant or guarantee a result, and in particular does not guarantee that his work as constructed will be fit for its purpose.

(2) An architect/engineer who also supplies goods does impliedly

take on such an obligation. "Supply" here requires something more than mere design (*Hawkins*).

(3) An architect/engineer may nonetheless take on express fitness for purpose obligations, e.g., as in *Greaves* (on the evidence) and *CGI Consultants* (because of the unusual relationship between architect and contractor).

3 LIABILITY FOR THE PROVISION OF COSTS ESTIMATES

Architects and engineers are frequently called upon to provide estimates of the likely costs of the project. If the works eventually cost more than the estimate, the issue is whether there was negligence in the provision of the estimate (which is usually all that a given figure will be, since a professional will rarely have given, or be held to have given, a guarantee of price).

These cases tend to turn on their own facts. Important criteria are:

—the amount by which the actual costs exceed the estimate,
—the context in which the estimate was given, including any qualifications,
—whether the reasons for the increase were matters which the professional should have brought to the client's attention.

This last criterion is particularly significant for the professional. It is important for the client to be aware of the factors that might cause an increase. This is particularly apparent from *Nye Saunders & Partners* v. *Alan Bristow* (1987) 37 BLR 92 (CA).

The facts were that a firm of architects were retained by the defendant to prepare a planning application and provide services in connection with the renovation of the defendant's mansion and installation of a swimming pool. The defendant made it clear that he had approximately £250,000 to spend. In February 1974 the architects provided a written estimate of £238,000 which they had in fact obtained from an independent quantity surveyor. By September 1974 the projected costs had risen to some £440,000, and Mr Bristow aborted the project and terminated the architects' retainer. The architects then sued for their fees.

The main reason for the increase was inflation in building costs. Mr Bristow was an experienced businessman who might be thought to have taken into account the possible effects of inflation. Nevertheless, the architect was held to have been negligent in failing to warn him of the possibility of inflation.

Two factors appear to have influenced the Court of Appeal. First, the trial judge had been impressed by the expert evidence that it was not proper practice for architects to omit a warning about inflation when giving estimates. Secondly, Mr Bristow had consistently sought, and obtained, the architects' confirmation over several months that the estimate still stood, and its accuracy was therefore clearly of great importance to him. Although the Court of Appeal accepted it as "sensible and prudent" of the architects to consult a quantity surveyor about costs, it was held that such consultation did not operate to discharge their obligation to warn Mr Bristow of the possible effects of inflation.

In this case, the architects were plaintiffs suing for their fees and the Court of Appeal were not called upon to deal with the counterclaim. The issues of what damages arise in these cases is however an interesting one. The problem also arises where an architect, engineer or quantity surveyor under-estimates quantities when preparing bills for a project. If a project is aborted, as in *Nye*, the claim would be primarily for wasted costs. If the project proceeds, it is difficult to see how the increased costs *per se* can be recovered as damages since, except in a very rare case where a professional can be held to have warranted a price, the plaintiff would always have had to pay the increased price, even if the professional had provided a proper estimate. Two possible heads of damage are:

(a) Sometimes an earlier indication of the correct cost would have enabled certain savings to be made, e.g., when the estimates have led to a contractor's claim for loss and expense or damages as well as to claims for the payment for the extra work. In such cases, there seems to be no reason why the loss and expense could not be recoverable from the professional as damages

(b) There may well be a claim for an abatement of at least some of the professional's fees (see below).

4 OBLIGATIONS DURING THE CONSTRUCTION PERIOD

Architects and civil engineers are often appointed as supervising officers or contract administrators on building or engineering contracts, usually under one or other of the standard JCT or ICE forms of contract. Their obligations will involve such matters as certifying payments due to the contractor, awarding extensions of time, considering claims for loss and expense, supervising work generally, issuing certificates at practical completion and a final certificate at the end of any maintenance period and many others. In such cases, where the architect is generally the agent of the employer, it is implicit in his contract with the employer that he will act fairly as against the contractor, "holding the balance between his client and the contractor" (Lord Reid in *Sutcliffe* v. *Thackrah* [1974] AC 727). Duties owed direct to the contractor or third parties generally are considered at the end of this section. The following obligations are each considered in turn:

(a) Certification

In *Sutcliffe* v. *Thackrah* (above) the House of Lords confirmed that architects acting as certifiers enjoyed no quasi-arbitral immunity from action in negligence from their clients. The first instance decision of Judge Stabb QC contained observations on the architects' duties as certifier, particularly in relation to defective work. These observations were not themselves the subject of the appeal to the Court of Appeal and House of Lords and are therefore good law.

Judge Stabb QC first outlined the duties of the architect in relation to his supervision:

"I think that the degree of supervision required of an architect must be governed to some extent by his confidence in the contractor. If and when something occurs which should indicate to him a lack of competence in a contractor, then, in the interest of his employer, the standard of his supervision should be higher. No-one suggests that the architect is required to tell a contractor how his work is to be done, nor is the architect responsible for the manner in which the contractor does the work. What his supervisory duty does require of him is to follow the progress of the work and to take steps to see that those works comply with the general requirements of the contract in specification and quality."

He then went on to consider a specific question: to what extent can an architect, when issuing interim certificates, disregard defective work in arriving at the valuation of that work? (In practice the actual measurement and valuing is often carried out by a quantity surveyor on the architect's behalf.)

It might seem that such work should always be taken into account, but over-payment in one interim certificate can usually be corrected in the next, and in this case the architect had not reason to think that the defects would not be remedied. Faced with rival experts who argued on the one hand for a strict approach to the effect that an architect should not pass any defective work; and on the other, that the process of interim certification was a rough and ready or approximate one, Judge Stabb decided that, although prolonged or detailed inspection at an interim stage was not practicable "more than a glance round" was to be expected. In particular the architect should notify the quantity surveyor of any work which he classified as not properly executed, so as to give the quantity surveyor the opportunity of excluding it from the valuation. A strict approach was therefore the correct one. The judge noted that, although certificates could generally be corrected on the next valuation, that would not be so if the contract was prematurely terminated for some reason or if the contractor became insolvent.

In *Townsend* v. *Stone Toms & Partners* (1984) 27 BLR 26 (CA) the Court of Appeal endorsed the view that if an architect deliberately over-certifies work which he knew had not been done properly, this was a clear breach of his contractual duty. In this case it was no argument for the architect to say that he believed that the retention would cover the cost of making good defects of which he was aware. This was a clear breach of his mandate from the client.

In *Lubenham Fidelities and Investments Co. Ltd* v. *South Pembrokeshire District Council* (1986) 33 BLR 39 (CA) the Court of Appeal was prepared to consider that an architect who had deliberately misapplied the contractual provisions intending to deprive the contractor of sums due to him might be liable to the contractor in tort (see also *John Mowlem & Co. Plc* v. *Eagle Star Insurance Co. Ltd* (1992) 62 BLR 126 (QBD) which is dealt with later). The court also held that an employer under a JCT 63 form of contract was not in breach of contract so long as he paid the sum certified. However, an arbitrator should bear in mind that his payment certificates may still be challenged in arbitration under the standard forms of contract.

(b) Supervision

The following words of Lord Upjohn in *East Ham Corporation* v. *Bernard Sunley & Sons Ltd* [1966] AC 406 at page 443 have consistently been cited in court cases as authoritative of architects' supervisory obligations in building contracts:

"As is well known the architect is not permanently on the site but appears at intervals, it may be of a week or a fortnight, and he has, of course, to inspect the progress of the work. When he arrives on the site there may be very many important matters with which he has to deal: the work may be getting behind-hand through labour trouble; some of the suppliers of materials or the sub-contractors may be lagging; there may be physical trouble on the site itself, such as, finding an unexpected amount of underground water. All these are matters which may call for important decisions by the architect. He may in such circumstances think that he knows the builder sufficiently well and can rely upon him to carry out a good job; that it is more important that he should deal with urgent matters on the site than that he should make a minute inspection on the site to see that the builder is complying with the specifications laid down by him . . . It by no means follows that, in failing to discover a defect which a reasonable examination would have disclosed, in fact the architect was necessarily thereby in breach of his duty to the building owner so as to be liable in an action for negligence. It may well be that the omission of the architect to find a defect was due to no more than an error of judgment, or was a deliberately calculated risk which, in all the circumstances of the case, was reasonable and proper."

So:

(a) mere failure to discover a defect does not necessarily imply negligence;

(b) the overall management of the project is important;

(c) it may be reasonable to allocate time to urgent matters rather than to inspecting minute details; and

(d) the trustworthiness of the builder is a factor to be taken into consideration in deciding on the level of supervision.

In *Corfield* v. *Grant* (1992) 59 BLR 102 (QBD) Bowsher J described the project, a hotel conversion as an "inadequately controlled muddle" and said that the plaintiff architect was in continuous breach of contract. The need for co-ordination was particularly important in this project where work could never be progressed in an orderly way stage by stage, and where the employer was particularly anxious to move speedily. Since the project required different degrees of attention at different times, what was adequate, said Bowsher J, was not to be tested by the number of hours worked on site or elsewhere by the architect, but by asking whether it was enough—"the proof of the pudding is in the eating". Here the architect had not supervised and controlled properly.

In addition, the project demanded that the architect have an experienced assistant. The inexperience of the particular assistant in this case was compounded by the architect's failure to give clear instructions or have a detailed plan of action for him.

In *Corfield* the defendant made some 28 allegations of negligence against the architect, most of which are of no great significance. One, however, may be noted. The judge held that it was not negligent to fail to include in the specification a schedule of rates for dayworks (which would have defined and limited to some degree the rates that the contractor could claim for additional work) though it would have been better to have done so. However it was negligent to certify interim payments on a "general impression" of the value of the works, especially on a project where the builder was "inclined to high charges".

In *Kensington Chelsea & Westminster Area Health Authority* v. *Wettern Composites* (1984) 31 BLR 57 (QBD) the first defendants were sub-contractors for the supply and erection of pre-cast concrete mullions of a hospital conversion. Expert evidence indicated that the defects in fixing were "startling". The vertical supports of some 85 per cent of the mullions examined, and the horizontal supports in 25 per cent, were unsatisfactory. Judge Smout QC noted three particular factors that led to his finding the architects liable for negligent supervision:

(a) the architects had been alerted relatively early on to the poor workmanship and lack of frankness of the sub-contractors;

(b) the fixing of the mullions was work that, by its nature, could be speedily covered up in the course of erection. That made close supervision all the more essential;

(c) the burden of supervision was greater where, as here, poor workmanship should result in physical danger.

Although regarding the point as without clear authority, the judge also held that the fact of the employer appointing a clerk of works did not reduce the architects' obligations, even though the clerk of works was providing "constant supervision". However, Bowsher J held the clerk of works 20 per cent liable (and the architects 80 per cent).

The case is also of interest in answering the following question: to what extent can a fellow professional in the employer's team discharge his responsibility to his client to warn of defects by simply notifying the architect or supervising officer? Here the structural engineers were also sued. Bowsher J made clear that the structural engineer's duties would not normally extend to supervision of the fixing of the mullions. Their duty was "to notify the architect as to those defects in the fixings of which they had knowledge". It was not their job to supervise others to put things right. That was the duty of the architect and the clerk of works. The structural engineers had discharged their duty by in fact writing to the architect setting out their misgivings about the fixing, a warning that went unheeded.

It appears that a breach of the duty of an architect to supervise will be harder to prove where there is deliberate concealment or covering up by the contractor—*Gray* v. *T P Bennett* (1987) 43 BLR 63 (QBD). In this case a 10-storey reinforced concrete building was designed so that concrete projections or nibs provided support for the brick cladding. Some 17 years after construction, and after bulges had appeared in the brickwork, the concrete panels were opened up. It was discovered that about 90 per cent of the nibs had been "hacked back or butchered" to which the experts giving evidence applied epithets such as "appalling", "destructive" and "mindless vandalism".

The judge concluded that the only possible explanation on the evidence was that the operatives fitting the brickwork onto the nibs had been engaged in a deliberate policy to conceal from the architect what the judge described as "destruction on a massive scale". That being so, the architect was not negligent in failing to discover what was going on on his routine visits.

Interestingly, the judge also held that even if the architect had been in breach of his duty, the deliberate act of the fixers was the true cause of the damage that necessitated the remedial works. It was not reasonably foreseeable by the architect that any failure by him to supervise properly would have led to such a loss, since it was not reasonably foreseeable that the operatives would have behaved as they did.

Finally, is the architect under a lower duty of supervision if the contract price is relatively low and if the project is being "built down" to a price? It appears that the answer is in the affirmative, except that there are certain minimum standards that are required from the architect whatever the price. The authority is *Cotton* v. *Wallis* [1955] 3 All ER 373 when the Court of Appeal took into account the low price in assessing the conduct of the architect. The principle was applied in *Brown & Brown* v.

Architects and engineers—professional negligence

Gilbert-Scott & Another (1992) 35 Con LR 120 in the Official Referees' Court, where it was held that although the plaintiffs required a low-budget conservatory, (and "if you buy a Mini Minor you cannot expect to have a car with all the attributes of a Rolls Royce and the same must be true of building works", as the judge put it), the architect was in breach of his duty in failing to be present at crucial points including, for example, the laying of a damp-proof membrane. This was particularly so bearing in mind the inexperience of the second defendant, the young builder engaged on the recommendation of the architect to carry out the work. It will be remembered that this was one of the factors that Lord Upjohn isolated in *Sutcliffe* (*supra*).

(c) Termination of the employment of the contractor, or to advise on termination

West Faulkner Associates v. *Newham LBC* (1992) 31 Con LR 105, a decision of Judge Newey QC in the Official Referees' Court is a clear warning to architects that the proper administration of a building contract may require firm action and, where appropriate, determination of the contractor's employment.

In this case, the Borough Council engaged William Moss Construction to renovate 150 dwellings on a housing estate. The contract period was 9 weeks. This was in fact exceeded by some 28 weeks. Efforts to speed the contractors up were unsuccessful. The judge described the overrun on the various blocks of houses as "enormous" even taking into account some failure by the Council to supply information on time. The Council, who were particularly concerned at the plight of the tenants who had been temporarily removed while the works were being carried out, expressed some surprise that the architect did not feel able either to determine the contract or to threaten the determination. The architects, and indeed their quantity surveyors, said that it was generally difficult to terminate on grounds of failure to proceed "regularly and diligently", a relevant ground under the contract.

Despite repeated concern by the Council, they continued to maintain this position and followed the advice of their "very timorous" quantity surveyors (as the judge described them).

Acknowledging that the architects were without authoritative guidance as to what "regularly and diligently" meant, the judge nonetheless held that they were in breach of contract in failing to serve a notice which, under this contract, would have given Moss 14 days to mend their ways or face a second notice determining the contract. He held that this was "not a marginal case". They knew how badly the work was proceeding on site, how seriously the tenants were being affected and that the Council were being placed in an increasingly difficult and embarrassing position.

(d) Abatement of fees for negligence

It is well established that in sale of goods cases the buyer is entitled to abate the sale price by reason of defects in the goods (*Mondel* v. *Steel* (1941) 1 BLR 106 (Exch). Abatement must be distinguished from set off. The party abating in respect of defective goods is not setting of by way of a cross action, but simply defending himself by showing how much less the subject matter of the action as worth by reason of the breach of contract.

There is some authority that the principles of abatement do not apply to cases of professional negligence. In *Hutchinson* v. *Harris* (1978) 10 BLR 19 (CA) the plaintiff engaged the defendant architect under the RIBA conditions of engagement for a conversion of her house. The parties fell out with each other, and the trial judge found that the defendant architect was negligent in passing defective work and certifying payment and supervising. He awarded the plaintiff £1,375 being the cost of the remedial works, but gave judgment for the defendant architect on the counterclaim for £800, the balance of her fees. The plaintiff appealed.

The plaintiff argued on appeal that the counterclaim for fees should have been abated because of the architect's negligence. The Court of Appeal held that the doctrine of abatement did not apply to cases involving professional services, distinguishing one case (*Sincock* v. *Bangs (Reading)* [1952] JBL 562) in which such abatement had apparently been allowed. However, there seems to be no reason in principle why such fees should not be capable of abatement to the extent that no services had been performed by the architect or engineer. The real concern of the Court of Appeal in *Hutchinson* v. *Harris* was that the plaintiff might be doubly compensated if she obtained not only the remedial costs but also an abatement of fees due to the architect. It is perhaps the principle of double compensation that most requires consideration in these types.

In any case, presumably where there is a complete "failure of consideration" by the professional (i.e., where his service is so poor as to amount to no service at all), no fees will be due whatsoever on ordinary principles of contract law. Even there however, the principle of double compensation must be considered. The plaintiff is to be put in the position in which he would have been had the professional performed his task properly.

(e) Obligation to advise on issues of law

There is authority that an architect or engineer may be liable for failing to advise his client on the law. In *B L Holdings Ltd* v. *Robert J Wood & Partners* (1978) 10 BLR 48 (QBD) Gibson J held an architect liable in negligence for communicating incorrect information to his clients. The information was that the local planning authority would not take parking into account in determining whether or not an "office development permit" was required for planning permission. The defendants had obtained this information from the local authority themselves, and were somewhat surprised at it, but did not mention the fact to their clients. Gibson J held not only that a few architects would have been misled by the local authority but that so might some lawyers, and accepted that it might be "hard" to require of an architect that he know more law than the planning authority.

The Court of Appeal in fact overturned the decision on the facts, but they did not disapprove the statements of Gibson J, and it seems that an architect or engineer may at least come under an obligation to advise his client to take legal advice, at appropriate points in a project.

5 EVIDENCE

It seems to be fairly well established in cases involving the professional negligence of architects and engineers that expert evidence will be required at court to persuade the judge that the standard of the professional in question has fallen below that of the reasonably competent professional. In *Worboys* v. *Acme Investments Ltd* (1969) 4 BLR 133 (CA) it was suggested to the court by counsel that in certain classes of case the court could find a breach of professional duty without having the usual type of evidence as to what constituted lack of care of the professional man in question. The court accepted that there may be some cases in which it would not be necessary to adduce such evidence – for example if an architect had simply omitted to provide a front door to the premises. Such cases will be fairly explicit and readily ascertainable breaches of contractual obligations.

Similarly, in *Nye Saunders* v. *Alan Bristow* (*supra*) the Court of Appeal rejected an alternative ground that had been held by the trial judge to the effect that disclosure of the risk of inflation was "so obviously necessary" to enable the client to make an informed decision that no reasonably prudent architect would have failed to make it. That ground had been based on parts of a speech by Lord Bridge in the medical negligence case of *Sidaway* v. *Board of Governors of the Bethlem Royal Hospital* [1985] AC 871. However, the Court of Appeal held that that case was limited to the specific application of certain aspects of medical negligence, in particular the "doctrine of informed consent", and that the decision to uphold the trial judge in *Nye Saunders* was not to be based on that part of his judgment.

It will be important to ensure that the experts in question are from the same field as the professional whose negligence is being alleged. In *Investors in Industry* v. *South Bedfordshire District Council* (*supra*) the Court of Appeal felt that little reliance could be placed on expert evidence from three engineers that was given in relation to the alleged negligence of an architect. The evidence related to a profession other than their own.

6 DUTIES TO THIRD PARTIES

This section covers duties owed in the tort of negligence ie outside the law of contract.

Following *Murphy* v. *Brentwood District Council* [1990] 3 WLR 414, which overruled *Anns* v. *Merton London Borough Council*, the scope for claims for third parties in negligence against architects or engineers is much restricted. In the absence of the third party suffering physical injury or damage to property other than the property that is the subject of the alleged negligence[2] there will be no liability in negligence, since the loss suffered is classified as pure economic loss.

However there may still be liability to a third party under:

(a) the doctrine of negligent misstatement—*Hedley Byrne* v. *Heller & Partners* [1964] AC 465; or

(b) the Defective Premises Act 1972 in respect of dwellinghouses.

Each is considered in turn.

A claim for negligent misstatement requires a "special relationship" of proximity between the architect/engineer and the person acting on negligent misstatement. Pure economic loss is, and always has been, recoverable under this doctrine. The court will consider the following criteria set out by the Court of Appeal in *James McNaughton Paper Group* v. *Hicks Anderson & Co* (1990) CA:

(i) the purpose for which the statement is made;

(ii) the relationship between the parties;

(iii) the size of the class of which the plaintiff is a members;

(iv) the state of knowledge of the defendant;

(v) whether the plaintiff was entitled to rely on the misstatement.

This sort of liability could arise when the architect/engineer offers advice to any third party involved with the building project.

One interesting consequence of the Murphy decision is that plaintiffs often now seek to widen the definition of what amounts to a "statement" for the purpose of *Hedley Byrne* v. *Heller*. In *Lancashire & Cheshire*

---

2. And allowing for claims under the so-called "complex structure" theory propounded in *D & F Estates* v. *Church Commissioners*, though, apparently, not endorsed in Murphy itself. This is the theory that in the case of a complex structure, the requirement for liability that there be damage to "other property" of the plaintiff can be found by treating various parts of the structure effectively as separate property. Lord Bridge was also prepared, in Murphy, to consider damage caused by defects such as an exploding boiler or electrical malfunction as being outside the category of pure economic loss.

Architects and engineers—professional negligence

Association of Baptist Churches Inc v. *Howard & Seddon Partnership (a firm)* [1993] 3 All ER 467, the plaintiff employed the defendant architect to design a sanctuary for a church. The design of the defendant was defective and the sanctuary suffered from condensation problems. The claim by the plaintiff in contract was statute barred. The judge allowed a concurrent claim in tort to proceed, but since the loss was purely economic, this could only be pursued if, as the plaintiff argued, the act of providing to the plaintiff the plans containing the defective design was capable of amounting to a "representation" for the purpose of *Hedley Byrne*. The judge held that it was not.

Hiron v. *Pynford South Ltd* (1991) 60 BLR 78 (QBD) suggests that courts will be reluctant to find sufficient proximity between an architect and another party where that other party has his own advisers.

The Hirons (first plaintiffs) engaged Lewis (fourth defendants) to advise them after their house suffered subsidence damage. The Hirons claimed on their house insurance policy against Legal & General (L&G) (second plaintiffs in the action). L&G engaged Olley as structural engineers to advise about underpinning. Pynford Services Ltd (the second defendant) undertook a site investigation and Pynford South Ltd (the first defendant) carried out the remedial works, both employed by the Hirons. Olley approved the remedial work scheme for their direct client L&G. Lewis approved the scheme similarly for their direct clients, the Hirons. Olley supervised the remedial work.

In dealing with the Hirons/Lewis and the L&G/Olley "own adviser" relationships, Judge Newey QC, while acknowledging that concurrent liabilities in contract and tort were possible, was disinclined to find any tortious liability here. He then dealt with the Hirons/Olley "cross adviser" relationship. He held generally that no duty was owed in tort and that there was insufficient proximity for *Hedley Byrne* purposes. He gave the following reasons:

(a) Olley were engaged by L&G whose interests were not precisely the same as those of the Hirons. L&G would wish to pay no more than was strictly necessary, while the Hirons simply wanted their house underpinned.

(b) Although Olley were aware of the Hirons, they had no direct communications with them.

(c) The Hirons had their own advisers who, although building surveyors and not engineers, would have considerable experience of subsidence.

For the same reasons, Lewis owed no duty to L&G.

Section 1 of the Defective Premises Act 1972 states:

"A person taking on work for or in connection with the provision of a dwelling . . . owes a duty—

(a) if the dwelling is provided to the order of any person common to that person; and

(b) ... to every person who acquires an interest ... in the dwelling; to see that the work which he takes on is done in a workmanlike, or as the case may be, professional manner, with proper materials and so that as regards that work the dwelling will be fit for habitation when completed."

The use of the words "professional manner" indicate that professionals are included as possible defendants.

Miles Charles Thompson v. *Clive Alexander & Partners* (1992) 8 Con LJ 199 an Official Referees' decision, provides some encouragement for architects and engineers. The defendants argued that there could be no breach purely by reason of defective workmanship and materials. What was required was defects substantial enough to render the dwellinghouse unfit for habitation.

Judge Esyr Lewis QC, following an earlier Court of Appeal decision (*Alexander* v. *Mercouris* [1979] 1 WLR 1270 (CA), agreed. The statute could not have been intended to compensate persons in respect of defects which merely reduced the value of the dwellinghouse rather than rendered it unfit for habitation. It should however be noted that in *Hancock* v. *Brazier (Anerley) Ltd* [1966] 2 All ER 901 it was suggested that the require-ment of fitness for purpose added nothing to the requirement that the work should be done in a workmanlike manner and with proper materials.

Liability under this Act is likely to be more one of the promising avenues for claims made by owners of dwellinghouses other than the original owners.

It had been thought that the Defective Premises Act 1972 effectively did not apply to the (approximately) 97 per cent of new dwellings covered by the National House Builders Council warranty scheme, which 10 year protection for new dwellings, but it appears that this is no longer the position.[3]

Duties to contractors

Because of *Murphy*, the contractor can in principle take action against the architect on the building contract only:

(a) where he has suffered physical injury or damage other than pure financial loss; or

(b) where he can mount a claim for negligent mis-representation under *Hedley Byrne*.

3. Section 2 exempts "approved schemes" from all remedies. It had been through that the NHBC scheme was an approved scheme. It now appears however that at some stage before 1988 an agreement was concluded between the Secretary of State and the NHBC that this would not be so—see Duncan Wallace QC, "Anns beyond repair", 1991 LQR 243.

As to the first of these, case law indicates that the architect owes few duties to a contractor even where personal injury or damage to other property can be shown. In *Clayton* v. *Woodman* (1962) 4 BLR 65 (CA), the plaintiff, an experienced bricklayer employed by the contractor, made criticisms on site to the architect regarding his design and suggested that rather than try to incorporate a gable into a new building, it would be better to pull it down and build a new wall. The architect rejected the suggestion, decided that the gable was safe, and ordered a chase to be cut along the base of the gable. This was done but the gable then collapsed, seriously injuring the plaintiff. The Court of Appeal held that the architect held no duty to the bricklayer. What seems to have been of importance to the court were the considerations

(a) that the architect was acting on the instructions of his client, the employer and owed his primary obligations to him. Indeed it was suggested that he would have been in breach of his duties to the employer if he had decided not to cut the chase;

(b) that it was the builder's responsibility to provide a safe system of work for his operatives.

Further, in *Oldschool* v. *Gleeson (Construction) Ltd* (1976) 4 BLR 105 (QBD) Judge Stabb QC stated:

"I take the view that the duty of care which an architect or a consulting engineer owes to a third party is limited by the assumption that the contractor who executes the works acts at all times as a competent contractor. The contractor cannot seek to pass the blame for incompetent work onto the consulting engineer on the grounds that he failed to intervene to prevent it."

The situation might be different, Judge Stabb felt, if the architect's design was so faulty that no competent contractor could have avoided damage in carrying it out.

As to the second of these, the possibility of *Hedley Byrne* liability as between contractor and architect arises most usually in the issue of whether a contractor can claim in negligence against an architect for incorrect certification, in particular under-valuation, under the building contract. Until 1988 it had seemed that a claim could be maintained in negligence by a contractor against an architect for negligent certification. The authority was an *obiter dictum* of Lord Salmon in *Arenson* v. *Arenson* [1977] AC 405. That case concerned the duty of care owed by an architect to his client in negligently over-certifying a sum due. But Lord Salmon went on to say:

"[The architect] might however have negligently certified that less money was payable than was in fact due and thereby starve the contractor of money. In a trade in which cash flow is especially important this might have caused the contractor serious damage for which the architect could have been successfully sued."

This view was subsequently followed in two first instance decisions namely *Shui On Construction Ltd* v. *Shui Kay Co. Ltd* (1985) 4 Con LJ 305, a decision of the Hong Kong Crown Court; and *Michael Salliss & Co. Ltd v. Calil* (1987) 4 Const LJ 125, a decision of Judge Fox-Andrews QC. In the second of these, Judge Fox-Andrews again stressed the importance of cash flow to the contractor.

It now appears however that, unless the Court of Appeal decision in *Pacific Associates* v. *Baxter* (1988) 44 BLR 33 (CA) is reconsidered, an architect or engineer will rarely owe a duty to a contractor for negligent under-certification.

Pacific were contractors under a FIDIC engineering contract for the dredging of a lagoon in the Persian Gulf. Halcrow were the engineers under the contract. Pacific claimed extensions of time and additional expense. The application was rejected by Halcrow. Pacific commenced arbitration proceedings against the employer which resulted in a settlement of some £10 million. They then pursued Halcrow for the balance of the claim of some £45 million. The Court of Appeal struck the claim out as disclosing no cause of action.

The decision is a difficult one. The reasons given by the three judges were not the same. The matter was complicated by two other factors. The court seemed to have placed at least some significance on a disclaimer clause in Halcrow's contract with the employer.[4] One interpretation of the *Hedley Byrne* doctrine requires a "voluntary assumption of responsibility" by the maker of the statement (although in other cases duties have been imposed without this requirement). It was said by Lord Devlin in *Hedley Byrne* itself that a party could not be said to be assuming a voluntary responsibility if, at the same time, he was disclaiming responsibility as against the party with whom he was in a contractual relationship. Thus in this case, the court felt that Halcrow could not have voluntarily assumed any responsibility for their actions.

The second and more important factor was the existence of the arbitration clause in the FIDIC contract. (This was certainly of great significance for Purchas and Russell LJJ.) It was seen as providing the proper means for the contractor to recover any monies that might be due to him. This perhaps provides the best means of distinguishing *Pacific*, i.e., the point can be raised in cases where the contract with the contractor and employer contains no arbitration clause. However, such cases will be rare where the standard forms of building contract are used.

Pacific Associates has wider consequences. For example in the Canadian case of *Re Edgworth Construction Ltd* v. *N D Lea & Associates Ltd* (1991) 54 BLR 11, engineers prepared specifications and drawings and submitted them to the Ministry which incorporated them in tender documents. They had no control over the use made by the Ministry of these

---

4. Though see Duncan Wallace QC in his article "Charter for the Construction Professional?" at page 207 of the 1990 *Construction Law Journal* for a contrary view.

documents (this was significant). The defendants were not named as the engineer in the contract and had no control over the use made by the Ministry of these documents. The plaintiffs, who won the tender, alleged that the design had been negligently prepared, and sued for negligent misstatement. Their claim was struck out on the grounds of lack of proximity and reliance and foreseeability. In any case, it was held that when the designs, plan and specification were incorporated into the tender documents, they became representations of the Ministry to prospective bidders, and ceased to be representations of the defendants. Further the defendants had no direct relationship with the plaintiffs and no opportunity to define what risks it was prepared to assume. Pacific Associates was specifically referred to by the court in coming to these conclusions.[5]

To conclude, it seems that the possibilities of claims by a contractor against the architect or engineer, aside from physical injury or damage, can only be under the following heads:

(a) in cases were Pacific can be distinguished, e.g., where there is no arbitration clause;

(b) in cases involving dwellinghouses, under the Defective Premises Act 1972 (see above);

(c) where the architect has acted deliberately to defraud the contractor (see *Lubenham, supra*);

(d) for the torts of wrongful interference with economic interests or conspiracy.

Grounds (c) and (d) may be possibilities in the light of *John Mowlem & Co. Plc* v. *Eagle Star Insurance Co. Ltd* (1992) 62 BLR 126 (QBD). In this case Mowlem were contractors under a management contract to Carlton Gate. They obtained an arbitration award against them for some £12 million. Carlton Gate then went into receivership. Mowlem launched an action against the architect for three "economic torts" as follows:

(a) inducing/procuring a breach of contract;

(b) wrongful interference with economic interests, i.e., interference by the architect with Mowlem's certification process under Mowlem's contract with Carlton Gate;

(c) conspiracy.

The architect applied for the action to be struck out as disclosing no cause of action. Judge Loyd QC struck out the claim under (a). The contractor would have to show that the architect had allegedly yielded to the interference in breach of contract by the employer, and that it had

5. The Ontario Court of Appeal, in upholding a contractor's claim against an engineer in *Auto Concrete Curb Ltd* v. *South Nation River Conservation Authority* (1994) 10 Constr. LJ 1 at p.37, has suggested that both *Pacific Associates* and *Edgeworth Construction Ltd* are of limited application.

procured Carlton Gate effectively to interfere with itself. This would be artificial. However, Judge Loyd QC allowed the action to proceed on grounds (b) and (c).

The decision is only authority for the view that such economic torts will not actually be struck out. A contractor will still face formidable difficulties. Head (b) will require a deliberate mis-application of the relevant certification clauses with the intention of depriving a contractor of a sum to which it would be entitled. Similarly, head (c) requires a deliberate conspiracy between the architect and employer to injure the contractor unlawfully. Even if matters such as these could be proved on the particular facts of any case, there is still one further problem. If the plaintiff cannot show that a proper certification would have actually led to payment before the employer became insolvent—at least on the balance of probabilities—his claim will still fail as a matter of causation of loss.

7 DAMAGES

In architects'/engineers' professional negligence cases, the test for remoteness of damage will be as set out in the leading case of *Hadley* v. *Baxendale* (1854) 9 Ex 341. This states that the damages which a party is entitled to receive for breach of contract should be such as may fairly and reasonably be considered either as arising naturally, i.e., according to the usual course of things from the breach (first limb); or such as may reasonably be supposed to have been in the contemplation of the parties at the time when they made the contract as the probable result of the breach of it (second limb). It is not proposed to discuss the general principles of damages here but rather to consider certain matters that are perhaps peculiar to actions for professional negligence against architects and engineers.

It is necessary to consider the issues of:

    (a) apportionment;
    (b) betterment;
    (c) other relevant heads.

Each is considered in turn.

(a) Apportionment

Architects' and engineers' cases are frequently multi-party cases in which the professionals along with contractors and sub-contractors will be joined. It is important to treat separately:

    (i) the position as regards the successful plaintiff and the defendants; and

121

(ii) the position between the defendants *inter se* in terms of their contribution to the plaintiff's loss.

Under (i) the plaintiff may recover in full against all defendants, for example. He cannot of course recover twice over, or anything more than his actual loss, but a judgment against all defendants in full gives him the right to enforce his judgment against all defendants. Conversely, he may recover only partially against one defendant, and fully against others.

Apportionment under (ii) does not affect the plaintiff's rights in the least. It simply deals with the rights of the defendants against each other to recover whatever sums any one of them may have to pay in the event that the plaintiff chooses to enforce his judgment against that one. It is typical in multi-party actions for the defendants to issue contribution notices against each other, claiming contributions under the Civil Liability (Contribution) Act 1978. This gives courts power to apportion losses as between the defendants where the defendants are held liable to the plaintiff for the same loss.

There are no hard and fast rules of apportionment but it may be useful to group together some of the cases dealing with the point.

In *Eames* v. *North Hertfordshire District Council* (1980) 18 BLR 50 Judge Fay QC found a council liable for the negligence of its building inspector, architect/designer liable for his negligent design, specialist contractors negligent for their work and developers negligent for failing to ascertain properly whether the land in question could safely have its present building built on it (liability in some of these cases would now be unlikely following *Murphy*). Judge Fay QC noted that in considering the local authority's liability in cases following *Eames* he had expressed the view "that the blameworthiness of the policeman who fails to detect the crime is less than that of the criminal himself" and said that he had in typical cases arising out of negligent passing of defective foundations held a local authority to be 25 per cent to blame and the builder 75 per cent. This percentage allocation is of course not a rule of law, but may have some precedent value, or operate as a guide, in cases where joint liability is found against a wrongdoer, and another party who should have supervised or overseen the work of the wrongdoer.

In *Kensington LBC* v. *Wettern* it will be recalled that in failing to supervise a contractor the architect was held 80 per cent liable, that the employer's clerk of works was held 20 per cent liable. Finally, in *Holland Hannen and Cubitts* it will be recalled that, on the facts, the Court of Appeal reallocated the apportionment of liability of the trial judge to allocate more responsibility to the design team rather than to the sub-contractor and that sub-contractor's consultant.

(b) Betterment

Costs of rectification will frequently be claimed in cases involving architects' and engineers' negligence. The question often arises as to what extent the plaintiff is entitled to recover costs incurred in building to a better standard than he originally had. In *Richard Roberts Holdings Ltd* v. *Douglas Smith Stimson Partnership & Others* (1988) 46 BLR 50 (QB) Judge Newey said:

"If the only practicable method of overcoming the consequences of a defendant's breach of contract is to build to a higher standard than the contract had required, the plaintiff may recover the cost of building to that higher standard."

He went on to say however that if a plaintiff chose to build to a higher standard than was strictly necessary, then unless the new works were so different as to break the chain of causation, the plaintiff would get the cost of the works less a credit to the defendant for the betterment.

In *The Board of Governors of the Hospitals for Sick Children* v. *McLauchlan & Harvey Plc* (1987) 19 Con LR 25 Judge Newey QC again reiterated the importance of reasonableness. After stating that the plaintiff could only recover reasonable costs he added:

"Reasonable costs do not, however, mean the minimum amount which, with hindsight, it could be held would have sufficed."

Reference should also be made to the Court of Appeal of New Zealand case of *Bevan Investments* v. *Blackhall & Struthers* (1977) 11 BLR 78 (CA).

This case involved the faulty design of a recreation centre. A new scheme was put forward using as much as possible of what had already been built. The plaintiff however was unable to obtain sufficient finance to enable the project to be continued and in view of the litigation, and the architect's persistent denial of liability and assertion that the building as designed had been capable of completion, there was some uncertainty as to whether damages would be recovered, and in the circumstances it was decided that nothing could be done until the litigation was concluded.

The architect was found liable in negligence. The court stressed that the measure of loss should be the amount required to rectify the defects complained of so as to give the building owner the equivalent of a building substantially in accordance with the contract, and since in this case the only practicable action was to complete according to the modified design, the cost of doing so was the reasonable measure of damages, but that in calculating those damages, credit should be given for the hypothetical additional cost of a proper and initial design in order to avoid any element of betterment.

It was also stated that the assessment should be computed at the date of trial, either because of the principle that damages were to be assessed by reference to the date when the reinstatement works could reasonably be carried out, and it was reasonable to postpone until the issues of liability and damages were settled; or because such damage was not too remote because it was foreseeable that the company might be unable to complete until trial. Clearly the plaintiff was properly compensated by being awarded his damages at the trial date. In many building cases, where there is building price inflation, to be awarded damages at the time of the loss, rather than at the date of trial, even allowing for interest on such damages, will not operate to compensate the plaintiff.

(c) Other relevant heads

(i) Distress and inconvenience

Damages under this head will generally only be awarded where the contract itself has some form of pleasure as its subject matter, e.g., contracts for holidays etc.[6] Building contracts do not fall into this category, and neither, by analogy, do contracts of employment between architects or engineers and their employers. In *Hutchinson* v. *Harris* (1978) 10 BLR 19 (CA), the Court of Appeal suggested that general damages could be awarded in a professional negligence action against an architect, though declined to award them in that case. However the attitude of the courts has probably changed since 1978 and the better view may be represented by Staughton LJ in *Hayes* v. *Dodd* [1990] 2 All ER 815, a solicitor's negligence case:

"... the object of the contract was not comfort or pleasure or the relief of discomfort, but simply carrying on a commercial activity with a view to profit."

Where damages are awarded in negligence cases against architects and engineers, they are likely to be minimal—see for example the Court of Appeal case on surveyors' negligence, *Watts* v. *Morrow*, where the plaintiff's damages were reduced from the £4,000 awarded by the trial judge to each plaintiff, to £750 each.

(ii) Cost of surveyors' fees etc.

In *Hutchinson* v. *Harris* (1978) 10 BLR 19 (CA) the plaintiff tried to claim damages for her surveyor's fees in pursuing the litigation. It was held that these could be recoverable only as part of a costs order, and thereafter on taxation of costs, and not as damages.

(iii) The opportunity of obtaining cheaper quotations

In *Corfield* v. *Grant*, the hotelier who had employed an architect, who was held liable for some degree of negligence, obtained damages for the loss of the opportunity of obtaining competitive quotations. His allegation was that because of the architect's delay (which was found in law) he had lost

---

6. *Addis* v. *Gramophone Co. Ltd* [1909] AC 488. *Bliss* v. *S E Thames RHA* [1987] ICR 700.

the opportunity to obtain competitive quotations, since he had to work speedily and obtain whatever quotation he could. Judge Bowsher QC awarded damages on the principle of *Chaplin* v. *Hicks* [1911] 2 QB 786, i.e., on the basis of the loss of an opportunity of obtaining cheaper quotations. In this particular case the hotelier claimed £1,944 being 10 per cent of the price paid for kitchen equipment, on the basis that had he had more time, he would have been able to obtain a 10 per cent discount. The judge noted that he should only have a proportion of £1,944 to correspond to the possibility of obtaining the discount, and assessed damages on a broad basis under that head at £500.

Damages for lost opportunities have been awarded in other professional negligence actions, e.g., *Kitchen* v. *Royal Air Force* [1958] 1 WLR 563.

(iv) Damages for under-estimates of likely costs

See the discussion above in respect of *Nye Saunders* v. *Bristow*.

CONCLUSION

An examination of the law relating to negligence against professionals shows that it is not possible to divorce the issue of liability from insurance aspects. When considering liability in the tort of negligence in particular, issues of public policy prevail and the courts are charged with the task of assessing upon which party the burden of liability should fall. Most professions insist that their practitioners are insured in any event and thus, ultimately the cost of insurance falls upon the clients of the professional who are responsible for the payment of the fees.

The 1990s has given rise to a more sobering experience for a number of professionals. This follows from the halcyon days of the late 1980s. Professionals involved in various aspects of property such as surveyors, architects and property lawyers have been especially severely affected. Statistics show that the reduction in size of the two former professions has been serious and dramatic. Yet there exists an ironic contradiction. The number of claims made against professionals increases in times of recession. This has been especially true of surveyors who have faced a high volume of claims over allegations of excessive valuations. Underwriters have had no alternative other than to increase premiums in order to generate funds to replenish depleted reserves. The profession has, consequently, been faced with having to fund additional insurance premiums from income which may be significantly reduced. The increase in claims has given rise to a greater willingness on the part of underwriters to take advantage of defences such as material non-dislosure or breach of warranty. As a consequence, brokers need to be vigilant. Should a claimant be faced with such a defence by his insurers during the course of his investigation, he will have to consider whether or not his broker has been at fault by failing in any of his duties or responsibilities.

As the courts appear to be dealing with the last of the claims against surveyors arising from the dramatic fall in property prices, which for the most part peaked in or around 1990, the Commercial Court is currently bracing itself for the volume of substantive litigation being brought by names at Lloyd's against those responsible for running and managing

Conclusion

specific Lloyd's syndicates. This litigation promises to be both lengthy and complex.

There has been no impetus toward the concept of no fault liability. In November 1990 it was reported that a private member's bill which sought to provide "*no fault*" compensation for victims of medical accidents, was defeated in Parliament. It was supported by the then Labour opposition, but was defeated by the Government. The then Minister for Health, Kenneth Clarke, stated that while he considered such schemes to be attractive, he nonetheless thought that they posed serious problems. The bill received the support of the Medical Defence Union. The difficulty must be that such a scheme could lead to a dangerous lowering of standards and would furthermore single out the medical professions as being distinguishable from other professions.

Whilst it remains to be seen whether or not the Lord Chancellor will finally endorse and approve proposals for solicitors acting on a "*no win no fee*" basis, it is hoped that even if such proposals were to be adopted, it will not lead to a rash of speculative claims against professionals.

ROYAL INSTITUTION OF CHARTERED SURVEYORS PROFESSIONAL INDEMNITY COLLECTIVE POLICY©

EFFECTED THROUGH RICS INSURANCE SERVICES LIMITED

IN CONSIDERATION of the Insured named in the Schedule hereto having paid the premium set forth in the Schedule to the Insurers who have hereunto subscribed their Names (hereinafter referred to as "the Insurers").

THE INSURERS HEREBY SEVERALLY AGREE each for the proportion set against its name to indemnify the Insured (as defined herein) in accordance with the terms and Conditions contained hereunder or endorsed hereon,

PROVIDED THAT:

1. the total liability of the Insurers shall not exceed the limits of liability expressed in the said Schedule or such other limits of liability as may be substituted therefore by memorandum hereon or attached hereto signed by or on behalf of the Insurers,

2. the liability of each of the Insurers individually to the Insured in respect of any claim for indemnity and any contribution towards the Insured's costs shall be limited to the proportion set against each Insurers' name.

For the avoidance of doubt it should be noted that the limit of indemnity and the excess applies to all the Insureds jointly and for this purpose only the Policy is a joint Policy.

SCHEDULE

Definitions

1. "PROFESSIONAL BUSINESS" shall mean:
   (a) those services which are normally undertaken by members of the Royal Institution of Chartered Surveyors or as otherwise declared to Insurers hereof and performed in the conduct of business by or on behalf of the Firm(s) named in the Schedule.

(b) advice given or services performed by any Insured whilst holding an individual appointment but if as a Director or officer of a company only in relation to services performed in connection with buildings and/or property and/or land, such services being of the same nature as in (a) above being services normally performed by the Director or officer for clients of the Firm(s) named in the Schedule providing the fees (if any) relating to those services undertaken by any Insured holding an individual appointment are taken into account in ascertaining the gross earnings of the Firm(s).

In the event of any dispute or disagreement arising between the Insured and the Insurers as to the correct interpretation of the definition of Professional Business the facts shall be submitted to the President for the time being of The Royal Institution of Chartered Surveyors or his nominee whose decision shall be final and binding on both parties.

2. "The INSURED" shall mean any of the following:

(a) Those persons named in Question 4 of the last completed proposal form and any other person or persons who have subsequently become Partner(s)/Director(s) in the Firm(s) prior to the expiry of the Policy Period specified in the Schedule

(b) Any former Partner(s)/Director(s) of the Firm(s) for services performed for and on behalf of the Firm(s) including retired Partner(s)/Director(s) remaining as Consultants to the Firm(s)

(c) Any person who is or has been under a contract of service for and/or on behalf of the Firm(s)

(d) The Estates and/or legal representatives of any of the persons noted under (a), (b) or (c) hereof in the event of their death, incapacity, insolvency or bankruptcy

(e) Any Firm(s) named in Item 1 of the Schedule.

"FIRM(S)" shall mean the Firm(s) named in the Schedule or the predecessors in business of the said Firm(s) as disclosed to Insurers.

"DOCUMENTS" shall mean deeds, wills, agreements, maps, plans, records, books, letters, certificates, computer system records, forms and documents of whatsoever nature whether written, printed or reproduced by any other method (other than bearer bonds, coupons, bank notes, currency notes and negotiable instruments).

"POLICY PERIOD" shall mean the Period of Insurance specified in the Schedule.

Whereas the Insured, as defined herein, have made to Insurers a written proposal bearing the date stated in the Schedule containing particulars and statements which it is hereby agreed are the basis of this Policy and are to be considered as incorporated herein:

Insuring clauses

NOW WE, THE INSURERS TO THE EXTENT AND IN THE MANNER HEREINAFTER PROVIDED, HEREBY AGREE:

1. Civil liability

To indemnify the Insured against any claim or claims first made against them or any of them during the Policy Period in respect of any civil liability whatsoever or whensoever arising (including liability for Claimants' costs) incurred in the course of any PROFESSIONAL BUSINESS carried on by the Insured.

Where a series of such claims arise from a breach of or repeated breaches of a single duty or identical duties owed and arising from a single engagement all claims within that series shall for the purpose of the limit of indemnity (Condition 7) and the excess (Condition 8) under this Policy be treated as a single claim.

Provided that any and all such claims arising from a single survey and/or valuation shall for the like purpose be treated as a single claim under this Policy.

2. Fidelity

To indemnify the Insured against their own direct loss or losses which, during the Policy Period, they shall discover they have sustained by reason of any dishonesty or fraud of any past or present Partner, Director or Employee of the Firm(s) named in the Schedule, provided always that:
   (a) such dishonest or fraudulent act(s) are carried out by the person(s) concerned with the manifest intent to cause such loss to the Insured or to obtain improper personal gain either for themselves or in collusion with others.
   (b) no indemnity shall be afforded hereby to any person committing or condoning such dishonesty or fraud.
   (c) the annual accounts of the Insured have been prepared and/or certified by an Independent Accountant or Auditor.
   (d) any dishonesty or fraud committed by a person or persons acting in concert shall for the purposes of this Policy be treated as giving rise to one loss.
   (e) such loss or losses shall include Accountants' fees incurred as the result of such loss up to £15,000 or such amount as agreed by Insurers.
   (f) any monies which but for such dishonesty or fraud would be due to such person from the Insured, or any monies of such person held by the Insured, shall be deducted from any amount payable under this Policy.

Appendix 1

3. Loss of documents

To indemnify the Insured against reasonable costs and expenses of whatsoever nature incurred by the Insured in replacing or restoring DOCUMENTS either the property of or entrusted to or lodged or deposited with the Firm(s), having been discovered during the Policy Period to have been damaged, lost or mislaid and which after diligent search cannot be found.

Special institution conditions

1. (a) Insurers will not exercise their right to avoid this Policy where there has been non-disclosure or mis-representation of facts or untrue statements in the proposal form, provided always that the Insured shall establish to Insurers' satisfaction that such non-disclosure, mis-representation or untrue statement was free of any fraudulent intent.

(b) However, in the case of a claim first made against the Insured during the period of this Insurance where

   (i) they had previous knowledge of the circumstances which could give rise to such claim and

   (ii) they should have notified the same under any preceding Insurance, then, where the indemnity or cover under this Policy is greater or wider in scope than that to which the Insured would have been entitled under such preceding Insurance (whether with other Insurers or not), Insurers shall only be liable to afford indemnity to such amount and extent as would have been afforded to the Insured by such preceding Insurance.

2. Where the Insured's breach of or non-compliance with any condition of this Policy has resulted in prejudice to the handling or settlement of any claim Insurers shall be entitled to reduce the indemnity afforded by the Policy in respect of such claims (including costs and expenses) to such sum as in Insurers' reasonable opinion would have been payable by them in the absence of such prejudice.

3. In the event of any dispute or disagreement between the Insured and Insurers regarding the application of these Special Institution Conditions, such dispute or disagreement shall be referred by either party for arbitration to any person nominated by the President for the time being of the Royal Institution of Chartered Surveyors.

Exclusions

The Policy shall not indemnify the Insured against:

1. any claim or loss where the Insured are entitled to indemnity under any other Insurance(s) except in respect of any excess beyond the amount which would have been payable under such Insurance had this Policy not been effected.

2. any claim or circumstance that may give rise to a claim which has been notified to any Insurance Intermediary or Insurer pursuant to any other Policy or certificate of insurance attaching prior to the inception of this Policy or disclosed on the completed proposal form that shall form the basis of this contract.

3. any claim or loss arising out of any dispute between the Insured and any present or former Employee or any person who has been offered employment with the Insured.

4. any claim or loss arising out of the death or bodily injury or disease of an Employee under a contract of service with the Firm(s) whilst in the course of employment for or on behalf of the Insured.

5. any claim brought by a Firm, company or organisation controlling the Insured Firm(s) or of which any Partner(s)/Director(s) of the Firm(s) have control unless such claim or claims originates from an independent third party.

6. any claim or loss arising out of the use of any motor vehicles by the Insured in circumstances in which provisions of the Road Traffic Acts apply.

7. any claim or loss arising out of the ownership by the Insured of any buildings, premises or land or that part of any building leased, occupied or rented by the Insured.

8. any claim or loss arising out of any dishonesty or fraud of any person after discovery by the Insured, in relation to that person, of reasonable cause for suspicion of fraud or dishonesty.

9. any claim or loss arising out of any trading losses or trading liabilities incurred by any business managed or carried on by the Insured, including loss of any client account or business.

10. any liability for any amount of liquidated damages or which arises out of any express guarantee assumed by the Insured under a contract or agreement which would not otherwise have attached in the absence of such contract or agreement.

11. any claim or loss (including loss of value) arising directly or indirectly from pollution. This exclusion shall not apply where such claim or loss arises from the Insured's negligent structural design or specification or failure to report a structural defect in a property but cover shall only extend to that part of any claim or loss which relates to the cost of re-designing, re-specifying, remedying and/or rectifying the defective structure but shall not include the cost of remedying and/or rectifying any loss or damage to the land.

For the purposes of this exclusion, pollution shall mean pollution or contamination by naturally occurring or man made substances, forces or organisms or any combination of them whether permanent or transitory and however occurring.

12. any claim or loss arising out of the enforcement of any judgment

originally obtained in any court of the United States of America/Canada or any territories which come under the jurisdiction of the United States of America/Canada.

13. any claim or loss arising out of survey/inspection and/or valuation reports of real/leasehold property unless such surveys/inspections and/or valuations shall have been carried out by

    (a) A Fellow or Professional Associate of the Royal Institution of Chartered Surveyors (RICS); or

       A Fellow or Associate of the Incorporated Society of Valuers and Auctioneers (ISVA); or

       A Fellow or Associate of the Faculty of Architects and Surveyors (FFAS); or

       A Fellow or Associate of the Royal Institute of British Architects (RIBA); or

       A Fellow or Associate of the Royal Incorporation of Architects of Scotland (RIAS); or

    (b) anyone who has not less than five years experience of such work; or

    (c) any other person delegated by the Insured to execute such work as part of their training subject always to:

       (i) supervision of such work by a person qualified in accordance with (a) above or

       (ii) agreement in writing having been obtained from the Insurers prior to cover being granted.

14. any claim or loss whether directly or indirectly caused by, or contributed to by, or arising from:

    (a) ionising radiation or contamination by radioactivity from any nuclear fuel or from any nuclear waste from the combustion of nuclear fuel or the radioactive toxic explosive or other hazardous properties of any explosive nuclear assembly or nuclear component thereof; or

    (b) war, invasion, acts of foreign enemies, hostilities (whether war be declared or not), civil war, rebellion, revolution, insurrection, military or usurped power or confiscation or nationalisation or requisition or destruction of or damage to property by, or under the order of, any government or public or local authority.

General conditions

1. The Insured shall not admit liability for, or settle any claim, or incur any costs or expenses in connection therewith, without the written consent of the Insurers who shall be entitled at any time to take over and conduct in the name of the Insured or the said Firm(s) as the case may be, the defence or settlement of any such claim. Nevertheless, neither the

Insured nor the Insurers shall be required to contest any legal proceedings unless a Queen's Counsel (to be mutually agreed upon by the Insured and the Insurers) shall advise that such proceedings should be contested.

2. The Insured shall give to the Insurers as soon as possible details in writing of:

    (a) any claim or claims made against them;

    (b) the discovery of any loss to them which may be the subject of indemnity hereunder.

3. The Insured shall give to Insurers notice in writing as soon as possible during the Policy Period of:

    (a) any circumstance of which the Insured shall first become aware during the Policy Period which may give rise to a claim against them:

    (b) the discovery of a reasonable cause for suspicion of dishonesty or fraud on the part of a present Partner, Director or Employee of the Firm(s) whether giving rise to a claim or loss under this Policy or not.

    (c) any threatened or actual proceedings under the Property Misdescriptions Act 1991.

Provided notice has been given in accordance with this Condition then any subsequent claim made against the Insured or any loss discovered by the Insured shall be deemed to have been made or discovered during the Policy Period.

4. Whether notice has been given in accordance with General Condition 2 or 3 the Insured shall give such full co-operation to Insurers as they shall reasonably require.

5. If any payment is made under this Policy in respect of a claim and the Insurers are thereupon subrogated to the Insured's rights of recovery in relation thereto it is agreed that the Insurers shall not exercise such rights against any Employee of the Insured unless such claim has been brought about or contributed to by the dishonest, fraudulent, criminal or malicious act or omission of the Employee.

6. If the Insured shall make any claim under this Policy fraudulently or knowing the same to be fraudulent as regards amount or otherwise this Policy shall become void and all claims hereunder shall be forfeited.

7. The liability of the Insurers shall not exceed for any one claim by the Insured uder this Policy the sum specified in item 4 of the Schedule except that their liability for or in respect of the replacing or restoring of computer system records shall not exceed £50,000 any one claim and £150,000 in the aggregate.

Insurers shall in addition indemnify the Insured in respect of all costs and expenses incurred with their written consent in the defence or settlement of any claim which falls to be dealt with under Insuring Clause 1 of this Policy, provided that if a payment in excess of the amount specified in Item 4 of the Schedule to this Policy has to be made to dispose of such a claim, the Insurers' liability for such costs and expenses shall be of such proportion hereof as the amount specified in Item 4 of the Schedule to this Policy bears to the amount paid to dispose of that claim.

Insurers may in addition indemnify the Insured in respect of 80% of costs and expenses incurred with their prior written consent in the defence of any proceedings brought under the Property Misdescriptions Act 1991 but only where the Insurers believe that defending such proceedings could protect the Insured against any subsequent or concurrent civil action arising from professional services undertaken by the Insured giving rise to such proceedings. Any subsequent or concurrent civil action arising out of any proceedings notified hereunder shall be deemed to be notified hereunder.

8. If an amount is specified under Item 5 of the Schedule this amount shall be borne by the Insured at their own risk, and Insurers Liability shall only be in excess of this amount.

The amount specified under Item 5 of the Schedule shall not be applicable to:
  (a) claims or losses falling under Insuring Clause 3 of the Policy.
  (b) claims arising out of any libel or slander.
  (c) costs and expenses incurred with Insurers' written consent, such consent not to be unreasonably withheld.

9. The proper law for the interpretation of this Policy is English Law. the Courts of England and Wales alone shall have jurisdiction for hearing and determining any litigation arising out of or in connection with the interpretation of this Policy and any arbitration proceedings shall be heard and determined solely in England in accordance with English Law and procedure.

Notice pursuant to General Condition 2 and 3 shall be deemed to be the receipt of notice by:

RICS Insurance Services Limited Plantation House
31–35 Fenchurch Street London EC3M 3DX.

who will be Insurers' Agents for this purpose.

J.C. MORTIMER
Managing Director

APPENDIX 2

RIBA INSURANCE AGENCY LTD (APIA–RIBA/87 WORDING)

A. Definitions and Interpretation

1. "Assured" shall mean:
   (a) Any person or Firm for whom indemnity has been requested in the proposal form;
   (b) Any other person who has been or during the Period of Insurance becomes a partner director or principal of the Firm;
provided that liability arises directly out of Professional Business carried out by that person in the name of the Firm.

2. "Firm" shall mean the Assured Firm described in the Schedule.

3. "Professional Business" shall mean the business described in the Schedule.

4. "Geographical Limits" shall mean the area described in the Schedule.

5. "Period of Insurance" shall mean the period shown in the Schedule.

6. "Limit of Indemnity" shall mean the sum shown in the Schedule.

The liability of Insurers in respect of Section 1 shall not exceed the Limit of Indemnity in respect of each and every claim (or series of claims from the same originating cause) but where any claim circumstance or event is notified to Insurers which is the same as or arises out of or is connected with any claim circumstance or event notified at the same time or previously such claim circumstance or event shall not be separate for the purposes of assessing the Limit of Indemnity available to the Assured.

The liability of Insurers in respect of Section 2 shall not exceed in the aggregate the sum shown in the Schedule.

7. "defence costs" shall mean all costs and expenses incurred with the written consent of the Insurers in the investigation, defence, or settlement of any claim circumstance or event and the costs of representation at any inquiry or other proceedings which have a direct relevance to any claim circumstance or event which (but for the Excess) form the subject of indemnity by Insurers.

8. "Excess" shall mean the first amount of each claim (or series of claims from the same originating cause) shown in the Schedule.

9. "document" shall mean deeds, wills, agreements, maps, plans, records, written or printed books, letters, certificates or written or printed documents or forms of any nature whatsoever (excluding any bearer bonds or coupons, bank or currency notes or other negotiable paper)

137

and/or magnetic tape or other like means of recording information for use with any computer record system.

10. "claim" shall mean any claim made against the Assured.

11. "claimant" shall mean the party making such claim.

12. "circumstance or event" shall mean any circumstance or event which is likely to give rise to a claim.

13. "United Kingdom" shall mean England, Wales, Scotland, Northern Ireland, Isle of Man and the Channel Islands.

14. Any marginal note is for information purposes only and shall not be incorporated in or construed as part of the Policy.

15. Words in the singular include the plural and words in the plural include the singular.

B. Basis of Contract

The Assured [as defined in A.1 (a)] having made to Insurers a written proposal on the date stated in the Schedule which together with any other related particulars and statements that have been supplied in writing are the basis of the contract, and having paid to Insurers the premium stated in the Schedule, is indemnified subject to the Policy terms and conditions for any claim made during the Period of Insurance arising only out of the exercise and conduct by or on behalf of the Assured of the Professional Business within the Geographical Limits.

Section 1

C. Professional Liability

The Assured is indemnified against any claim made during the Period of Insurance for which the Assured shall become legally liable to pay compensation together with claimant's costs, fees and expenses in accordance with any judgment award or settlement made in the United Kingdom (or any order made anywhere in the world to enforce such judgment award or settlement in whole or in part) in consequence of:

    (a) any breach of the professional dury of care owed by the Assured to the claimant which term is deemed to include a breach of warranty of authority;

    (b) any libel, slander or slander of title, slander of goods or injurious falsehood;

    (c) the loss, destruction of or damage to any document in the care, custody and control of the Assured or for which the Assured is responsible (except to the extent insured by D. Section 2).

Costs Clause

In addition to the Limit of Indemnity the Insurers will pay defence costs provided that if a payment greater than the Limit of Indemnity available from Insurers has to be made to dispose of a claim, Insurers' liability for defence costs associated with such claim shall be that proportion of the defence costs as the Limit of Indemnity available from Insurers for such claim bears to the amount required to be paid to dispose of the claim.

Section 2

D. Additional Protection

The Assured is indemnified for reasonable and necessary costs and expenses first incurred during the Period of Insurance by the Assured arising out of the Professional Business in the United Kingdom and with the prior written consent of Insurers:

(a) in replacing, restoring and reconstituting any document which is the property of the Assured or for which the Assured is responsible;

(b) in the prosecution of any injunction and/or proceedings for compensation arising out of infringement of any copyright vested in the Assured provided always that there is no indemnity hereunder in respect of any costs that may be awarded against the Assured.

E. General Exclusions

The Policy shall not indemnify the Assured in respect of:

Excess

1. The Excess.

Consortium

2. Any claim arising out of the Professional Business carried out by the Assured for and/or in the name of any consortium or joint venture of which the Assured forms part unless specifically endorsed hereon.

Transport Property

3. Any claim arising out of the ownership, possession or use by or on behalf of the Assured of any aircraft, watercraft, hovercraft or motor vehicle or trailer, or any buildings, premises or land or that part of any building leased, occupied or rented by the Assured, or any property of the Assured.

Appendix 2

Disclosed Circumstance

4. Any claim arising out of any circumstance or event which has been disclosed by the Assured to any insurer prior to the inception of this Policy.

Employment

5. Any claim arising out of injury, disease, illness or death of the Assured or any person working under a contract of employment apprenticeship or service with the Assured, or any claim arising out of any dispute between the Assured and any present or former employee or any person who has been offered employment with the Assured.

Trading Liability

6. Any claim arising out of or in connection with any trading loss or trading liability incurred by any business managed by or carried out by or on behalf of the Assured.

Fraud and Dishonesty

7. Any claim directly or indirectly contributed to or caused by any dishonest, fraudulent, criminal or malicious act or omission of any partner director or principal of the Assured.

Warranties, Penalties

8. Any claim arising out of performance warranties, penalty clauses or liquidated damages clauses unless the liability of the Assured to the claimant would have existed in the absence of such warranties or clauses.

Non-Contribution

9. Any claim for which the Assured is or but for the existence of this Policy would be entitled to indemnity under any other insurance except in respect of any amount which exceeds that which would have been payable under such other insurance had this Policy not been effected.

Nuclear and War Risks

10. Liability for any claim:
   (i) directly or indirectly caused by or contributed to by or arising from (a) ionising radiations or contamination by radioactivity from any nuclear fuel or from any nuclear waste from the combustion of nuclear fuel, (b) the radioactive toxic explosive or other hazardous properties of any explosive nuclear assembly or nuclear component thereof;

(ii) directly or indirectly occasioned by or happening through or in consequence of war, invasion, acts of foreign enemies, hostilities (whether war be declared or not), civil war, rebellion, revolution, insurrection, military or usurped power.

Penal Damages

11. (i) Any penal, punitive, exemplary or aggravated damages whenever identifiable as such.

(ii) Any additional damages under Section 17(3) of the Copyright Act 1956.

F. General Conditions

Surveys

1. No indemnity is provided by C. Section 1(a) for claims arising out of any survey and/or valuation report rendered by or on behalf of the Assured unless the Assured has complied with the following conditions:

(a) the report is made in writing and;

(b) the survey and/or valuation is made by

(i) a partner director or principal in the Firm or a member of the Assured's staff who is a Fellow or Professional Associate or Member of the Royal Institute of British Architects or of the Royal Institution of Chartered Surveyors or is a Registered Architect who has not less than one year's experience in undertaking structural surveys and/or valuation work such experience being related to the subject matter of the report or

(ii) any member of the Assured's staff who has not less than five years' experience in undertaking structural surveys and/or valuation work such experience being related to the subject matter of the report and;

(c) except in the case where a report is provided to a Building Society, Insurance Company, Bank or other such institutional lender upon a standard report form provided to the Assured for that purpose the Assured has incorporated in the report the following reservations:

"We have not inspected woodwork or other parts of the structure which are covered, unexposed or inaccessible and we are therefore unable to report that any such part of the property is free from defect."

Where the Assured considers that High Alumina Cement may be present in a building the following paragraph is also to be added:

"Furthermore, we must stress that we have not carried out any investigation to determine whether High Alumina Cement was used during the construction of the building inspected and we are therefore unable to report that the building is free from risk in this respect. In view of the possible potential danger connected with High Alumina Cement we strongly recommend that the appropriate investigations, inspections and tests be carried out immediately by a suitably qualified engineer."

(d) any report and/or test made subsequent to the date of this Policy in connection with High Alumina Cement is carried out only by a suitably qualified engineer and presented in writing.

Notification Procedures

2. The Assured shall as conditions precedent to their right to be indemnified under:

(a) C. Section 1 of this Policy, give notice in writing to Insurers as soon as possible of any claim or of the receipt of notice from any person of an intention to make a claim.

(b) D. Section 2(a) of the Policy, give notice in writing to Insurers within seven days of discovery if during the currency of the Policy they shall discover that any document has been destroyed or damaged or lost or mislaid.

(c) D. Section 2(b) of the Policy, give notice in writing to Insurers as soon as possible when a situation comes to their notice which requires or may require any step to be taken to protect their own or Insurers' interests.

3. The Assured shall give during the period of Insurance full details in writing as soon as possible of any circumstances or event of which the Assured shall first become aware during the Period of Insurance. Any such circumstance or event notified to Insurers during the Period of Insurance which subsequently gives rise to a claim shall be deemed to be a claim made during the Period of Insurance.

4. Notice to Insurers to be given under this Policy shall be deemed to be properly made if given in writing to RIBA Insurance Agency Ltd, at the address shown in the Schedule.

Non Admission of Liability

5. The Assured shall not admit liability and no admission, arrangement, offer, promise or payment shall be made by the Assured without Insurers' written consent.

Insurers' Rights

6. Insurers shall be entitled, if they so desire, to take over and conduct in the name of the Assured the investigation, defence or settlement of any

claim circumstance or event and shall have full discretion in the conduct of the same. The Assured shall give all such assistance as Insurers may reasonably require for this purpose, but the Assured shall not be required to contest any legal proceedings unless a Queen's Counsel (or by mutual agreement between the Assured and the Insurers a similar authority) shall advise that such proceedings could be contested with the probability of success.

7. In the event that Insurers shall be advised by their solicitors or on the advice of their solicitors' counsel that it is prudent to do so, Insurers shall be entitled to make a payment of the amount available from Insurers from the Limit of Indemnity to the Assured in exoneration and total discharge of any further liability of any kind whatsoever by the Insurers to the Assured under this Policy. It shall be deemed to be proper payment in exoneration and discharge of the Insurers' liability hereunder to the Assured if the Insurers pay these monies to the RIBA Insurance Agency Ltd.

Applicable Law

8. This contract is governed by the laws of England and any dispute or difference arising hereunder between the Assured and Insurers shall be referred to a Queen's Counsel of the English Bar to be mutually agreed between Insurers and the Assured or in the event of disagreement by the Chairman of the Bar Council.

Subrogation Against Employees

9. Insurers shall not exercise any right of subrogation that may exist against any employee or former employee of the Assured unless Insurers shall have made a payment brought about or contributed to by the act or omission of the employee or former employee which was dishonest, fraudulent, criminal or malicious.

Additional Insurance

10. The Assured shall not effect insurance for any sum that exceeds the Limit of Indemnity without the prior consent of the RIBA Insurance Agency Ltd.

Fraud

11. If any request for indemnity is made and the same is false or fraudulent as regards the amount or otherwise this Policy shall become void and any indemnity hereunder shall be forfeited.

Appendix 2

G. Special RIBA Conditions

1. Insurers will not exercise their right to avoid the Policy nor will Insurers reject a request for indemnity when it is alleged that there has been:

(a) Non-disclosure of facts; or

(b) Misrepresentation of facts; or

(c) Incorrect particulars or statements; or

(d) Late notification of a claim; or

(e) Late notification of intention to make a claim; or

(f) Late notification of a circumstance or event.

Provided always that the Assured shall establish to Insurers' satisfaction that such alleged non-disclosure, misrepresentation or incorrect particulars or statements or late notification was innocent and free of any fraudulent conduct or intent to deceive.

2. When Insurers are so satisfied the following conditions shall apply:

(a) In any case of a claim and the Assured were previously aware of the claim or a circumstance or event, or in any case of the Assured being previously aware of an intention to make a claim or of a circumstance or event and the Assured could have notified the claim circumstance or event under any preceding policy of indemnity, then if the indemnity available from Insurers under this Policy is greater or wider in scope than that to which the Assured would have been entitled under such preceding policy of indemnity, Insurers shall only be liable to indemnify the Assured for such amount and on such terms as would have been available to the Assured under such preceding policy of indemnity; save that nothing in this clause shall entitle the Assured to indemnity wider or more extensive than is available to the Assured under this Policy (notwithstanding the terms of this clause).

(b) Where the Assured's conduct or breach of or non-compliance with any condition of this Policy has resulted in prejudice to the handling or settlement of any claim the indemnity afforded by the Policy in respect of such claim (including defence costs) shall be reduced to such sum as in Insurers' opinion would have been payable by them in the absence of such prejudice.

(c) No indemnity shall be available for any claim circumstance or event notified to Insurers after the Period of Insurance.

In the event of any disagreement by the Assured regarding the application of these Special Conditions, such disagreement shall at the Assured's request be referred to the person nominated by the President for the time being of the Royal Institute of British Architects for his consideration and intercession on the Assured's behalf if the facts are considered to warrant this by the person so nominated, and the Insurers agree to give due and proper consideration to any such intercession.

APPENDIX 3

MORTGAGE VALUATION: GUIDANCE FOR VALUERS
1 June 1992 (amended September 1992)

GUIDANCE NOTES FOR VALUERS ON THE VALUATION AND INSPECTION OF RESIDENTIAL PROPERTY FOR MORTGAGE PURPOSES ON BEHALF OF BUILDING SOCIETIES, BANKS AND OTHER LENDERS

These Notes are for the guidance of valuers and apply to inspections carried out on or after 1 June 1992 and, in respect of such inspections, supersede previous published guidance. The Council of Mortgage Lenders and the Building Societies Association were consulted during the production of these Notes.

1. The Valuer's Roles

1.1 The roles of the Valuer, who must have knowledge of and experience in the valuation of the residential property in the particular locality, are:

1.1.1 to advise the Lender as to the open market value (not a forced sale valuation) (see section 4.4) at the date of inspection;

1.1.2 to advise the Lender as to the nature of the property (see section 4) and any factors likely materially to affect its value;

1.1.3 if required by the Lender, to provide an assessment of the estimated current reinstatement cost in its present form (unless otherwise stated) for insurance purposes including garage, outbuildings, site clearance and professional fees, excluding VAT (except on fees).

1.2 The Valuer should not make a recommendation as to the amount or percentage of mortgage advance or as to the length of the mortgage term. Nor is it the Valuer's responsibility to give advice as to the suitability of the property for "second mortgage purposes".

2. The Valuer's Inspection

Subject to the Valuer's judgement, a visual inspection is undertaken of so much of the exterior and interior of the property as is accessible to the Valuer without undue difficulty. Accordingly it is to include all that part of

146

the property which is visible whilst standing at ground level within the boundaries of the site and adjacent public/communal areas and whilst standing at the various floor levels, as follows:

2.1 Main Building—External

Roof coverings, chimneys, parapets, gutters, walls, windows, doors, pipes, wood or metalwork, paintwork, damp proof courses, air bricks and ground levels.

2.2 Main Building—Internal

2.2.1 Parts not readily accessible or visible are not inspected, and furniture and effects are not moved, nor floor coverings lifted.

2.2.2 Subject to reasonable accessibility, the roof space is inspected only to the extent visible from the access hatch, without entering it.

2.2.3 Ceilings, walls, load bearers and floor surfaces are inspected except where covered or obscured. Readings should be taken with a moisture meter for rising dampness.

2.2.4 Cellars are inspected to the extent that they are reasonably accessible, but under floor voids are *not* inspected.

2.3 Services

The Valuer is to identify whether or not there are gas, electricity, central heating, plumbing and drainage services. Testing of services is *not* undertaken.

2.4 Outbuildings

Garages and other buildings of substantial permanent construction, and any structure(s) attached to the dwelling are inspected.

2.5 Site

The inspection should include the general state of boundaries, structures, drives, paths, retaining walls and the proximity of trees only to the extent that they are likely materially to affect the property's value.

2.6 Neighbouring properties

The nature, use and apparent state of repair of neighbouring properties in the immediate vicinity is considered only to the extent that they may materially affect the value of the subject property.

2.7 Flats, maisonettes or similar units forming part of a larger building or group of related buildings

The above provisions apply, but here "Main Building" means the building containing the proposed security but not including other buildings physically attached to it.

2.7.1 *Main Building—External:* The exterior of the proposed security and sufficient of the remainder of the Main Building to ascertain its general state of repair.

2.7.2 *Main Building—Internal:* The interior of the proposed security, the communal entrance areas within the Main Building from which the proposed security takes access and the communal area on the floor(s) of the proposed security. The roof space will only be inspected (as defined in paragraph 2.2.2) where access is directly available from within the subject flat.

2.7.3 *Outbuildings:* Garaging, car parking, other buildings (excluding sports complexes) of permanent construction and any other structures attached to the Main Building or which serve the proposed security.

3. The Valuer's Report

3.1 Subject to covering the matters referred to in section 1 above, reporting should be confined strictly to answering questions raised by the Lender.

3.2 If it is suspected that hidden defects exist which could have a material effect on the value of the property, the Valuer should so advise and recommend more extensive investigation by the intending Borrower prior to entering into a legal commitment to purchase or, in the case of a re-mortgage, as a pre-condition of the mortgage advance. It may be appropriate in exceptional circumstances to defer making a valuation until the results of the further investigations are known.

3.3 If it is not reasonably possible to carry out any substantial part of the inspection (see section 2 above) this should be stated.

3.4 Any obvious evidence of serious disrepair to the property or obvious potential hazard to it should be reported, as should any other matters likely materially to affect the value.

3.5 Where the Valuer relies on information provided, this should be indicated in the Report as also should be the source of that information.

3.6 The Lender should be informed of the existence of any apparently recent significant alterations and extensions so as to alert the Lender's legal adviser to any enquiries to be made.

3.7 Where the proposed security is part of a building comprising flats or maisonettes, the Valuer's Report should identify any apparent deficiencies in the management and/or maintenance arrangements observed during the inspection which materially affects the value.

3.8 Where the apparent sharing of drives, paths, or other areas might affect the value of the subject property, the Valuer should inform the Lender.

3.9 The form of construction should be reported, and where non-traditional the Valuer should advise accordingly, stating the type of construction and the source of this information if it is not apparent from the inspection.

3.10 Where the Valuer decides to report a necessity for works to be carried out to a property as a condition of any advance and the Valuer identifies the property as being:

3.10.1 of architectural or historic interest, or listed as such; or

3.10.2 in a conservation area; or

3.10.3 of unusual construction

the Valuer should advise that a person with appropriate specialist knowledge be asked to give advice as to the appropriate works unless, exceptionally, the Valuer believes he/she is competent to give advice which if adopted would not be detrimental to the property's architectural or historic integrity, its future structural condition or conservation of the building fabric.

3.11 In the case of new properties or conversions where the Valuer is obliged to base the valuation upon drawings and a specification, this fact should be stated in the Report.

4. The Valuation

4.1 Unless it is made apparent by an express statement in the Report the Valuer will have made the following assumptions and will have been under no duty to have verified these assumptions:

4.1.1 that vacant possession is provided;

4.1.2 that planning permission and statutory approvals for the buildings and for their use, including any extensions or alterations, have been obtained;

4.1.3 that no deleterious or hazardous materials or techniques have been used;

4.1.4 that the property is not subject to any unusual or especially onerous restrictions, encumbrances or outgoings and that good title can be shown;

4.1.5 that the property and its value are unaffected by any matters which would be revealed by inspection of the Contaminated Uses Land Register or by a Local Search (or their equivalent in Scotland and Northern Ireland) and replies to the usual enquiries, or by a Statutory Notice and that neither the property, nor its condition, nor its use, nor its intended use, is or will be unlawful;

4.1.6 that an inspection of those parts which have not been inspected or a survey inspection would not reveal material defects or cause the Valuer to alter the valuation materially;

4.1.7 that the property is connected to main services which are available on normal terms;

4.1.8   that sewers, main services and the roads giving access to the property have been adopted;

4.1.9   that in the case of a new property the construction of which has not been completed, the construction will be satisfactorily completed;

4.1.10 that in the case of a newly constructed property, the builder is a registered member of the NHBC or equivalent and has registered the subject property in accordance with the scheme concerned; and

4.1.11 that where the proposed security is part of a building comprising flats or maisonettes, unless instructed or otherwise aware to the contrary, the cost of repairs and maintenance to the building and grounds are shared proportionately between all the flats and maisonettes forming part of the block, and that there are no onerous liabilities outstanding.

4.2 Among the relevant factors to be taken into account in the valuation are:

4.2.1 the tenure of the interest to be offered as security, and if known the terms of any tenancies to which that interest is subject;

4.2.2 the age, type, accommodation, siting, amenities, fixtures and features of the property and other significant environmental factors within the locality; and

4.2.3 the apparent general state of and liability for repair, the construction and apparent major defects; liability to subsidence, flooding, and/or other risks. (Particular care is needed with non-traditional construction.)

4.3 Unless otherwise instructed any development value is to be excluded from the "open market valuation" and the Valuer will not include any element of value attributable to furnishings, removable fittings and sales incentives of any description when arriving at an opinion of the value. Portable and temporary structures are to be excluded also.

4.4 The definition of "open market value" is the best price at which the sale of an interest in the property might reasonably be expected to have been completed unconditionally for cash consideration at the date of the valuation assuming:

4.4.1 a willing seller;

4.4.2 that, prior to the date of valuation, there had been a reasonable period (having regard to the nature of the property and the state of the market) for the proper marketing of the interest, for the agreement of price and terms and for the completion of the sale;

4.4.3 that the state of the market, level of values and other circumstances were, on any earlier assumed date of exchange of contracts, the same as on the date of valuation; and

4.4.4 that no account is taken of any additional bid by a purchaser with a special interest.

5. Valuation for Insurance Purposes

In assessing the current reinstatement cost (see paragraph 1.1.3) the Valuer should have regard to the ABI/BCIS House Rebuilding Cost Index.

6. The Valuer's Record of Inspection and Valuation

6.1 The Valuer is advised to make and retain legible notes as to his/her findings and, particularly, the limits of the inspection and the circumstances under which it was carried out.

6.2 The Valuer is advised to keep a record of the comparable transactions and/or valuations to which he/she has had regard in arriving at his/her valuation.

7. The Variation of Instructions

All mortgage valuations should be in accordance with these Guidance Notes unless variations are notified to the Valuer in writing.

MODEL CONDITIONS OF ENGAGEMENT BETWEEN THE LENDER AND THE VALUER

1. The Valuer will carry out for the Lender's current fee an inspection of the proposed security, and report, in accordance with the current RICS/ISVA Guidance Notes for Valuers on the valuation and inspection of residential property for mortgage purposes on behalf of building societies, banks and other lenders, subject to any variations specified by the Lender in the issue of instructions.

2. The purpose of the report and valuation for mortgage is to enable the Lending Institution to assess the security offered by the property for the proposed loan and, where applicable, to enable the Directors to fulfil the requirements of Section 13 of the Building Societies Act 1986.

3. The report and valuation will be presented on the Lender's prescribed form or other type of form as may be agreed.

4. Before the Valuer proceeds, the Lender will take all reasonable steps to inform the Borrower as to the limitations of the inspection report and valuation, and will suggest that the Borrower commissions a more detailed inspection and Report before entering into a legal commitment.

5. Unless the parties otherwise agree in writing, all disputes arising out of this agreement shall be finally settled under English Law and the parties irrevocably submit to the jurisdiction of the English Courts, save that

Appendix 3

where the subject property is in Scotland, Scots Law shall apply and the Scottish Courts shall have jurisdiction.

Published with kind permission of

The Royal Institution of Chartered Surveyors
12 Great George Street, London SW1P 3AD, and
The Incorporated Society of Valuers and Auctioneers
3 Cadogan Gate, London SW1X 0AS

INSURANCE BROKERS REGISTRATION COUNCIL (CODE OF CONDUCT) APPROVAL ORDER 1978 (S.I. 1978 No. 1394)

Dated September 27, 1978 and made by the Secretary of State under the Insurance Brokers Registration Act 1977, ss.27(1) and 28(1).

1. This Order may be cited as the Insurance Brokers Registration Council (Code of Conduct) Approval Order 1978 and shall come into operation on October 20, 1978.

2. The Code of Conduct drawn up by the Insurance Brokers Registration Council pursuant to section 10 of the Insurance Brokers (Registration) Act 1977 is hereby approved as set out in the Schedule to this Order.

SCHEDULE. CODE OF CONDUCT DRAWN UP BY THE INSURANCE BROKERS REGISTRATION COUNCIL PURSUANT TO SECTION 10 OF THE INSURANCE BROKERS [REGISTRATION] ACT 1977

Words and expressions used in this Code of Conduct shall have the same meaning as are ascribed to them in the Act except that:

"insurance broker" means registered insurance broker and enrolled body corporate;

"insurer" means a person or body of persons carrying on insurance business;

"advertisements" or "advertising" means canvassing, the offer of services or other methods whereby business is sought by insurance brokers.

1. This Code of Conduct shall serve as a guide to insurance brokers and other persons concerned with their conduct but the mention or lack of mention in it of a particular act or omission shall not be taken as conclusive of any question of professional conduct.

In my opinion of the Council the objective of the Code is to assist in establishing a recognised standard of professional conduct required of all insurance brokers who should, in the interests of the public and in the performance of their duties, bear in mind both this objective and the underlying spirit of this Code.

Matters which might relate to acts or omissions amounting to negligence will be dealt with, if necessary, by the Courts but the Council acknowledges that gross negligence *or* repeated cases of negligence may amount to unprofessional conduct.

2. The following are, in the opinion of the Council, the acts and omissions which, if done or made by registered insurance brokers or enrolled bodies corporate constitute unprofessional conduct: namely any acts or omissions that breach the fundamental principles governing the professional conduct of insurance brokers set out in paragraph 3 below.

3. The principles mentioned in paragraph 2 above are as follows:

A. *Insurance brokers shall at all times conduct their business with utmost good faith and integrity.*

B. *Insurance brokers shall do everything possible to satisfy the insurance requirements of their clients and shall place the interest of those clients before all other considerations. Subject to these requirements and interests, insurance brokers shall have proper regard for others.*

C. *Statements made by or on behalf of insurance brokers when advertising shall not be misleading or extravagant.*

The following are some specific examples of the application of those principles:

(1) In the conduct of their business insurance brokers shall provide advice objectively and independently.

(2) Insurance brokers shall only use or permit the use of the description "insurance broker" in connection with a business provided that business is carried on in accordance with the requirements of the Rules made by the Council under sections 11 and 12 of the Act.

(3) Insurance brokers shall ensure that all work carried out in connection with their insurance broking business shall be under the control and day-to-day supervision of a registered insurance broker and they shall do everything possible to ensure that their employees are made aware of this Code.

(4) Insurance brokers shall on request from the client explain the differences in, and the relative costs of, the principal types of insurance which in the opinion of the insurance broker might suit a client's needs.

(5) Insurance brokers shall ensure the use of a sufficient number of insurers to satisfy the insurance requirements of their clients.

(6) Insurance brokers shall, upon request, disclose to any client who is an individual and who is, or is contemplating becoming, the holder of a United Kingdom policy of insurance the amount of commission paid by the insurer under any relevant policy of insurance.

(7) Although the choice of an insurer can only be a matter of

judgment, insurance brokers shall use their skill objectively in the best interests of their client.

(8) Insurance brokers shall not withhold from the policyholder any written evidence or documentation relating to the contract of insurance without adequate and justifiable reasons being disclosed in writing and without delay to the policyholder. If an insurance broker withholds a document from a policyholder by way of a lien for monies due from that policyholder he shall provide the reason in the manner required above.

(9) Insurance brokers shall inform a client of the name of all insurers with whom a contract of insurance is placed. This information shall be given at the inception of the contract and any changes thereafter shall be advised at the earliest opportunity to the client.

(10) Before any work involving a charge is undertaken or an agreement to carry out business is concluded, insurance brokers shall disclose and identify any amount they propose to charge to the client or policyholder which will be in addition to the premium payable to the insurer.

(11) Insurance brokers shall disclose to a client any payment which they receive as a result of securing on behalf of that client any service additional to the arrangement of a contract of insurance.

(12) Insurance brokers shall have proper regard to the wishes of a policyholder or client who seeks to terminate any agreement with them to carry out business.

(13) Any information acquired by an insurance broker from his client shall not be used or disclosed except in the normal course of negotiating, maintaining, or renewing a contract of insurance for that client or unless the consent of the client has been obtained or the information is required by a court of competent jurisdiction.

(14) In the completion of the proposal form, claim form, or any other material document, insurance brokers shall make it clear that all the answers or statements are the client's own responsibility. The client should always be asked to check the details and told that the inclusion of incorrect information may result in a claim being repudiated.

(15) Advertisements made by or on behalf of insurance brokers shall comply with the applicable parts of the Code of Advertising Practice published by the Advertising Standards Authority and for this purpose the Code of Advertising Practice shall be deemed to form part of this Code of Conduct.

(16) Advertisements made by or on behalf of insurance brokers shall distinguish between contractual benefits, that is those that the

contract of insurance is bound to provide, and non-contractual benefits, that is the amount of benefit which it might provide assuming the insurer's particular forecast is correct. Where such advertisements include a forecast of non-contractual benefits, insurance brokers shall restrict the forecast to that provided by the insurer concerned.

(17) Advertisements made by or on behalf of insurance brokers shall not be restricted to the policies of one insurer except where the reasons for such restriction are fully explained in the advertisement, the insurer named therein, and the prior approval of that insurer obtained.

(18) When advertising their services directly or indirectly either in person or in writing insurance brokers shall disclose their identity, occupation and purpose before seeking information or before giving advice.

(19) Insurance brokers shall display in any office where they are carrying on business and to which the public have access a notice to the effect that a copy of the Code of Conduct is available upon request and that if a member of the public wishes to make a complaint or requires the assistance of the Council in resolving a dispute, he may write to the Insurance Brokers Registration Council at its offices at 15 St. Helen's Place, London EC3A 6DS.

APPENDIX 5

ASSOCIATION OF BRITISH INSURERS: GENERAL INSURANCE BUSINESS—CODE OF PRACTICE FOR ALL INTERMEDIARIES (INCLUDING EMPLOYEES OF INSURANCE COMPANIES) OTHER THAN REGISTERED INSURANCE BROKERS (INTRODUCED JANUARY 1989)*

This Code applies to general business as defined in the Insurance Companies Act 1982, but does not apply to reinsurance business. As a condition of membership of the Association of British Insurers, members undertake to enforce this Code and to use their best endeavours to ensure that all those involved in selling their policies observe its provisions.

It shall be an overriding obligation of an intermediary at all times to conduct business with the utmost good faith and integrity.

In the case of complaints from policyholders (either direct or indirect, for example through a trading standards officer or citizens advice bureau), the insurance company concerned shall require an intermediary to co-operate so that the facts can be established. An intermediary shall inform the policyholder complaining that he can take his problem direct to the insurance company concerned.

A. General sales principles

1. The intermediary shall:—
    (i) where appropriate, make a prior appointment to call. Unsolicited or unarranged calls shall be made at an hour likely to be suitable to the prospective policyholder;
    (ii) when he makes contact with the prospective policyholder, identify himself and explain as soon as possible that the arrangements he wishes to discuss could include insurance. He shall make it known that he is:—
        (a) an employee of an insurance company, for whose conduct the company accepts responsibility; or
        (b) an agent of one company, for whose conduct the company accepts responsibility; or
        (c) an agent of two or up to six companies, for whose conduct the companies accept responsibility; or

* © Association of British Insurers, November 1988. Association of British Insurers, Aldermary House, Queen Street, London EC4N 1TT. TEL: 071–248 4477.

157

      (d) an independent intermediary seeking to act on behalf of the prospective policyholder, for whose conduct the company/ companies do not accept responsibility;

  (iii) ensure as far as possible that the policy proposed is suitable to the needs and resources of the prospective policyholder;

  (iv) give advice only on those insurance matters in which he is knowledgeable and seek or recommend other specialist advice when necessary; and

  (v) treat all information supplied by the prospective policyholder as completely confidential to himself and to the company or companies to which the business is being offered.

2. The intermediary shall not:—

  (i) inform the prospective policyholder that his name has been given by another person, unless he is prepared to disclose that person's name if requested to do so by the prospective policyholder and has that person's consent to make that disclosure;

  (ii) make inaccurate or unfair criticisms of any insurer; or

  (iii) make comparisons with other types of policy unless he makes clear the differing characteristics of each policy.

B. Explanation of the contract

The intermediary shall:—

  (i) identify the insurance company;

  (ii) explain all the essential provisions of the cover afforded by the policy, or policies, which he is recommending, so as to ensure as far as possible that the prospective policyholder understands what he is buying:

  (iii) draw attention to any restrictions and exclusions applying to the policy;

  (iv) if necessary, obtain from the insurance company specialist advice in relation to items (ii) and (iii) above;

  (v) not impose any charge in addition to the premium required by the insurance company without disclosing the amount and purpose of such charge; and

  (vi) if he is an independent intermediary, disclose his commission on request.

C. Disclosure of underwriting information

The intermediary shall, in obtaining the completion of the proposal form or any other material:—

(i) avoid influencing the prospective policyholder and make it clear that all the answers or statements are the latter's own responsibility; and

(ii) ensure that the consequences of non-disclosure and inaccuracies are pointed out to the prospective policyholder by drawing his attention to the relevant statement in the proposal form and by explaining them himself to the prospective policyholder.

D. Accounts and financial aspects

The intermediary shall, if authorised to collect monies in accordance with the terms of his agency appointment:—

(i) keep a proper account of all financial transactions with a prospective policyholder which involve the transmission of money in respect of insurance;

(ii) acknowledge receipt (which, unless the intermediary has been otherwise authorised by the insurance company, shall be on his own behalf) of all money received in connection with an insurance policy and shall distinguish the premium from any other payment included in the money; and

(iii) remit any such monies so collected in strict conformity with his agency appointment.

E. Documentation

The intermediary shall not withhold from the policyholder any written evidence or documentation relating to the contract of insurance.

F. Existing policyholders

The intermediary shall abide by the principles set out in this Code to the extent that they are relevant to his dealings with existing policyholders.

G. Claims

If the policyholder advises the intermediary of an incident which might give rise to a claim, the intermediary shall inform the company without delay, and in any event within three working days, and thereafter give prompt advice to the policyholder of the company's requirements concerning the claim, including the provision as soon as possible of information required to establish the nature and extent of the loss. Information received from the policyholder shall be passed to the company without delay.

H. Professional indemnity cover for independent intermediaries

The intermediary shall obtain, and maintain in force, professional indemnity insurance in accordance with the requirements of the

Association of British Insurers as set out in the Annex, which may be updated from time to time.

I. Letters of appointment

This Code of Practice shall be incorporated verbatim or by reference in all Letters of Appointment of non-registered intermediaries and no policy of the company shall be sold by such intermediaries except within the terms of such a Letter of Appointment.

ANNEX. CODE OF PRACTICE FOR THE SELLING OF
GENERAL INSURANCE PROFESSIONAL INDEMNITY
COVER REQUIRED FOR NON-REGISTERED
INDEPENDENT INTERMEDIARIES

As from 1st January 1989 (new agents) and by 1st July 1989 (existing agents) all non-registered independent intermediaries must take out and maintain in force professional indemnity cover in accordance with the requirements set out below.

The insurance may be taken out with any authorised UK or EEC insurer who has agreed to:—

(a) issue cover in accordance with the requirements set out below;

(b) provide the intermediary with an annual certificate as evidence that the cover meets the ABI requirements, this certificate to contain the name and address including postcode of the intermediary, the policy number, the period of the policy, the limit of indemnity, the self-insured excess and the name of the insurer;

(c) send a duplicate certificate to ABI at the time the certificate is issued to the intermediary;

(d) inform ABI, by means of monthly lists, of any cases of non-renewal, cancellation of the cover mid-term or of the cover becoming inadequate.

The requirements are as follows:—

A. Limits of indemnity

The policy shall at inception and at each renewal date, which shall not be more than 12 months from inception or the last renewal date, provide a minimum limit of indemnity of either:—

(a) a sum equal to three times the annual general business commission of the business for the last accounting period ending prior to inception or renewal of the policy, or a sum of £250,000 whichever sum is the greater.

In no case shall the minimum limit of indemnity be required to exceed £5m, and a minimum sum of £250,000 shall apply at all times to each and every claim of series of claims arising out of the same occurrence, or

(b) a sum equal to three times the annual general business commission of the business for the last accounting period ending prior to inception or renewal of the policy, or a sum of £500,000 whichever sum shall be the greater.

In no case shall the minimum limit of indemnity be required to exceed £5m.

B. Maximum self-insured excess

The maximum self-insured excess permitted in normal circumstances shall be 1% of the minimum limit of indemnity required by Paragraph A(a) or A(b) above as the case may be. Subject to the agreement of the professional indemnity insurer, the self-insured excess may be increased to a maximum of 2% of such minimum limit of indemnity.

C. Scope of policy cover

The policy shall indemnify the insured:—

(a) against losses arising from claims made against the insured:
  (i) for breach of duty in connection with the business by reason of any negligent act, error or omission; and
  (ii) in respect of libel or slander or in Scotland defamation, committed in the conduct of the business by the insured, any employee or former employee of the insured, and where the business is or was carried on in partnership any partner or former partner of the insured; and
  (iii) by reason of any dishonest or fraudulent act or omission committed or made in the conduct of the business by any employee (other than a director of a body corporate) or former employee (other than a director of a body corporate) of the insured; and
(b) against claims arising in connection with the business in respect of:—
  (i) any loss of money or other property whatsoever belonging to the insured or for which the insured is legally liable in consequence of any dishonest or fraudulent act or omission of any employee (other than a director of a body corporate) or former employee (other than a director of a body corporate) of the insured; and
  (ii) legal liability incurred by reason of loss of documents and costs and expenses incurred in replacing or restoring such documents.

161

Appendix 5

D. General business only

The above requirements relate only to the intermediary's general insurance business.

CODE OF PRACTICE FOR LLOYD'S BROKERS*

Introduction to Code of Practice for Lloyd's Brokers

1. The intention of Lloyd's in promulgating codes of practice is to assist in establishing a recognised standard of professional conduct for all members of the Lloyd's community who should, in discharging their duties as such, bear in mind both the provisions and the underlying spirit and intent of these codes.

2. The Code of Practice for Lloyd's Brokers is intended as an explanatory statement of the principles which are expected to apply to the conduct of Lloyd's brokers.

3. Lloyd's brokers and their partners, directors and employees who are individually registered under the Insurance Brokers (Registration) Act 1977 are also subject to the Code of Conduct drawn up under that Act. The three fundamental principles of that code are:

   A.   Insurance brokers shall at all times conduct their business with utmost good faith and integrity.

   B.   Insurance brokers shall do everything possible to satisfy the insurance requirements of their clients and shall place the interests of those clients before all other considerations. Subject to these requirements and interests, insurance brokers shall have proper regard for others.

   C.   Statements made by or on behalf of insurance brokers when advertising shall not be misleading or extravagant.

4. Under the terms of the Lloyd's Brokers Byelaw (No. 5 of 1988) the Council must be satisfied on the registration or the review of the registration of a Lloyd's broker that the Lloyd's broker is a "fit and proper" person. In making that assessment the Council may have regard to the observance by the Lloyd's broker of any relevant Lloyd's codes of practice.

5. Lloyd's brokers are the agents of their clients and, as such, they are subject to the general law as it applies to agents. The provisions of the

---

* Issued by The Council of Lloyd's on 6 July 1988, under paragraph 20 of the Lloyd's Brokers Byelaw (No. 5 of 1988). This Code of Practice came into force on 1 November, 1988. © Lloyd's of London, 1988.

Code of Practice are not intended in any way to derogate from that general law.

6. It is recognised that the practice described in this Code may be at variance with the law or legally established custom or practice applicable elsewhere than in England and Wales. In such circumstances, departure from the Code may be appropriate.

7. This Code applies only to the insurance activities of Lloyd's brokers. A Lloyd's broker is a partnership or body corporate permitted by the Council to broke insurance business at Lloyd's.

Code of Practice for Lloyd's Brokers

Unless the context otherwise requires, for the purposes of this Code of Practice the term "Lloyd's broker" includes the individuals engaged in the insurance activities of the Lloyd's broker as well as the partnership or body corporate permitted by the Council to broke insurance business at Lloyd's.

The paragraphs inset in italics are the examples given in the IBRC Code of Conduct of the application of the three fundamental principles of that Code. These examples are relevant in this Lloyd's Code because Lloyd's brokers and their partners, directors and employees who are registered insurance brokers in the UK are subject to the IBRC Code.

1. Relationship with client

1.1 When a Lloyd's broker establishes a relationship with a client, he should take appropriate steps to see that the client understands the Lloyd's broker's role.

1.2 A Lloyd's broker should understand the type of client with which he is dealing (including whether the client is a private individual, a business, another insurance intermediary or a reassured) and the extent of the client's awareness of risk and insurance and take that knowledge into account in his dealings with the client. A Lloyd's broker should take appropriate steps to see that the client is aware that local law may affect his insurance requirements.

> *(1) In the conduct of their business insurance brokers shall provide advice objectively and independently.*
>
> *(4) Insurance brokers shall on request from the client explain the differences in, and the relative costs of, the principal types of insurance which in the opinion of the insurance broker might suit a client's needs.*

1.3 Misunderstandings as to the scope of authority and instructions are far less likely to arise where they are set down in writing. Therefore, in the absence of accurate written instructions from a client as to coverage sought, a Lloyd's broker should, where it is reasonably practicable, confirm instructions in writing promptly, including appropriate reference to recommendations made by the Lloyd's broker but declined by the client.

1.4 A Lloyd's broker should not act for one client if he is aware that by so doing he could materially prejudice the performance of his obligations to another client.

2. *Remuneration*

2.1 A Lloyd's broker should, if requested by a client, disclose the amount of brokerage and the nature and where practicable the amount of commission or other remuneration he receives as a result of effecting an insurance for that client.

2.2 A Lloyd's broker will have to consider whether he is likely to receive any brokerage by effecting reinsurances of an original insurance. This type of remuneration will not normally be received by a Lloyd's broker in his capacity as agent of the original client and will not, therefore, normally be disclosable if the original client enquires. This will, however, depend on the circumstances of the particular transaction.

  (6) Insurance brokers shall, upon request, disclose to any client who is an individual and who is, or is contemplating becoming the holder of a United Kingdom policy of insurance the amount of commission paid by the insurer under any relevant policy of insurance.

  (10) Before any work involving a charge is undertaken or an agreement to carry out business is concluded, insurance brokers shall disclose and identify any amount they propose to charge to the client or policyholder which will be in addition to the premium payable to the insurer.

  (11) Insurance brokers shall disclose to a client any payment which they receive as a result of securing on behalf of that client any service additional to the arrangement of a contract of insurance.

2.3 A Lloyd's broker should deduct and retain any commission from the amount of a claim collected for a client only where this is the recognised practice for the type of insurance concerned and if the Lloyd's broker intends to deduct and retain any such commission the proportion should be disclosed to the client prior to the Lloyd's broker undertaking to effect the insurance.

2.4 Where it is the normal practice to return commissions pro rata to any return premiums, any intention on the part of a Lloyd's broker to depart from this practice should be advised to the client when the Lloyd's broker accepts his instructions to place the risk.

3. *Confidentiality of client information*

  (13) Any information acquired by an insurance broker from his client shall not be used or disclosed except in the normal course of negotiating,

maintaining, or renewing a contract of insurance for that client or unless the consent of the client has been obtained or the information is required by a court of competent jurisdiction.

3.1 A Lloyd's broker may wish to compile statistics or otherwise use information gained from the operation of the accounts of various clients, in order to broke a risk for a particular client to insurers. In each case, the Lloyd's broker should consider what information he may properly use and great care must be taken that a client about whose account information is being used is not adversely affected by it. Although calling upon his general knowledge and experience of other clients' affairs would normally be permissible, the disclosure by a Lloyd's broker of information revealing the identities of clients and specific details of their affairs without their informed consent is not permissible, unless such information is already available to the market generally.

3.2 The duty to maintain the confidentiality of information can be overridden in certain limited and specific circumstances. For example, the Lloyd's Information and Confidentiality Byelaw (No. 4 of 1983) empowers the Council of Lloyd's (or other person acting under its authority) to require Lloyd's brokers to produce information including that relating to the affairs of their principals and clients. That provision thus permits confidential information to be legitimately imparted by a Lloyd's broker in circumstances other than those set out in the IBRC code.

3.3 A Lloyd's broker should take appropriate steps to maintain the security of confidential documents in his possession.

4. Choice of insurers

> *(5) Insurance brokers shall ensure the use of a sufficient number of insurers to satisfy the insurance requirements of their clients.*
>
> *(7) Although the choice of an insurer can only be a matter of judgement, insurance brokers shall use their skill objectively in the best interests of their client.*

4.1 A Lloyd's broker should not allow any shareholding or other connections which he has with any insurance company, non-Lloyd's underwriting agent, coverholder or Lloyd's syndicate to prejudice the performance of his duties to his clients. In this context, connections with a Lloyd's syndicate would include the participation by partners, directors or employees of the Lloyd's broker in the syndicate as Members of Lloyd's of the placing of Members of Lloyd's on the syndicate by a Members' Agent which is connected with the Lloyd's broker.

4.2 Except for certain compulsory classes of insurance, it is not illegal under English law for an insurance for a client based in the UK to be effected outside the UK with an insurer which is not authorised to carry on insurance of the class concerned in the EEC. If, however, a Lloyd's broker suggests to such a client that such an insurance should be placed with such an insurer, he should, if he believes that it would be appropriate having regard to the client's experience of insurance, advise the client in writing that:

(a) the management and solvency of the insurer are not supervised by the appropriate authority in any EEC member country;

(b) notwithstanding that the client may be an individual who would otherwise fall within the protection of the Policyholders Protection Act 1975, in the event of the failure of the insurer, no protection would be afforded to the client by that Act if the insurer was not suitably authorised in the UK; and

(c) the client may have difficulties in bringing proceedings and/or executing a judgment against the insurer.

The client's written acknowledgement of such advice should be sought.

4.3 Where a client's instructions concerning the choice of an insurer override a Lloyd's broker's advice, the Lloyd's broker should inform the client that this is contrary to the Lloyd's broker's advice and seek the client's written acknowledgement thereof.

5. Disclosure to insurers

5.1 It is the duty of the Lloyd's broker and his client to disclose all material circumstances within their knowledge and to give a fair presentation of the risk to insurers.

5.2 A Lloyd's broker should explain to a client the duty of good faith and the obligation to disclose all circumstances material to the risk which he wishes to insure and the consequences of any failure to make such disclosure.

5.3 Other than in exceptional circumstances, a Lloyd's broker should not complete a proposal form on behalf of a client. If the Lloyd's broker does so complete a proposal form he should disclose that fact to the insurers.

(14) In the completion of the proposal form, claim form, or any other material document, insurance brokers shall make it clear that all the answers or statements are the client's own responsibility. The client should always be asked to check the details and told that the inclusion of incorrect information may result in a claim being repudiated.

5.4 Slips and other placing information presented to insurers should be clear and unambiguous and the Lloyd's broker's relevant personnel should be competent to answer the insurer's reasonable questions about the risk. A Lloyd's broker should be prompt to convey insurers' requests for further information to the client.

5.5 If a Lloyd's broker has reason to believe that the disclosure of the material facts by the client is not true, fair and complete, he should request the client to make the necessary true, fair and complete disclosure. In the absence of such agreement, the broker should consider whether he should decline to continue acting for the client and what obligations he has to insurers or any regulatory authority.

5.6 In cases where two Lloyd's brokers act jointly on a placing, they should each take appropriate steps to see that there is a clear mutual understanding of their respective duties to the client. Both Lloyd's brokers should also take appropriate steps to see that the client and insurers know each Lloyd's broker's responsibilities.

6. Documentation

>*(9) Insurance brokers shall inform a client of the name of all insurers with whom a contract of insurance is placed. This information shall be given at the inception of the contract and any changes thereafter shall be advised at the earliest opportunity to the client.*

6.1 Cover notes and other written evidence of cover issued by a Lloyd's broker should be signed by suitably senior personnel. It is good practice for such documents to be signed by someone of seniority who was not involved in the placing but who has checked that the placing has been properly effected instead of or as well as the person responsible for the placing. This latter practice will not normally need to be followed in respect of temporary motor insurance cover notes.

6.2 A Lloyd's broker should only advise a client that any proportion of an insurance has been effected when that proportion has been accepted by insurers.

6.3 A Lloyd's broker should provide his client with prompt written confirmation that an insurance has been effected and the terms thereof. If the full wording is not included with the confirmation, the Lloyd's broker should forward it as soon as possible.

6.4 Subject to any lien that he may legitimately exercise, a Lloyd's broker should pass on promptly to a client any written evidence or documentation relating to a contract of insurance arranged for that client which the client may reasonably require. Where the Lloyd's broker exercises a lien and withholds documents, he should inform the client accordingly.

>*(8) Insurance brokers shall not withhold from the policyholder any written evidence or documentation relating to the contract of insurance without adequate and justifiable reasons being disclosed in writing and without delay to the policyholder. If an insurance broker withholds a document from a policyholder by way of a lien for monies due from that policyholder he shall provide the reason in the manner required above.*

7. Accounting

7.1 At an early stage in the business relationship, a Lloyd's broker should advise a client of his obligations to the Lloyd's broker and insurers concerning the timely payment of premiums.

7.2 Any insurance monies handled by a Lloyd's broker have to be kept in Insurance Broking Accounts. The operation of these accounts is the responsibility of the Lloyd's broker and he receives and retains any interest or investment income earned on them. A Lloyd's broker should apply due diligence to the collection and payment of all insurance monies.

7.3 A Lloyd's broker should have proper regard for the settlement due date agreed with the insurers for any contract of insurance.

7.4 A Lloyd's broker should remit money received and due to clients promptly. Where a risk is placed with a number of insurers, and claims monies are remitted to the Lloyd's broker at different times, the Lloyd's broker will need to consider whether, having regard to the amount received and the time when the balance will be received, and any other relevant factors such as amounts owed by the client to the Lloyd's broker, he should pass on to the client such proceeds as he has received as soon as possible rather than await the balance and make payment in full.

8. Binding authorities

(N.B. In this section, "binding authorities" does not include limited binding authorities where reference has to be made to one or more leading insurers before a risk is bound.)

8.1 It is insurers' practice, particularly in certain classes of business, to grant underwriting authority to a Lloyd's broker under a binding authority. The primary purpose of this practice is to facilitate prompt and efficient acceptance of business. If a Lloyd's broker is in a position to place business from his own clients under the binding authority, that Lloyd's broker has a potential conflict of interest. A Lloyd's broker should not accept business from a client under a binding authority granted to him if to do so would not be in the client's best interests.

8.2 Where a Lloyd's broker accepts his own client's risk on behalf of insurers under a binding authority granted to him, he should disclose this to the client. Where the client so requests, a Lloyd's broker should inform him of all financial advantages to the Lloyd's broker of the use of the binding authority.

8.3 At the time of accepting a binding authority a Lloyd's broker should remind the insurers who are granting that authority that the Lloyd's broker's first duty will be to his existing and future clients rather than to the insurers granting the authority.

9. Claims

9.1 A Lloyd's broker should explain to his clients their obligations to notify claims promptly and to disclose all material facts.

9.2 If a Lloyd's broker has reason to believe that the notification of the facts of a claim by a client is not true, fair and complete, he should request him to make the necessary true, fair and complete disclosure. In the absence of such agreement, the broker should consider whether he should decline to continue acting for the client and what obligations he has to insurers or any regulatory authority.

9.3 A Lloyd's broker should take appropriate steps in connection with claims notified by clients to see that all information properly required by insurers is promptly provided to them.

9.4 A Lloyd's broker should give prompt advice to his client of insurers' requirements concerning notified claims.

9.5 On receipt of insurers' decision on the settlement or otherwise of a claim, a Lloyd's broker should promptly inform the client.

9.6 A Lloyd's broker should not, without the fully informed consent of both parties, act for both his client and insurers during the claims settling process if by doing so he would be undertaking duties to one principal which are inconsistent with those owed to the other. In any event, a Lloyd's broker who receives or holds on behalf of the insurers concerned an adjuster's report or similar document relating to an insurance claim made by his client should only do so on the basis that the information in the report may be imparted to the client.

9.7 A Lloyd's broker has a potential conflict of interest where he has an insurer's authority to settle claims. If he cannot reconcile the client's best interests with the obligations to the insurer concerned, he should refer the claim to the insurer for instructions.

9.8 In circumstances where the interests of two or more clients of a Lloyd's broker might conflict (e.g., where one is the first party and one the third party in an accident), the Lloyd's broker should take appropriate steps so that the interests of each can be fairly represented.

10. Renewals

The client should be aware of the date of expiry of his insurance from the insuring documentation. It should nevertheless be normal practice for a Lloyd's broker to seek from his client whose insurance is approaching expiry instructions concerning the renewal of that insurance and to remind the client of the duties of good faith and disclosure.

11. Transfer of client

> *(12) Insurance brokers shall have proper regard for the wishes of a policyholder or client who seeks to terminate any agreement with them to carry out business.*

On transfer of a client to another Lloyd's broker, the prior Lloyd's broker should if so instructed by the client and subject to the payment of any monies owed by the client to the prior Lloyd's broker make available to the new Lloyd's broker all such documentation to which the client is entitled and which is reasonably necessary for the new Lloyd's broker to discharge his duties to that client.

12. Servicing

A Lloyd's broker should provide any relevant service requested by his client in relation to any insurance placed for that client notwithstanding the expiry of the insurance contract, unless the Lloyd's broker is properly satisfied that the client has instructed a new broker to assume all such obligations and that the new broker has accepted such instruction.

13. Complaints

13.1 A Lloyd's broker should have a procedure so that complaints by clients and insurers are at the appropriate stage dealt with at a suitably senior level and other than by the personnel involved in the matter giving rise to the complaint. Upon a receipt of a complaint, a Lloyd's broker should give notification to the client of the complaints procedure which he operates. The notification should incorporate a reference to the right of a complainant to write to the Council of Lloyd's.

> *(19) Insurance brokers shall display in any office where they are carrying on business and to which the public have access a notice to the effect that a copy of the Code of Conduct is available upon request and that if a member of the public wishes to make a complaint or requires the assistance of the Council in resolving a dispute, he may write to the Insurance Brokers Registration Council at its offices at 15 St. Helen's Place, London EC3A 6DS.*

13.2 A Lloyd's broking company or partnership should add the following paragraph to the notice required by IBRC Practice Note (No. 2) to be displayed in its office and display that notice in a prominent position in the reception area of its office:

> *This Company/Partnership and those described above as "At Lloyd's" are insurance brokers acting under the statutory authority of the Council of Lloyd's to whom the complaints or disputes may be referred.*

14. Supervision of staff

> *(3) Insurance brokers shall ensure that all work carried out in connection*

with their insurance broking business shall be under the control and day-to-day supervision of a registered insurance broker and they shall do everything possible to ensure that their employees are made aware of this Code.

14.1 A broker should either operate his own training programmes or make use of training programmes such as those operated by Lloyd's Training Centre and the Chartered Insurance Institute, participation in which will maintain and improve the competence of all involved in the Lloyd's broking business.

14.2 A Lloyd's broker should take appropriate steps to see that its staff are aware of legal requirements, including the law of agency, affecting their activities.

14.3 A Lloyd's broker should take appropriate steps to see that his staff are aware of the standards expected of them by this Code of Practice.

15. Competence

A Lloyd's broker should not handle classes of business in which he is not competent.

16. Use of Lloyd's name

16.1 A Lloyd's broker should not permit businesses over which he has control to misuse Lloyd's name.

16.2 A Lloyd's broker should be careful not to do or permit to be done anything that would prejudice the regulatory status of insurers in any jurisdiction.

(2) *Insurance brokers shall only use or permit the use of the description "insurance broker" in connection with a business provided that business is carried on in accordance with the requirements of the Rules made by the Council under sections 11 and 12 of the (1977) Act.*

(15) *Advertisements made by or on behalf of insurance brokers shall comply with the applicable parts of the Code of Advertising Practice published by the Advertising Standards Authority and for this purpose the Code of Advertising Practice shall be deemed to form part of this Code of Conduct.*

(16) *Advertisements made by or on behalf of insurance brokers shall distinguish between contractual benefits, that is those that the contract of insurance is bound to provide, and non-contractual benefits, that is the amount of benefit which it might provide assuming the insurer's particular forecast is correct. Where such advertisements include a forecast of non-contractual benefits, insurance brokers shall restrict the forecast to that provided by the insurer concerned.*

(17) *Advertisements made by or on behalf of insurance brokers shall not be*

restricted to the policies of one insurer except where the reasons for such restriction are fully explained in the advertisement, the insurer named therein, and the prior approval of that insurer obtained.

(18) When advertising their services directly or indirectly either in person or in writing insurance brokers shall disclose their identity, occupation and purpose before seeking information or before giving advice.

INDEX

Index

Damage, latent, 27, 37–40
Damages, 40–41
  in cases concerning architects or engineers, 121–125
  apportionment, 121–122
  betterment, 123–124
  and insurance brokers, assessment of liabilities, 82–83
  surveyors, assessment of liabilities, 65–67
Damages, exemplary, 31, 40–41
Damages, punitive, 41
Delegation, 9, 99–102
Disclaimers, scope, 57–60, 64–65, 119
Distress, 68, 124
Doctors, question of specialist liability, 4–5
Duty of care, *see* Care, duty of

E & O brokers, 85–86
Economic loss, 28–29
  and architects or engineers, 115–116
  and errors and omissions brokers, 86
  and negligence, 13, 14, 16
  and surveyors, 53–56
Embezzlement, compensation by professional bodies, 37
Engineers, 7–8, 95
  duties to contractors, 14–16, 117–121
  negligence
    and costs estimates, 106–107
    damages, *see* Architects, negligence, question of damages
    design liabilities, *see* Architects, negligence, design liabilities
  duties to third parties, 115–121
  obligations during construction period, 107–114
    advice on issues of law, 113–114
    supervision, 111
  question of evidence in court, 114–115
  See also Architects
Errors and omissions brokers, 85–86
European Union, and regulation of insurance intermediaries, 92–93
Exclusion clauses, scope, 56–57
Experience, relevance to negligence claims, 4
Expert witnesses, 7–8, 33–34

Fees, 1
  abatement, 113
  and damages, 124
Financial guarantees, and insurance brokers, 86–87
Financial loss, and errors and omissions brokers, 86
Financial services, question of insurance brokers' conflict of interest, 92

Fraud, compensation by professional bodies, 37

Inconvenience
  and damages, 124
  surveyor's liability, 68
Indemnity, professional, 43–47, 50
Injury, physical, question of liability, 117–118
Insolvency, where creditor has claim under insurance, 51, 52
Insurance brokers, 22–24, 83–84
  duties, 77–94
    and common law, 78–84
      question of agency status, 78–80
      re-insurance, 80–81
    statutory and voluntary regulation, 91–93
  use of standard forms, 49
  See also Underwriters
Insurance Brokers Registration Council, Code of Conduct, 84, 153–156
Insurance Brokers Regulation Council, Code of Conduct, 91
Insurance companies, Association of British Insurers Code of Practice, text, 157–162
Insurance policies, "claims made" contrasted with "events occurring", 43
Insurer, change of, resulting problems, 43–47
Interim insurance, contract of, 78

Judges, immunity from suit, 33
Judgment, error of, compared with negligence, 6

Law Society, question of duty of care, 36
Liability, voluntary assumption of, and surveyors, 56–57
Life insurance, regulation of brokers, 91–92
Lloyd's, claims against, 36, 127–128
Lloyd's brokers
  Code of Practice, 92, 163–173
  duty of care owed to clients and employers, 20–21

Mareva injunctions, application, 52
Material facts, importance of disclosure, 89
Material non-disclosure, 47–50, 77, 89–90
Medical practitioners, *see* Doctors
Misrepresentation, insurance brokers' liabilities, 84
Mortgage Valuation: Guidance for Valuers, text, 146–152
Multi-party actions, and apportionment of damages, 121–122